Spiritual Classics
from the late
twentieth century

compiled and introduced by

ANN LOADES

National Society/Church House Publishing

National Society/Church House Publishing
Church House
Great Smith Street
London
SW1P 3NZ

ISBN 0 7151 4859 1

First published in 1995 by The National Society and Church House Publishing

Cover design by Leigh Hurlock
Page design and typesetting by Church House Publishing
Printed in Great Britain by Biddles Ltd, Guildford and King's Lynn

CONTENTS

Preface

This anthology is simply one person's attempt to make selections from a particular range of Christian spirituality in the latter part of our present century. All six authors whose prayers, reflections, preaching and teaching are included here are deeply preoccupied with how they themselves, and all of us in our interdependence on one another, may be orientated to God in our very different lives. Each of the six draws deeply on the Christian tradition. Each of them is actively engaged in handing that inheritance on to others so that they in turn can make it their own.

No anthology could represent every possible kind of spirituality at this period of history even within the limits of western culture. Reading the work of these six authors may encourage us to search for other examples to find resources for our own orientation to God, and our own 'traditioning', however modest that may be. Some will find that the most helpful kinds of writing for them are to be found in the work of novelists, playwrights and poets; others may need to turn almost exclusively to musicians and composers of music; yet others to artists in stained glass, in sculpture and painting. Some will need to revel in a mixture of any or all of these, or delight in the complexities of the non-human realm in which we find ourselves. If a spirituality is to be identifiably Christian, however, at some point or other, some form of connection with the Christian tradition will need to be discernible. Beyond that, perhaps we need only bear in mind that the 'fruit of the Spirit' includes 'love, joy, peace, patience, kindness, goodness, faithfulness, gentleness, self-control' (Galatians 5:22).

This anthology includes selections from the writings of three women and three men. All of them have enjoyed the immense privileges of access to learning – theology, ethics, philosophy, history, Scripture, sociology, anthropology, psychology – yet all have in common the capacity to be generous with their learning in many varied ways. Some of their writing is easier to read than other parts. Some of it narrates and reflects on deep pain, not least the pain of enduring and even embracing profound change in one's life. We have no reason to suppose that getting a taste for God will leave us just where or as we are, any more than at mid-life or in late life we are precisely the same person we were at five or fifteen years old. We change if we involve ourselves with one another. We change if we search for God, or make it possible for God in his searching to find us. We may have to make changes in our perception of God. Spirituality can have quite a lot to do with the practice of courage, whatever our age.

Each section begins with a brief outline biography so that readers may have a clue about the kind of context in which each author lives. The connections between the particular selections within the work of any one author have been kept as minimal as possible. Each section may be read on its own, separate from that of another. Readers may simply like to dip in here and there, and see what they find. What the six authors have in common becomes clear, whatever the mode of reading; that is, apart from private prayer and reading Scripture, prayer and Scripture as part of engagement with worship and various forms of liturgy and the liturgical texts themselves, matter together with various kinds of institutional and political engagement. Spirituality for them is not about consciousness-raising, personal development or whatever. These may be accidental by-products of an orientation towards a deep and passionate pre-occupation with God, but they are not its goal. Transformation for conviviality, living-with-others, being graced into life in society and church alike might be nearer the mark.

1

Helen Oppenheimer

GENEROSITY

H elen Oppenheimer is a writer on Christian ethics and theology who in 1993 was given a Lambeth DD for her work. This is her first qualification in theology. Her mother and her headmistress, as it happens, had put their heads together when Helen as a sixth former had thought of reading English at university, and between them they encouraged her to read PPE – Politics, Philosophy and Economics at Oxford, and it was in philosophy and ethics that she was to find profound satisfaction, not least because at the time she was studying for her undergraduate and postgraduate degrees, philosophy was undergoing some major and stimulating changes. She and her husband could have lived in South Africa, but her homes have been in Oxford and Jersey. In the former place, she was roped into a group of theologians and philosophers who treated her as one of them, and encouraged her first papers. She put ethics back on the syllabus at Cuddesdon Theological College (where Janet Martin Soskice was to teach) and one of the fruits of this period was her book, *The Character of Christian Morality* (1965). A later and major work was her book, *The Hope of Happiness: A Sketch for a Christian Humanism* (1983). She has made a significant contribution over the years to our understanding of how to integrate theology and ethics together, not least when writing about marriage, and she has had a long association with some of the Church of England's Commissions of one kind or another, bringing her own distinctive voice to the discussions. She has preached many sermons, not least in the days when it was even less common to find a woman doing so than it is now. Her commitment to the significance of the presence of

1

women as well as men in the lay as well as the ordained ministry of the church is part and parcel of a deeply 'orthodox' Christian faith, exhibited most recently in her latest book, *Finding and Following: Talking with Children about God* (1994), written, as she says in her preface, for adults who have some influence with children, which means almost all of us. Without labouring the point (which should emerge almost of itself from the following readings from her work) generosity to one another and the hope of fulfilment and the sheer *joie de vivre* we might suppose to be characteristic of a Christian expectation of resurrection are marks of her approach to thinking about how we relate to God and one another.

In these pages which lead us through some of Helen Oppenheimer's spirituality we reflect on different levels of the ways we relate to one another and to Christ and God through the material world, to be relished in itself and in the way it gives us a foretaste of a resurrection life with God. In our next section, from the writings of Janet Martin Soskice, we can find both Christian conviction, but also a spirituality which has, at least as represented here, a sharper focus on women's spirituality. And finally, in this half of the book which introduces us to women's spirituality in our time, we have Margaret Spufford's personal experience of her own physical pain, of her daughter's life, and her reflections on 'creation' and its meaning. This gives her spirituality a particular focus on the relation between incarnation, sacrament and pain of an explicitly liturgical kind.

Fellowship

Here are some paragraphs on Fellowship originally published in Theology, *and then reprinted in a collection on* The Sacred Ministry, *of great value not least in these days when much is unreflectively said in Christian circles about* koinonia. *Spirituality, whatever it means in a particular life, is fostered in and with others in all the complexities of our relationships, and these are of different sorts and of different levels.*

There is a most urgent need for an applied theology of the Body of Christ: and if this theology is going to turn out to be much too difficult for the ordinary Christian to understand, then it must be said that there is something wrong with it. Of course it may be a deep mystery which one is not yet holy enough to enter into, but that is another matter from sheer intellectual abstruseness. No doubt there are also great stretches of Christian theology which just are abstruse as well as mysterious: would we not expect the doctrines of the Trinity and the Incarnation to be beyond our intelligence? Nothing forbids us to study intellectually the science of God, but nothing guarantees that we shall get very far, for we may well suppose that God is infinitely clever as well as infinitely holy, and can lead his own life without our comprehension. But such doctrines as the Church and the Atonement should surely not take human understanding out of its depth so quickly. If they are true they must be capable of emerging into the experience of the ordinary Christian, not in so far as he is intelligent but in so far as he is becoming holy. If these doctrines are beyond most of us, it is as if the applied sciences of cooking or bringing up children were beyond the ordinary woman. Ought a book about the Body of Christ, then, to enlighten a vicar on how to run his parish? In general the answer must be Yes, for the same reason as the answer to the converse question, Ought a PCC to discuss theology? must be Yes. The Body of Christ, when it becomes specific *is* the local church; the agenda of the PCC, whether or not this is realised, *is* theology.

The epistles of St Paul may be called in evidence here. The tendency of the Apostle to weave together high speculation about the Body of Christ with seemingly prosaic administrative arrangements, with the interchange of social goodwill and with practical moral exhortation, might not in itself provide a precedent for the future conduct of Church affairs. We might after all conceive ourselves to have developed our thinking and drawn useful distinctions which in early days were only implicit. But the authority and liveliness, adding up to a kind of inescapable authenticity, in St Paul's procedure of weaving the strands together, compared with the deadness and limpness of our own tendency to draw them apart, surely gives one to think. When he shoots from one live metaphor to another and brings them to bear upon Christian living, do we really want to turn metaphor into technicality and then insulate the resulting theory from contact with practical affairs?

The next temptation is for this Pauline authenticity to lose itself in glibness. In reaction against making technicalities of the great metaphors of the Church it is fatally easy to make slogans of them. There is a fashionable line of thought each step of which is attractive but which skims along the surface of great matters, arriving so quickly and easily at its destination that not much is gathered on the way. We are the Body of Christ and severally members thereof, and this means us, in ordinary parish life. This seems a simple method of exorcizing the false individualism whose church services were inward-looking and whose service to the world was self-righteous and probably paternalistic. In fellowship with one another we can 'be the Church' and this fellowship will automatically supply the needed link between religion and the world.

In the Christian life it is not deep and subtle relationships which matter but a simple, though of course costly, orientation of the will. The *agape* on which Christian fellowship is based is nothing to do with feelings but with turning towards one's neighbour, any neighbour, and treating him as the child of God, as a Thou and not an It. To such exhortations we are all accustomed and heaven forbid that we should repudiate the insights they summarise. But to stop short at this stage is almost inevitably to set forth Christian fellowship as a matter of quantity of relationships rather than quality, to eliminate selfishness not by positive enlargement of capacity for love, but by loss of depth. A great deal that is written and said today about community, I-Thou relationships and the love of the neighbour seems dangerously to ignore the magnificent multiplicity and intricacy of the ways in which human beings can enter into relationship with one another.

Of course the good Samaritan, the man who sees humanity even in the potentially alien or repulsive, and who acts on this perception at considerable trouble to himself, is a key Christian figure. Perhaps he was late home to his own Samaritan family for the sake of this stranger. One might call him a model example of seeing the essentials of a situation, of getting his priorities right, and by his true neighbourliness he showed up some false neighbours. But he is not thereby a pattern for every kind of Christian relationship; and in particular, for the fellowship of the Body of Christ he is a pattern only in a negative way. There is nothing to suggest that he went about looking for strangers to be kind to in preference to entering into more profound relationships, nor that he would have been a very well-integrated Samaritan if he had. There could be stages in Church history when the members of Christ's body would do well to take more note of the Johannine figures of Lazarus and his sisters or the beloved disciple, at least to the extent of learning that the Lord was evidently not afraid of, or hostile towards, specific relationships, however urgently he warned his followers against selfish exclusiveness.

Why then should one suppose that the Church is at present in such a stage, and that the perpetual dangers of false emphasis are not being incorrectly located? Many examples could be given: trivial examples admittedly, but inevitably so when the malady being diagnosed is a form of chronic triviality.

For instance, there are several prevalent forms of misunderstanding between clergy and people which surely spring from a fundamental unreality in actual Christian fellowship. The normal reaction of parishioners to a new way of doing things which they do not find congenial is not to approach the vicar to explain their objections or find out what the changes mean: they silently and with a deadly politeness stay away from the services. This would hardly be the inital reaction of the members of a family whose mother failed to supply them with suitable meals.

A similar lack of communication is apt to occur over infant baptism. Of course, public baptism of infants means what it says, and of course a large part of the significance of the rite is the making the child a member of the Christian Church. But in our mobile society the chances are not high that a particular person will lead much of his life in the particular Christian community in which he happens to be born and baptised. To the child's parents, deeply concerned with their new baby's welfare, the real community to which they and their baby belong is the large or small group of relations and friends who will still be theirs wherever fortune takes them to live. If an artificial concourse of benevolent neighbours however Christian is proposed as a substitute for those most nearly concerned in witnessing the ceremony of making their child a member of Christ they will sense a falsehood, even if they are unable to put this awareness into words. A parish baptism which it is impossible for grandparents, aunts and uncles from elsewhere to attend can represent as sharp a cleavage of theology from life as an exclusive Saturday chris-tening hidden from the public gaze.

All this matters, because what is happening is that the vocabulary of fellowship is being debased. A man may not be gregarious because, for instance, he is acutely shy, seriously overworked, recently bereaved or seldom in one place for long, and such reasons do not necessarily impair his Christian faith. A patronal festival may be hopefully described as a great occasion, but it is a rare patronal festival which rouses or should arouse such keen enjoyment as a human birthday party. It makes a poor thing of the Body of Christ to blur such differences and to seem to reduce it to such inessential manifestations. Particularly if heaven itself is to be interpreted in terms of personal relationships with God and one another, it is imperative not to have an impoverished understanding of what a personal relationship can be. It is therefore necessary to insist that the kind of fellowship which can be scheduled to happen in parish halls is not better or more authentic than the kind which spontaneously occurs on a family outing or between friends discussing far into the night, or colleagues working hard to get something done. Any of these might be doors into or distractions from the kingdom of heaven.

What the Church urgently needs at the present time is a theology of friendship. As long as 'fellowship' is treated on the one hand as a sort of watered-down friendship and on the other hand is simultaneously set up as superior to the real thing, the vigour of the Body of Christ is bound to be impaired. The trouble spreads well beyond Church circles, and the word 'friend' is itself becoming similarly debased. One hears of people who become 'prisoners' friends', no doubt doing admirable liaison work between those in prison and the outer world, but who are sensibly advised not to reveal their own telephone numbers for fear of impinge-ment upon their private lives. Likewise the task of the Samaritans is to 'befriend', in necessary distinction from the somewhat different role of the professionals in these social fields; but when a human being is set on his feet again, his friend moves on to the next person who needs him. A much more sensitive and perhaps intricate apparatus of words and ideas is needed to allow us to do justice to the true complications and subtleties of such relationships. At the same time those who simply are friends in the basic meaning of the word have no need to try to assimi-late their relationship precisely to any of these helping roles.

The object of the exercise should not be to glorify friendship or any other deep human relationship as simply self-justifying or an end in itself. One would have to reckon not only with 'I have called you friends' (John 15:15) but with 'If ye love them which love you, what reward have ye? Do not even the publicans do the same?' (Matthew 5:46). There is scant comfort in the New Testament for those who confine their love to one small circle however dear. The present plea is not for a headlong flight from public civilities to private affections, but for a refusal to substitute either for the other, an appreciation of the range and depth of human capacities for love and goodwill, an exploration of the potentialities of personal relationships in Christian understanding.

True Christian fellowship may well turn out to be something like happiness or originality, lost as soon as it is directly sought but flourishing strongly as soon as self-conscious attention is removed from it. If a parish devotes itself to providing for real needs, worship primarily because that is what it is constituted to do, instruction when people are ignorant, sociability when they are lonely, fund-raising when money is needed, social service when people are in trouble and there is no one to help them, even on occasion political support in oppression, then 'fellowship' will look after itself. What matters is to be careful not to confuse means and ends, not to arrange 'occasions' for their own sake and then try to find people to partake in them, not to assimilate every sort of need to every other. Above all, it is surely the function of the Church to back people up in their own Christian lives, to let them know that they need not be alone.

A modern catch-phrase is 'acceptance' but this can come to seem thin and unfeeling. Tolerance of other people's failings is a great deal, but in the Body of Christ it is rightly felt not to be enough: hence many of our self-conscious efforts after something better. A more useful catch-phrase might be 'appreciation', a real attempt to grasp what people are trying to do and be, not just to put up with but to see the point of their peculiarities. If they could feel that the Church was behind them (generally but of course not invariably as exemplified by their parish and its vicar) in their attempts to walk with God and deal with everyday life, then the coffee cups and all they represent would, so to speak, fall into place. The prospect of growing up together 'unto a perfect man, unto the measure of the stature of the fulness of Christ' could come to seem much less unrealistic.

The Sacred Ministry, pp400-408

Friendship

These paragraphs on Friendship are from Helen Oppenheimer's book, Marriage, *1990.*

Is talking about reciprocity any more than a grandiose way of saying that a husband and wife should be friends? It was brought into the argument to introduce some flexibility into the notion of married people complementing each other. The biological difference between the sexes is neither to be ignored nor presumed upon. Being a man, or being a woman, leaves a lot to be worked out about our social roles; and the idea of reciprocity emphasises that the working out is to be done together. Traditional headship is not even ruled out, provided that the exacting Pauline description of it is taken with rare seriousness (Ephesians 5:21-33). So we come to speak of a sort of give and take based on contrast and likeness.

But friendship too is well described in this sort of way: so why should reciprocity be supposed to have a special relevance to marriage? With a little care one can take hold of this criticism, and instead of being much concerned to rebut it, make it the foundation of what remains to be said. Suppose reciprocity belongs in marriage just because marriage at its best depends upon friendship and cannot be properly understood without it?

There is some disentangling to be done to avoid some characteristic twentieth century muddles about love and friendship. Freud's lesson that human beings are sexual beings has been well and truly taken to heart, though it is a pity to be so dazzled by it that we cannot see anything else. Meantime liberal Christians are glad to have learnt the lesson of the importance of 'personal relationships', which are sometimes taken to mean almost the same as love. It is partly insight, partly confusion, to try to add these two ways of thinking up to an enlightened Christian conclusion by making the double affirmation that human relationships are fundamentally sexual, and that good sexual relationships need stability. So marriage, which provides the necessary stability, can be glorified as the supreme example of personal relationship. One hopes in this way to be traditional and modern at the same time. A good deal of naïvety about men's and women's dealings with one another can be suitably avoided, and a good many worthwhile things can be said about the relationships of husbands and wives, but the price to be paid is quite heavy. Not only is the notion of celibacy hard to fit into this scheme; but because people are determined to show themselves unafraid of sexuality, they become unable to value any friendship which lacks overtly sexual expression.

So friendship comes to be thought of as just a kind of cooled-down 'love', filling a gap when people have not arrived at real, adult, sexual relationships. Children have 'best friends' much as they keep rabbits in hutches. People are 'just good friends' when they are drawing back from being 'in love'. We 'befriend' the lonely and unfortunate, who are missing real 'personal relationships'.

Then with good but confused intentions some religious people demote friendship in another way by treating it, not as cooled-down sex, but as warmed-up neighbourliness. 'Friendship' and 'fellowship' become almost synonymous, and in some current church usage both are shadows of what they could mean. The biblical concept of fellowship is enfeebled to mean hardly more than politeness, and friendship is tethered to it because of a sort of fear of real friendship which makes favourites.

But real friendship is more important than these misunderstandings allow it to be. It is not something to make do with or to fall back upon. For human beings it is an end in itself rather than a means to some other end, whether sexual, economic, political or even religious. It enhances other relationships just because it has its own reality. Friendship is more than friendliness, though friendly people are ready to make friends. It is the particular and mutual appreciation of another man or woman as that very man or woman, not just as another person in general. Friendship shows itself primarily in the enjoyment of one another's company. Helping one's friends, or being helped by them, is secondary to affectionate communication.

Once all this has been said about friendship, it can then be happily applied to marriage as the characteristic sort of friendship which the human pairbond has developed. Having said that marriage is the joining of the lives of a man and a woman, we can explain that what makes sense of their choosing to belong to each other, including their physical union, is their mutual individual valuing of each other. If, the other way round, we try to characterise all personal relationships in terms of sexuality, we may be able to say all sorts of good things about marriage, but other kinds of friendship are left looking like sexual relationships deprived of sex.

When friendship is not given significance in its own right we shall miss opportunities for human happiness, and exaggerate unhappy trends. There will be less spontaneity in expressing all kinds of human affections for fear of stereotyped sexual assumptions. All warm relationships will tend towards one model, tyrannical if it becomes a monopoly.

There will be more marriages based entirely upon physical attraction rather than upon liking. There will be more isolation of young couples as all in all to each other. Homosexual people will find themselves more typecast. There will be more pressure on people, young or older, to rate themselves according to their sexual prowess.

Now that people are becoming so concerned about the divorce rate and are wondering, often vainly, whether better marriage preparation would be the way to bring it down, it is worth pointing out that just as growing up with happily married parents is more use than any number of educational courses, so growing up knowing what friendship means is a similar kind of strong basis.

The best time to educate people for marriage is long before they are old enough to understand it. The time when the parents who gave them birth are no longer their whole world, and the people they will fall in love with are somewhere in the future, has been called the 'latency phase'. But human relationship is far from latent. They are busily entering into a heritage of human communication, and especially they are discovering what it is to make friends. They are loving and fickle, vulnerable and resilient. They are developing a capacity which can enhance the rest of their lives and bring them enjoyment, solace, encouragement and delight. They are learning about loyalty and disloyalty, co-operation and rivalry, patience and impatience, sympathy and envy, in what we hope are reasonably manageable doses. Older people can help by giving all this the importance it deserves. Friendship can be learnt as young as speech. We need not think of it as any more childish than language. If we want a good foundation for faithful marriage we can look here.

Marriage, pp107-109

Grievances[1]

'Grievances' was first published in Theology *in 1988. It is placed here because how we do or do not deal with the wrongs we inflict on one another is central to fellowship and friendship alike.*

> *Do I not hate them, O Lord, that hate thee . . .? Yea, I hate them right sore: even as though they were mine enemies.* [2]

Tего is the magnificent psalmist who took the wings of the morning. For him, condoning evil was a more serious fault than cherishing grudges. He bore witness that he had not neglected to put God's enemies in the category of the 'hateable'.

Since his day, things have changed. God has made a new covenant with his chosen people. They are commanded now to get rid of this category of the 'hateable', get rid of it altogether, not just reorganise it.

Some moral theologians insist that God's love is 'unconditional'. In one sense we know perfectly well that it is not. God's people today have been told as clearly as God's people of old that something *is* required of them. The condition upon which they may receive his mercy is not virtue, nor even amends, but mercy to one another. Unless people forgive, their own sins cannot be forgiven. This priority was set up before the Lord died or rose again, before there was a doctrine of atonement and a Church to try to understand it.

So we turn our backs upon the straightforward partisanship of the psalmist. An enemy is there to be forgiven, to be blessed and prayed for. In a way, he is the most promising kind of neighbour, the test and guarantee of one's unselfishness.

Thomas Traherne put our Christian duty before us with persuasive vigour:

> *Yet you must arm yourself with Expectations of their Infirmities, and resolve nobly to forgive them: not in a sordid and Cowardly manner, by taking no notice of them: nor in a Dim and Lazy manner, by letting them alone: but in a Divine and Illustrious manner by chiding them meekly, and vigorously rendering and showering down all kinds of Benefits.*[3]

That would make an encouraging peroration to a practical discourse on forgiveness. Of course that is what it must be like to forgive, and we can do it if we try; or can we? What we have so far is a hopeful way of setting out a problem, not an answer: a destination not a route, still less a short cut. Some of us are troubled by both the practice and the theory of forgiveness.

What is it to forgive? We easily reject several inadequate accounts. Forgiveness is different from letting someone off from a punishment: we sometimes believe that punishment is still necessary, and often it is irrelevant. Forgiveness is more than *saying* 'I forgive you': to say anything may not be the point at all. It is more than abstaining from revenge: yet what is this 'more'? The manufacture of forgiving feelings cannot be necessary. Forgiveness is supposed not to depend upon conditions: but what is this transaction which requires neither party to do anything in particular?

We must repudiate the insidious conviction that a Christian is meant to be a doormat. Pious people meekly, indeed weakly, accept oppression, and set about forgiving their enemies not in Traherne's 'Divine and Illustrious manner' but sometimes with a spinelessness that destroys sympathy, sometimes with a smugness that seems to endow 'the meek shall inherit the earth' with an ironical and intolerable meaning far from beatitude. Turning the other cheek is distorted into yet another recipe for salvation, uncreative in human terms and not even loving. Shaw held this paradoxical new legalism up to mockery in his portrayal of the converted fighter Ferrovius in *Androcles and the Lion*.

It is bad enough to see people miserably failing to stand up for *themselves*. It is worse to see them almost corruptly condoning harms that have been done to other people, and all in the name of religion. We warm to King Clovis who on being instructed in the passion story exclaimed, as Gibbon recounted it, 'with indiscreet fury', "Had I been present at the head of my valiant Franks, I would have revenged his injuries." ' [4] We do not warm to people who make light of other people's wrongs, even in the name of the gospel: compassionate anger is more human and more moral, and it grieves us not to be able to call it more Christian.

But may not forgiveness be one of those things hidden from the wise and understanding and revealed to babes? Real forgiveness, human or divine, seems unsuitable for cool dissection. Ought we not simply to be asking God for his help?

The case is not quite so straightforward. In the prayer we have been taught to make, we do not *ask* our heavenly Father to help us to do this difficult feat of forgiving: we tell him we are doing it. We let it be made a condition for his mercy upon us. So if we are in moral and intellectual confusion about what it is we are supposed to be doing, our situation is an awkward one. It is no good saying sadly like a character in a poem by Browning:[5]

> *I would we were boys as of old*
> *In the field, by the fold:*
> *His outrage, God's patience, man's scorn*
> *Were so easily borne!*

We need to do more thinking to extricate ourselves from various entanglements.

The intellectual difficulty is that forgiveness is either unjustified or pointless.[6] When the sinner is not sorry, forgiveness is only condonation. If the sinner is truly sorry, there is nothing now to forgive.[7] It may be replied that what forgiveness does is anticipate repentance. It goes to meet a change of heart in the offender, gambling generously upon his restoration. So, as exemplifying 'an attitude of *trust* in the world',[8] forgiveness can be ethically defended, when it happens. But how can we set about achieving it?

We know of course that the complete answer is to hate the sin and love the sinner. But when 'hating the sin' is put into practice it can mean anything from the relentless ferocity of the persecutor to the vague regret of the worldly associate. These are a long way from forgiveness. And when we turn to 'loving the sinner', it is too easy to slip into what has been aptly called 'knee-jerk liberalism', that dreary automatic justifying of other people which is not much more constructive than obsessive self-justification. John Donne in his poetical litany asked to be delivered from

> *indiscreet humility*
> *Which might be scandalous*
> *And cast reproach on Christianity.*

It might indeed.

At this stage people begin to talk about forgiveness as restoring right relationships; and such understanding is, literally, heavenly. Far be it from me to give any impression of belittling it. The questions I am asking are about the bits that on earth are left over: the damage done by the unknown criminal, the casual but bitter offence caused by someone who does not in the least want one's friendship, the heartlessness of the bureaucrat, the insensitivity of the political opponent, the unreliability of the charmer who must not be trusted any more, the patronising smugness of the prig who is not human enough to transgress; and all these still more bafflingly when it is other people who are being made to suffer. It is impertinent in the old sense of 'irrelevant' and in the newer sense of 'presumptuous', to imagine ourselves establishing happy relationships where the truth is so intractable. So Donna Elvira might dream of forgiving Don Giovanni.

What we need is to 'will people's good' and a saint can give this real content. For some of us, this can seem at times like an empty formula, or worse, a tacit invitation to play God. If this one repented and that one relented, how we would welcome them back into the fold!

All this while we are skirting round the most fundamental answer, that what forgiveness does with evil is quench it, meet it with patient endurance so that the poison spreads no further. 'The buck stops here' is an uncouth but fair summary of an essential part of the theology of atonement. The miserable cycle of hurt and hate can be stopped, and Christians of all people ought to be able to partake in its stopping. It would be defeatist to deny that they can and do, from St Stephen praying, 'Lord, lay not this sin to their charge', to prisoners of conscience in this century who refuse to let bitterness overcome them.

Of course that kind of forgiveness is the true solution, but the worst is the corruption of the best. What is more real in most people's experience than the inspiring patience of a saint is the disheartening damage that ensues when rage pent up in the name of forbearance bursts out in the end, the unkind half-meant things that say themselves; and, no better, the sour or sickly diminishment of people who cannot be angry. Sitting on safety valves is not a good sort of religious exercise. We may come to believe in despondency that 'Only God can forgive sins'.

If the serenity of real sanctity has to be achieved as a condition for even asking for our own sins to be forgiven, our state is parlous. Each of these valid answers to our theoretical and practical difficulties about the meaning of forgiveness – hate the sin but not the sinner, restore relationships, quench the evil – leaves a residue of human inadequacy. Each of them is deeply true, at a stage we cannot say we are yet in. To solve the problems would be to have reached the next stage; but at least one can take a nearer look at them.

First then, can one make any approach to hating the sin and loving the sinner? One can stop trying to find Pickwickian meanings for the love of enemies, when really one finds them simply detestable. It is more practical to focus one's mind on the intellectual conviction that strange as it may seem God loves the sinner. One can be so anthropomorphic as to consider that a breach between brothers and sisters is a hurt to their parent, whatever the rights and wrongs of the question. To look upon a hostile human being as a child of God is neither to try to play God oneself nor just to suppress one's own indignation. It could be the beginning of a way to dislodge implacable resentment. Whatever forgiveness is, it must be easier to do it for someone's sake than on principle.

Secondly, it is true that sometimes relationships *can* be restored after offence. To see what this can mean, we can try putting ourselves at the receiving rather than the giving end, so we could get a sight of the notion of forgiveness on its home ground.

What do I need when I need to be forgiven? At least that question comes before the problem of how I can be grand and good enough to forgive other people. Surely the answer is, indeed, *justification by faith*. People ask in various ways for mercy, meaning all sorts of things like another chance, or a formal pardon, or help with the mess they have made, or a reconciliation. But whatever we ask for or are too proud or timid to ask for, what we crave for after all is justification, being in the right. If 'being in the right' sounds Pharisaical, as it does, we can use Catholic or Protestant jargon and talk about 'being in a state of grace' or 'being right with' God and one another. The point about forgiveness is that this human craving is not hopeless. Not all righteousness is self-righteousness. The truth that some people know instinctively and that the Protestant reformers rediscovered as a revelation worth living and dying for, is that justification *is* to be had but is not to be earned.

What people need, whether from God or from one another, is not to have to justify themselves by their works. They need to be set up and treated as if they mattered. They need to be attended to as complete human beings, without their failings being treated as characteristic or their good behaviour bargained over. If they are treated so, they will need less forgiving. In other words, they need grace. It is a pity to shrink the idea of 'grace' into a technicality. It is as it were the light one person sheds on another. If God's grace is sunlight, human grace is the real though derived light of the moon; but the ghostly coolness of moonlight is a poor illustration of the main point here, the sustaining reality of an uncensorious but not unexacting personal regard. So forgiveness (divine or human) is the way grace (divine or human) is projected upon badness. What it costs is another story. The present purpose is to show that we are not talking about a peculiar activity in which human beings usurp the prerogative of God.

The prerogative of God is to justify the *un*godly, when human grace has reached the end of its tether. What is to happen when forgiveness is, humanly speaking, out of the question? Where is 'justification' to get a purchase where honesty finds only deep misery or bitterness or the sort of abiding coldness where grace is in eclipse?

The third answer, the one we need most, to the question of what forgiveness means, that unconquerable love can somehow *quench* the evil, is the answer that seems furthest from us. If this quenching is something that only God can do, where does our forgiving come in and how does it matter?

Let us be realistic enough to acknowledge the objective existence of wrongs. In dealing with evil, forgiveness is facing something real.

> *Abel's blood for vengeance*
> *Pleaded to the skies.*[9]

Blood has no vocal chords. It is easy to think of this as a metaphor through and through, especially when we are trying to disapprove of what the metaphor means. Let us for a change go along with the metaphor and assert that there really are states of affairs which 'cry out' for justice. Grievances are at least as real as sins. The downtrodden in the Old Testament knew they had a case against their enemies in the heavenly court. The righteous man begged God for judgement, not in fear but in hope. Our confidence that God will pardon is presumption if we think it means that he will ignore. When it is other people's wrongs that are in question, it is offensive to suppose that nowadays God takes no heed of them.

Something has to be done with grievances, and pretending they do not exist is not doing something with them. The New Testament is not about the neglect of grievances but the enormous costliness of dealing with them. A simple penal theory of the atonement says rather too crudely that God in Christ took the punishment of sinners. There are more sensitive ways of elaborating upon the faith that God is not less than a just judge, but more. However in his creative mercy God brings all things to good, the fact that some of his children are bitterly aggrieved is, so to say, part of his problem. Simply to pardon offenders over the heads of the people they have hurt is to condone. Somehow he will 'make atonement' whatever it costs.

If our grievances are real, they are our very own, and nobody has the right to confiscate them if we want to cherish them. It is a real question what to do with them. If we are disposed to try to forgive we can, not ignore, but *sacrifice* our grievances. A sacrifice is not merely destroyed: it is offered up. To forgive could be to forgo the enjoyment of a real grievance by making a present of it. We can positively entrust our wrongs to God. Old Testament believers could assure themselves that God would at last vindicate them. Under the new covenant we may be sure that he will do nothing so simple, that somehow or other he will justify the ungodly. Forgiving is giving him a free hand. It is not presumptuous to see oneself and one's own injuries as part of God's problem. If St Paul could hope to fill up what was lacking in the sufferings of Christ, in due modesty we can take the chance not to add to the cost of atonement.

Theology 91, pp33-38

Temperance

This piece was first published in Theology *in 1962, and then in a collection called* Traditional Virtues Reassessed. *Quite apart from what Helen Oppenheimer has to say about this particular 'hinge' virtue, the last paragraph in particular introduces us to three of her concerns in spirituality; the material world as God's gift to us; the significance of the 'sacramental' for our lives; and above all, the promise of 'resurrection' with all the possible implications that may have for our lives here and now.*

Nowadays there is a feeling that we must apologise for the cardinal virtues, vindicate them, refurbish them, show that they are worthwhile after all. Temperance particularly, with its Babylonian captivity to total abstinence, seems to stand in need of reassessment.

The natural first move is to go back to the beginning and look with hopeful interest at the ideal of the golden mean. Nothing too much: neither asceticism nor self-indulgence, neither fanaticism nor flippancy, neither passion nor aloofness: this seems an eminently sane and admirable programme with which to confront the notoriously rudderless and bewildered modern man. There is no doubt that, properly presented, temperance in the ancient and honourable sense of moderation in all things can appear profoundly attractive. If people fail to find it so, there are several ways in which its charms may be drawn out. One way is to use the adjective 'temperate', less contaminated by unwanted associations, instead of the noun; another is to dwell on the horrors and miseries of immoderation, so as to make the tautology 'excess is excessive' take hold on the imagination; another is simply to reflect, lazily but gratefully, how agreeable life can be when moderation is practised by those about one. Among people who have the habit to any degree of taking stock of their surroundings there can be few who have never had occasion either to admire or to wish for the virtue of temperance, whether in matters of food and drink, politics, personal relationships, business affairs or intellectual controversy.

To turn from these considerations to the Gospels is like being plunged into a cold bath. Instead of a sage of quiet wisdom and frugal habits we are confronted with a Lord whose character is dynamic to the point of being profoundly disturbing. His teaching gave his enemies some colour for saying not only 'He is dangerous', but 'He is possessed, he is raving. Why listen to him?' (John 10:20).

Far from being conspicuously temperate in food and drink, he was called a gluttonous man and a winebibber; he is said to have miraculously made available many gallons of wine for a wedding party; he constantly described the Kingdom of Heaven in terms of feasting and making merry; and he gave ordinary food a central place on the most solemn occasions, before and even after his resurrection. Far from being a convenient figurehead for political moderates, he truly predicted that his coming would bring not peace but a sword; he warned his followers to expect persecutions and endure without compromise; and he himself died a criminal's death at the hands of the civil power. Far from encouraging detachment in personal relationships, he formed close friendships himself; he was willing to evince warm indignation (Mark 1:41) and fierce anger on occasion; and he was not ashamed to weep or show himself deeply moved (Luke 19:41). Far from advising temperance in the business affairs of this world, he commended the merchant who would sell everything for one longed-for treasure, and gave high praise to the woman who lavished her expensive ointment upon him as a luxurious present. Far from exemplifying a notable moderation in controversy, he called his opponents hypocrites and children of the devil; he made much use of hyperbole and vividly provocative turns of phrase; and when he turned the traders out of the Temple his disciples were reminded of the text, 'Zeal for thy house will consume me'. (John 2:17).

There is of course another side to the picture. One must not forget the teaching about counting the cost, the exhortation to be wise as serpents but harmless as doves, the rebuke to the Sons of Thunder for wanting to call down fire from heaven, the refusal to take a political part, the silence before Pilate. But on balance the Gospels surely give a general impression not of moderation in all things but of enthusiasm. The strong new wine that breaks the old wineskins seems a more apt image for their teaching than the pure milk of the Word.

Nor is this really surprising. 'Moderation' and 'religion' are ideas which have never readily fitted together. To see this truth from the side of moderation is to admit the fact that religion is dangerous. To see it, on the other hand, from the side of religion is to admit that in the last resort moderation is not enough. To insist on moderation in *all* things, even the things that really matter, is to strike a false note that vitiates Shangri-La. It is to preach the false Gospel that to preserve one's detachment and refuse to become deeply committed is a safe and happy way to live.

If temperance is none the less to be counted as a Christian virtue, the ideal of moderation, for all its evident attractiveness to people of good will, cannot be said to supply an adequate interpretation of it. Nor is it the only nor even the most authoritative interpretation available. The Shorter English Dictionary defines temperance as 'rational self-restraint', and these two ideas, reason and control, together form the backbone of the virtue of temperance as traditionally conceived. Perhaps then all we need in the way of re-assessment is to follow the example of modern translators of the Bible and substitute 'self-control' for the older word (Galations 5:23). It may be pointed out that, unlike the ideal of moderation, the ideal of self-control does not collapse when pushed to the limit. We need it as much over the things that really matter as we do over small things. Moreover, if one's doubts about moderation arise from reading the New Testament, one may notice that the Gospel which depicts Christ least of all as a moderate, depicts him most of all as supremely self-controlled (e.g. John 11:42). We may well feel that we have found a genuine indubitable virtue which we can whole-heartedly commend to our contemporaries as both excellent and Christian.

But still dissatisfaction is not removed. How are we to 'commend' self-control? The suggestion is that it should be presented as a more adequate ideal than moderation, an ideal which can therefore be aimed at more unreservedly; and here is the difficulty. We may grant for the moment the adequacy of the ideal, and summon up an admirable picture of the temperate man who is not passion's slave, who can control his appetites and live freely according to choice not impulse. The question is whether this idea can be achieved by being aimed at. It is fair to say that when people *set* themselves to achieve self-control the strong-minded become Rigorists and the weak stumble and go under. It is true that the Rigorist achieves something; one may even say that he achieves self-control; but he achieves it in such a way as to vitiate it as a Christian ideal. He controls himself by reining himself in tightly, by never relenting, by constantly exercising his will. He cannot relax into temperance but only screw himself up to it: instead of being passion's slave he is virtue's slave, cut off from the glorious liberty of the children of God. To commend temperance in this fashion is not to encourage Christian living but to arrange a field-day for Pharisees.

Temperance then, like happiness and originality, appears to be the kind of elusive value which must not be aimed at directly; but perhaps this applies not only to temperance but to all the virtues. Pursued separately, for their own sakes, they tend to lead to frustration or to slavery;

but to point this out is after all only to acknowledge the commonplace Christian doctrine that a man cannot be good in his own strength but only by the power of the Holy Spirit.

Yet the commonplace needs to be acknowledged and indeed emphasised, particularly when we are dealing with a virtue like self-control where Pelagian implications seem built in the very word itself. It is well worth while to stress that we cannot add a cubit to our moral stature by taking thought but only (like good children) by taking sustenance, the kind of sustenance which the Gospel as a whole offers us. If we seek the Kingdom of Heaven first we may expect that 'all these things', not only earthly blessings but goodness and happiness, temperance and all the other virtues, will be added; but we cannot reverse this order. It is made very plain too that seeking the Kingdom is a much more drastic procedure than just trying to be virtuous. It means not living circumspectly, but dying to live, not controlling oneself but losing oneself, not giving up all but the necessities of life but giving up everything only to receive everything back again. Self-control does come into the picture, but it comes in characteristically as a fruit of the Spirit, not as something we can do for ourselves. The attempt to acquire virtues piecemeal can be a way of trying to fend off the total claim.

To try, on the other hand, to accept the total claim is not to repudiate the particular virtues. One is not expected to take a deep plunge into unknown existential depths, but rather to put oneself in the way of becoming the kind of whole person who will be capable of practising recognisable Christian virtues. Surely one of these will be temperance: not a lukewarm kind of moderation, not an inflexible kind of self-control, but the kind of virtue we associate with the idea of tempered steel, a steadiness, a reliability, a suitability for the purpose in hand.

Again we have depicted an admirable quality; and if again a criticism is to be made, this time it will be vagueness. The picture we have drawn is not quite specific enough. It is a little too much like a picture of virtue in general, not of Christian temperance in particular. Yet the idea of Christian temperance has after all a definite content of its own. It is concerned with the right understanding of the material world. At its best temperance is a characteristic attitude towards *things*, an attitude which will often be well described as moderate, an attitude which leads to self-control, but which cannot be completely summed up in either of these ways.

This attitude is, of course, to appreciate these things according to their true status as creatures of God, but it has a double aspect which it is a pity to blur. The material world is 'very good', not just fairly good;

21

but entirely subordinate to people. Christian temperance holds on to both these truths without losing either of them. It is happily exemplified by George Macdonald in a passage quoted by C S Lewis:

> Let me, if I may, be ever welcomed to my room in winter by a glowing hearth, in summer by a vase of flowers; if I may not, let me then think how nice they would be, and bury myself in my work. I do not think that the road to contentment lies in despising what we have not got. Let us acknowledge all good, all delight that the world holds, and be content without it.[10]

Material things, then, are neither to be repudiated nor idolised: they are to be accepted and given up. This is Christian temperance. 'Give and take' is a convenient cliché for temperance in the sense of moderation, but 'take and give' will stand very well as a summary of temperance in the more specifically Christian sense I am trying to describe. Temperance is to acknowledge the material world as God's gift, as raw material for our human wants, to value it and to give it up as occasion arises. Intemperance is to fail to value it or to refuse to give it up. The woman with the alabaster pot was practising temperance: she knew that the ointment was precious and she gave it away freely. When we receive Holy Communion we are practising temperance: we are accepting God's creatures as what they are given for, the pledges of his grace. When we say, 'I believe in the resurrection of the body' we are recognising a kind of divine temperance, acknowledging that the physical world is something to be given up in death and yet worthwhile taking up again in resurrection.

Traditional Virtues Reassessed, pp414-418

Spirit and body

Here, Helen Oppenheimer develops her spiritual concerns in connection with Christ's incarnation, and God's 'findability', from Theology *1990.*

Presence

The slogan that spirit needs body must sound alarming to people reared on the doctrine that God is a spirit 'without body, parts or passions'. It sounds less alarming as popularly expressed by St Teresa: 'Christ has no hands on earth but yours.' We are not trying to pronounce about what God, intrinsically, can or cannot be, but about how God can be found in our world. If the main meaning of presence is physical presence, then a world in which persons, divine or human, can be identified needs to be some kind of physical world.

So we approach the notion of a sacramental universe, a universe in which the physical is capable of being the vehicle of the spiritual. The idea of 'real presence' can be released from its liturgical context and take on a less technical and less polemical meaning. To spell this out, we must first assert that material things can be laden with meaning. To say that God makes a world is to say that God makes matter the bearer of spirit. It is characteristic of human beings, made in God's image, to endow matter with meaning: in artistic creation, in ceremonial, and not least in everyday activities, such as the giving of gifts. Material things are 'raw material' for spiritual significance. Conversely, spirit can be embodied, made flesh, and needs to be made flesh in order to be findable.

These ideas are drawn togther in Teilhard de Chardin's powerful image of the Mass on the world.[11] He found himself in the Steppes, with neither bread, wine nor altar for the exercise of his priestly function of invoking the particular presence of God. So he made the whole earth his altar, and for the elements of bread and wine he offered 'all the labours and sufferings of the world' for God's consecration.

'Consecration' is the notion to which all this has been leading. The sacramental principle is the principle that matter is capable of consecration. Each human being is a kind of walking sacrament: which is what we properly mean by saying that human life is 'sacred'.

One human being, we believe, has a unique consecration to carry the presence of God. The concept of incarnation is at the centre of this sacramental understanding. To justify this high Christology would need long arguments, but an idea can be partly justified by doing the work one asks of it. Incarnation is the answer to a question, the persistent question of God's findability. But to provide such an answer incarnation cannot be a 'bolt from the blue'. Incarnation would hardly make sense if it stood alone. The Word is made flesh in Jesus of Nazareth, but if God had no other manifestations, we should have no way of knowing what we were trying to talk about. Incarnation needs to be backed by a wider, but not too vague, recognition of God's presence before and after the coming of Christ. 'In many and various ways God spoke of old to our fathers by the prophets; but in these last days he has spoken to us by a Son'. (Hebrews 1:1-2). Of course it is a metaphor to say that God speaks, but it is better to take it too seriously than not seriously enough. God's Word, to be heard by us, is embodied in some way or other. His ancient people were aware of many theophanies.

When in the twentieth century we are challenged by the absence of God, we speak of God coming in Christ; but we need not suppose that God has left us for nearly two thousand years without a sign. If we have reason to believe that Jesus Christ was in a strong sense the embodied presence of God, then to call the Church Christ's Body and the extension of the incarnation is to move into metaphor but not into nonsense. We should not be afraid of metaphor. What matters is that metaphor is tied to reality. There was a human body and the body was killed. Whatever we go on to say about the rising again of that body, there is something literally physical at the heart of our faith.

To live one's own life and die one's own death in the name of Christ, even to hope to rise again through his power, has more than attenuated ghostly meaning. Part of its meaning is that we can be incorporated in the community which has the pledge of his continuing presence. 'Body' is only one metaphor for characterising that community. 'Temple' and 'city' are others. 'Vine' is another and so is 'olive' (Romans 11:24); and sometimes the organic and the inorganic metaphors run into each other (Ephesians 2:20-21). But the fact to which the metaphors try to point, that this community is founded upon God's presence in the world, is an assertion which is mysterious but not fanciful. Language is not stretched nonsensically to say that the Church is the body which is in touch, and that by partaking in the life of the Church we keep in touch with the God we worship and with one another. So we are incorporated as members of the Body. This is how talk about corporate agency is rooted.

Nourishment

The Eucharist, 'the' sacrament, is no magical rite but the continuation of the findability of our God, of God's real presence. There is no need to be fundamentalist about the details of the New Testament stories to believe that the Lord who lived and died and rose, ate and drank with his followers, established his right to give his word and his power to fulfil it, and left them this way of keeping in touch with him. Austin Farrer put it like this: 'He gave them the sacrament by eating with them; he made it their salvation by his death.'[12] The ideas of embodiment, presence and nourishment fit together here. Without belittling other aspects which have meant much to our fellow Christians, we may stress the continuity between the table-fellowship of Christ's ministry and the Last Supper; the Last Supper and the Eucharist; the Eucharist and the promised heavenly banquet in the Kingdom.

There is a danger of proving too much, of slipping into superstitious magic, or into legalism which constricts means of grace into 'proper channels'. We do not need a rigid doctrine of the Eucharist but a sacramental understanding of the creation. Teilhard de Chardin's Mass on the world is miles away from arguments about what constitutes consecration, and not far from the Quaker's refusal to use special sacraments lest they should seem to restrict God's presence in the whole created universe.

The Eucharist is not central for all of us. The Friend finds God's presence especially in the 'inner Light'. There are other believers for whom the ordinary nourishment of Christians is the Word. Two things need saying. First, that these sturdy unsacramental Christians do not get away from embodiment: the world must be heard or read. Second, the point of sacraments is not that they should be compulsory but that they should be available. They are an answer to the challenge that spirit needs body. The Eucharist is given, not forced upon us. For many Christians the liturgy in which the Church continues to 'do this', to break bread in continuity with the Lord's own breaking of bread, is the most straightforward case of the findability of the presence of God.

Members

The upshot is that God's people are identifiable, not by their pronouncements but by their corporateness. Their identity is theological not political. Instead of the hopeless task of trying to speak of their moral and social concerns with one voice, they have the greater but hopeful responsibility of being the presence, the findability, of God upon earth.

God can be found, reliably though not exclusively, in Christ's body on earth. Christians are identified by being incorporated in that body. The responsibility is onerous, because, whatever they say, they say in Christ's name. It is not their virtues nor the shape of their opinions but their belonging which makes them Christians. Christians are people who in one way or another have taken upon themselves the name of Christ.

This definition makes Christian *dissension* worse, because opponents cannot be simply repudiated and the body itself is distracted; but Christian *diversity* is justified because it is who we are, not what we say, that gives us our identity. We have roots not a platform.

The Church may or may not need to be told to 'keep out of politics'. On the one hand, the confidence that our Christian identity does not stand or fall with our opinions makes available to us the whole of human life, including politics and even party politics, to engage ourselves in with enthusiasm and detachment. There are no 'no go' areas for Christians or even for Churches, any more than there are for the God they represent. But on the other hand, we risk taking God's name in vain. Because we represent God in everything we do or fail to do, it is the more important not to imagine that we have God in our pocket. If we become identified with plainly self-interested policies or with one side of a controversial argument, that is how we are presenting God to the world. Our inertness or our ferocity is the way God's presence is mediated to our contemporaries; and a very distorting medium either of these can be. Our diversity can be much less misleading. The word 'many-faceted' comes to mind. The Church may be a prism breaking up the white light of God's dazzling majesty.

The fact that Christians are found among their contemporaries doing their human best is not a feeble accommodation to worldly standards nor an anonymous humanism, but a proper exercise of responsibility. They have no need to claim a monopoly of decency, integrity or goodwill; or even of sacrificial love. They have no need to decry other people's inspirations nor to dress up their own intuitions as inspiration. What distinguishes Christians is an answerability to someone beyond themselves, who is ultimately in control: not a 'hot line' but a source of nourishment empowering them to make their characteristic and responsible contributions.

Theology 93, pp133-141

Christian flourishing

Here we have the notion of 'sacramentality' in effect re-explored and reinterpreted in original ways. In Called to be Saints *which follows it, Helen Oppenheimer reminds us of our vocation and our aspirations.*

It may be useful to distinguish four logical stages in the development of Christian thought about flourishing. The first stage is a naive but wholesome grasp of the principle that human happiness matters, that morality is about happiness. The kingdom of heaven is above all utterly desirable, a pearl of great price, worth anything to achieve. The comprehension of this link between man's well-being and his well-doing reaches back well behind the Gospels into the whole Old Testament. It may be amply illustrated from the Psalter: the godly man is 'like a tree planted by the water-side: that will bring forth his fruit in due season' (Psalm 1). He only has to 'taste and see, how gracious the Lord is . . . The lions do lack, and suffer hunger: but they who seek the Lord shall want no manner of thing that is good' (Psalm 34). He may be temporarily hesitant because of the sins and offences of his youth and the present power of his enemies, but he trusts that 'His soul shall dwell at ease: and his seed shall inherit the land' (Psalm 25). This is because righteousness is rooted in the way things are. It goes with, not against, the grain of the universe.

Some of these examples leave it uncertain whether the flourishing of the righteous is being assumed or promised. The second stage is already implicit and constantly emerges into explicitness. It is a frank empirical puzzlement about why the facts so often seem to deny any such link between goodness and happiness. The wicked flourish like a green bay tree (Psalm 37) and God stands far off (Psalm 10) or even sleeps while his people are killed all the day long (Psalm 44). To this recurring problem there are at this stage three basic simple answers: to deny that there is any God, so that the problem never arises; to deny the empirical facts and persuade oneself that one has never seen the righteous forsaken nor his seed begging their bread (Psalm 37); and the answer which has frequently prevailed historically, to put the emphasis upon the next world so that to do good here is to flourish not necessarily now but hereafter. This last view has proved regrettably corruptible, in converse directions. On the one hand, 'reward' constantly tends to decline into 'sanctions' again. The longing for a good time coming when right shall prevail has sometimes produced a thoroughly materialistic and even vindictive conception of the way in which God is to set the record straight. On the other hand, the hope for pie in the sky notoriously tends to encourage believers to take up a negative or destructive attitude towards human flourishing, their own or other people's, in this life. 'Otherworldliness' has been directly responsible for much human misery; and moreover it plays straight into the hands of the rigid humanist utilitarian, who can look no further than immediate human happiness in making moral judgments.

The next stage is to look somewhat deeper than any straightforward linkage of goodness and material flourishing, to refuse the simple answers, and to find joy, blessing and the glory of God not only in a world to come but in the sufferings and struggles of this present world. Such a view has good claim to be regarded as characteristically Christian. It expresses itself in hints in the Old Testament (especially Isaiah 53; it sorts well too with Psalm 22 read in the light of the Passion) and comes out fully in the New: in the Beatitudes and especially in the closing chapters of the fourth Gospel, reaching a climax in the high-priestly prayer of Christ. The conception of Christ as reigning from the Cross and his followers as truly flourishing when they are united with his sufferings is having a notable revival today and many Christians for whom the next world seems to have receded entirely out of reach are able to find inspiration in it. It is a kind of immanentist understanding of 'God's will', as opposed to a transcendentalist conception of 'doing God's commands' as something to be set in opposition to 'maximising happiness'.

Yet this view in turn is corruptible, or at least partial. It is a gospel of the Cross not the Resurrection, with all the intellectual attraction of a good paradox, but tempting one to ignore one set of facts: not the evils of the world, far from it, but the affirmative strand in the actual gospels, the basis for believing in Christ at all. It reduces Christian morality in scope, by again divorcing it effectually from the concept of human flourishing. Christianity does go by way of suffering to glory, but to stick in the suffering is as false as to ignore it. To take the Man of Sorrows as the paradigm for Christian ethics is to substitute the falsity of a near-masochism for the falsity of complacency.

There is a moral not only a tactical danger in the Christian Church seeming to acquire a vested interest in the troubles of the world. The old otherworldliness said glibly that human miseries do not matter: the new this-worldliness appears to say that they are all that matters, that the

Almighty is only interested in squalor and social problems, that he is not so much a god of the gaps as a god of the glooms, that since he is willing to be present in the evil we must not look for him mightily to prevail over it.

Such a view needs, if the facts can support it, the Pauline corrective, that though 'the whole creation groaneth, and travaileth in pain together until now' yet 'the sufferings of this present time are not worthy to be compared with the glory which shall be revealed in us' (Romans 8:18). If this is naive in the last resort, so be it. It certainly needs a substantial apologetic; but if it cannot be maintained, Christianity is a shadow of itself.

If it *can* be maintained one may begin to foreshadow a Christian view of flourishing, which will need to be subtle in its linking and balancing of material and spiritual, this-worldly and other-worldly. The plain earthly meaning of flourishing will not have to be repudiated but rather transmuted into a still empirical but more profound concept of blessedness, to which the key will be idea of fulfilment.

Religious Studies 5, pp163-171

Called to be saints

If Christian morality can rightly be grounded in allegiance the New Testament assumption that all Christians are called to be saints is not as fantastic as it sounds. In all humility any Christian can take seriously the prospect of becoming holy, not by self-defeating effort but as the fruit of the Spirit.

It is a fact that to try to give up one's self is to land in moral and logical contradiction. Actually to give oneself up to something more interesting and important, to forget oneself without any self-conscious renunciation, is a much more common experience than Christians, preoccupied with 'being good', are apt to realise; though artists and lovers, parents and patriots can all testify to it. It is after all something as natural as this that Christianity both asks of one and enables one to perform. One is not set a moral syllabus to work through: one is taken out of oneself by being invited to respond to the most profound and comprehensive claim imaginable, the love of God.

Up to a point the gaiety of this approach needs to be emphasised. To think about oneself and one's rights and duties is tiring and boring. To be released from this slavery even for a little while and to begin to behave naturally as a child of God, is a way of relaxing and being refreshed: a kind of badly-needed holiday from oneself. In the end one can, I hope, even come to value oneself rightly, as the person God has made who means something to others, leaving behind the persistent limited subject of a kind of silent autobiography that one usually finds it all too easy to become.

But of course the gaiety is not the whole picture. To think about the love of God is to think about the Cross, and to think honestly about the Cross is to repent, though not in the sense of morbidly blaming oneself for what was done nearly two thousand years ago. One comes to realise what a world it was to which Christ came, and how much of a piece our own reactions, positive and negative, are with the reactions of the people he confronted directly. There is no need to say 'It would happen like that today'. It is enough to realise that we still act and think in the ways which made it happen then. We cannot but feel ourselves unworthy of this love and therefore our response to it, the response which takes us out of ourselves, must be solemn as well as joyful. Giving up oneself is a kind of death. It can be spontaneous and natural, not self-conscious and strained, but still it cannot in the circumstances be altogether light-hearted and gay.

From this kind of thought about Christian doctrine, specifically Christian morality can take its rise. As a test case, take the most famous of all Christian precepts: 'Love your enemies'. Is this not a contradiction in terms? Does it offer any authentic method of handling our natural human revengefulness? Christians are often persuaded to forgive on the tenuous ground that their enemy really means well or that gentleness will soften his heart, and are then bitterly disappointed when these hopes turn out to be quite unrealistic.

It needs to be said that the teaching of Christ is much tougher than this. He did not say, 'Your enemy is no enemy at all,' nor 'Forgive him to make him nice again', but 'Only so can you be children of your heavenly Father, who makes his sun rise on good and bad alike'. (Matthew 5:45). The Christian Church has been able to fill in the sequel, for these were not just words: 'While we were yet sinners Christ died for us'. (Romans 5:8). This means that the ground of Christian forgiveness is not any false idealism about human nature but the sober reflection, 'How dare we be more unforgiving than God?'

If somebody strikes one on the right cheek, or more probably in the modern world on the wing of one's beloved and gleaming motor car, the extension of one's personality, it seems in the fury of the moment just outrageous to be told that one ought not to be angry and resentful. That sort of behaviour ought to be punished: to pretend the contrary is simply hypocritical. Often the best one can do is to say grimly, 'I'd like to have the law on him but my Christian duty is to forgive him'. This leads to frustration for oneself, for duty is ill-adapted to control feelings, and at the same time offers a very unacceptable kind of forgiveness to one's adversary. But if in this kind of situation one considers, not sentimentally but frankly, that Christ died for dangerous drivers and for people like oneself, one's own rights and duties begin after all to seem curiously insignificant. One finds oneself able to say, 'Who am I to make a fuss about a wrong: the question is, what is the best thing to do next?' This is unforced and realistic, and does not equate Christian love with a particularly unpleasant kind of duty. Paradoxically enough one's duty may well turn out to be to report the accident; but the sting of bitterness has been drawn.

Christian morality, then, is a response to a given situation, not a special set of values or of supernatural commandments. In the strength of his allegiance to God, not by making greater and greater efforts, the Christian can so surpass himself that his conception of duty is transformed. He is inclined to say that this idea makes sense of his moral life; but now he must be careful not to go too fast.

To suggest that the moral lives of unbelievers fail to make sense harks back to the false understanding of Christian morality which tries to keep virtue as a monopoly of Christians. It is untrue that only Christians can surpass themselves. People who go and visit the elderly, teachers who give extra time to slow pupils, neighbours who look after children when their mother is in hospital, people who ignore better-paid jobs to become social workers, volunteers who undertake dangerous life-saving tasks: all these are doing more than could reasonably be required of them, but they are frequently doing it simply as well-disposed human beings, not particularly as Christians. They may easily not be pious people at all: the word that comes readily to mind to describe them is 'humane'. Nor are they extraordinary exceptions. We are grateful for such conduct, but not amazed. To some extent we take it for granted, for without it human life as we know it would hardly be possible.

Yet human nature also has its dark side. One is seldom able to take these admirable ways of behaving entirely for granted. Even in the midst of family life, still more in one's relationships with the outside world, one is constantly obliged for fall back upon justice. Sometimes even justice is a struggle. One is certainly in no position to demand anything more as a matter of right; and yet one knows all the time that it is going beyond justice that makes life worthwhile.

This is where the Christian Gospel comes in. It finds us as human beings able to appreciate but not entitled to expect of one another the quality of life which I have called 'transcendent'. It offers us this quality made actual in the life of Christ, and the possibility of a relationship with Him which can make it actual in our own. For a Christian the idea of 'transcendence', which he can learn to recognise from all the things that matter to him in the world, is perfectly fulfilled and indeed itself transcended in the love of God. Without God the things which engage one's personality, though still entirely valid in themselves, would be miscellaneous, unrelated, lacking what one might call a focus. This is the legitimate sense in which one can describe Christianity as 'making sense of morality'.

If there were no focus one would have to abide by it. It certainly must not be contended that we cannot get on without a focus and that therefore there must be one. That would be an entirely illegitimate 'argument for the existence of God'. None the less it is fair to say that Christianity, seen in this way as a system of personal relationships crowned by the love of God, has a sort of cogency which is profoundly satisfying not only to the emotions but to the intellect. The idea of Heaven becomes credible, not as the reward of merit but as the consummation of all we have been trying to attain in all our personal commitments, where we find all we have been looking for in everything we have valued. Far from being a corruption of our moral endeavours, it is the achievement of their goal. So presented, the Christian hope is not an illegitimate prop to morality which needs to be removed so that the building can be seen properly, but the keystone of the arch. The sceptic, often for reasons which one must respect, believes that there is no such keystone to be had and that such an ultimate fulfilment of relationships is not to be expected; but this means that his morality lacks final integration.

The Character of Christian Morality, pp72-76

Jesus Christ his only Son our Lord who shall come to judge

A slightly revised version of a talk given on March 29, 1992 for the BBC Radio 4 Sunday evening programme Seeds of faith, *in a Lenten series of women speaking about the Creed. The talks were illustrated with music and readings: this one included a medley of familiar hymns at the beginning: the 'Dies irae' from Verdi's* Requiem; *and 'Et in unum Dominum Jesum Christum' from Bach's* Mass in B minor *at the end. Here, Helen Oppenheimer re-emphasises her convictions about how Christ relates to our humanity, both women and men.*

Christians believe that Jesus Christ is the *Son* of God. Ought women to be bothered by this and feel left out? Let me say that I believe this doctrine and I do not think we need see it as sexist; but none the less the question is serious. I am speaking, not as an out-and-out feminist, but as someone who believes that women are people and that this obvious fact has been much neglected down the centuries. Human beings have got into bad habits of thinking and speaking. 'Mankind' strictly means both men and women; but saying 'man' and 'men' for hundreds of years has consolidated a tacit assumption that men are the real thing while women are somehow extra, even if not inferior.

Add to that the He-man and Superman ideal which merrily says 'Bang, you're dead' and looks on the kind gentle virtues as sissy, and you can see why some of us think it is time for some changes. Both women and men are learning to think and speak differently. I have to say that this is bound to be painful as well as beneficial. If you think, as I do, that words and speech are among the great glories of humanity, it will hurt when ancient ways of speaking are spoilt. Our time is a time of transition and times of transition are apt to be quite uncomfortable.

So what are we to do with traditional Christian language about the Son of God? If we are watching out for sexism so keenly that anything which mentions 'man' or 'Lord' puts us off, both men and women will be the poorer. I think it is also an impoverishment if heroism gets a bad name. Human beings are not made to be *all* gentleness and compassion. We cannot always manage without strength and certainly not without courage. When I see children thrilled by the idea of a Superman who comes zooming to the rescue, I want to channel this enthusiasm, not just quench it.

One thing which feminism risks losing is a great deal of good poetry. Let me give you two quite different examples: first, a verse from the Anglo-

Saxon poem 'The dream of the Rood'. As a twentieth century woman I do not want to deafen my ears either to its rhythms or to its values:

> *Then the young Hero – it was God Almighty -*
> *Strong and steadfast, stripped himself for battle;*
> *He climbed up on the high gallows, constant in his purpose*
> *Mounted it in sight of many, mankind to ransom.*[13]

Secondly, here is a poem called 'Christ in the universe', written at the turn of the century by Alice Meynell.[14] She makes no attempt to use inclusive language. Must we therefore write it off?

> *With this ambiguous earth*
> *His dealings have been told us. These abide:*
> *The signal to a maid, the human birth,*
> *The lesson, and the young Man crucified.*
>
> *But not a star of all*
> *The innumerable host of stars has heard*
> *How he administered this terrestrial ball.*
> *Our race have kept their Lord's entrusted Word . . .*
>
> *No planet knows that this*
> *Our wayside planet, carrying land and wave,*
> *Love and life multiplied, and pain and bliss,*
> *Bears, as chief treasure, one forsaken grave.*
>
> *Nor, in our little day,*
> *May his devices with the heavens be guessed,*
> *His pilgrimage to thread the Milky Way,*
> *Or his bestowals there be manifest.*
>
> *But, in the eternities,*
> *Doubtless we shall compare together, hear*
> *A million alien Gospels, in what guise,*
> *He trod the Pleiades, the Lyre, the Bear.*
>
> *O be prepared, my soul!*
> *To read the inconceivable, to scan*
> *The million forms of God those stars unroll*
> *When, in our turn, we show to them a Man.*

When I was young and began to go to Holy Communion I just accepted that solemn moment in the service when we said 'And was made man'. It never entered my head to understand it as 'made *male*'. What I most want to say today is this: the centre of Christian belief is that God became *human* and lived a human life. So I do not want to rewrite the Creeds; but they still need explaining. Maybe we shall have to take up saying, 'And was made human'. It will not sound so good but it should mean the same. Some women though go beyond this and hanker after the notion of God being made woman. To me, *that is* sexist.

In my youth it did not occur to me to worry that God came as a man and not as a woman. There were different problems then. Older people were inclined to think of Jesus Christ simply as God walking about on earth, knowing Who He was and dealing divinely with everyone He met. The 'He' would almost always have a capital H. The message was that He knew all along that everything was under control. I found myself thinking, 'It was all very well for Him. He knew his sufferings were going to be over on the third day. But what help is that to all of us?' We were told about the cross all right, but only to din into us how human sin caused it. It was not thought right to point out to children that life was not 'all very well' for Jesus at all. He was not calm and stoical but agonisingly afraid; and the Gospels do not suggest that Jesus always saw God's purposes clearly.

Christians now have a firmer grasp of the idea that Jesus Christ was a real human being who had to grow up, find things out for himself and sometimes feel his way. He could suffer emotionally as well as physically. So in writing 'he' with a small h, I believe we have a better idea of what the Creed means.

What makes and keeps me a Christian is being able to believe that the living and holy God, the Maker of everything, came into the world and experienced at first hand what it is like to be a creature. The Lord is risen indeed: but first he really died. We are not expected to worship a God who sits up on high rewarding or punishing people for the way they cope with conditions their Creator has never faced. We need never say, 'It's all very well for Him'. To me the very heart of the Gospel is the fact that Jesus on the cross experienced the ancient desolation which made him cry out, 'My God, my God, why hast thou forsaken me?' This means that the God we pray to even knows what it is like to lose touch with God.

Some of the suffering human beings undergo, in this world which God made, seem unbearable. Christianity does not offer any guarantee that the worst will not happen. The Christian faith is that when the worst does happen, as sometimes it will, God is there; and that then, on the other side of death, there is rising again.

Now a God who becomes human and knows the meaning of fear, and even of loss of faith, could be a man or a woman. I think it would be sexist to mind which: except that we must mind about historical truth and we know that in fact Jesus was a man. I can see various practical reasons why this made sense.

A Daughter of God could have taken up the cause of women, but the Son of God could do something more fundamental. He could be a model of how a man need not take advantage of power. He could show to sexist human beings how women should be treated, as real people to be taken seriously. Just look at the Gospels and see how straightforwardly Jesus talked to women. He neither dominates nor patronises. Many of his followers ever since have failed to live up to his revolutionary ordinariness.

Since Jesus was not threatened by women I feel no need to be threatened by the fact that he was a man. I believe that women may happily accept Jesus Christ as the representative *human being* – but something follows here. If Jesus can represent women as well as men, then when human beings are to represent *him*, women as well as men are eligible. I am sorry to say that some opponents of women priests have been denying this. Their argument is counter-productive. I used to think that women ought to go on being patient a while longer rather than bring such disunity upon the Church: until I heard it argued that only a man could be a priest because only a man could represent Jesus. This misunderstanding of the maleness of Jesus is serious. It casts too much doubt on the full humanity of women to be tolerated even in the name of unity. It is now urgent to make it clear to men and women that 'he was made man' truly means 'he was made human'.

Some people, even some women, seem to think that Jesus is male because God is male and females are somehow unworthy. Other people would like a more motherly God and feel at odds with Christianity for not providing us with a female Saviour. Feminism has opened up these questions and we cannot just ignore them. But I am certain that there is more to human life, and more to the Christian faith, than maleness and femaleness. If it is all reduced to arguments about gender, both men and women will be diminished. Rather than being an out-and-out Christian feminist, I call myself a Christian humanist: someone who believes, as a Christian, that *human beings* matter, that women and men in all their variety are children of God.

Julian of Norwich was a great theologian and mystic who was unfussed by being a woman. She called Jesus our mother and just as unselfconsciously she called him Lord. When I first read her *Showings* I was neither impressed nor shocked by the one any more than by the other. I certainly felt included among her fellow Christians for whose benefit, she emphasises, her book was written.

> *And with this our good Lord said most joyfully: See how I love you, as if he had said, my darling, behold and see your Lord, your God, who is your Creator and your endless joy; see your own brother, your saviour; my child, behold and see what delight and bliss I have in your salvation, and for my love rejoice with me.*

> *And for my greater understanding, these blessed words were said: See how I love you, as if he had said, behold and see that I loved you so much, before I died for you, that I wanted to die for you. And now I have died for you, and willingly suffered what I could. And now all my bitter pain and my hard labour is turned into everlasting joy and bliss for me and for you . . .*

> *This is the understanding, as simply as I can say it, of those blessed words: See how I loved you. Our Lord revealed this to make us glad and joyful.*[15]

What I hope feminism will do for us is enable more women to enter into and contribute to the full heritage of humanity. Women have characteristic insights to offer. I am not at all sure that they are less ferocious than men, but I think they are often less legalistic. Women who bring up children learn from experience that claiming rights can be destructive and that human beings are cherished by generosity. That could be a woman's message but it is also at the centre of the Christian message. Need women grudge the fact that these words were written by a man about a man?

> *Have this mind among yourselves, which you have in Christ Jesus, who, though he was in the form of God, did not count equality with God a thing to be grasped, but emptied himself, taking the form of a servant, being born in the likeness of men. And being found in human form he humbled himself and became obedient unto death, even death on a cross. Therefore God has highly exalted him and bestowed on him the name which is above every name, that at the name of Jesus every knee should bow, in heaven and on earth and under the earth, and every tongue confess that Jesus Christ is Lord, to the glory of God the Father.*[16]

In this letter by St Paul to the Philippians surely Christ's maleness is beside the point: what counts is God becoming human. Some feminists want to put a question mark against the title 'Lord': but surely that is defeatist. Must I cut myself off from all those human beings who call Jesus 'Lord' in reverent directness? I do not want to address him just as

'Jesus', not only becuase it sounds familiar but because for me it suggests a sort of sweet piety I cannot get on with.

The meanings of words shift. Nowadays people do not say to one another 'Yes, Lord' meaning 'Yes, sir'. They do not address 'Lord Somebody' simply as 'Lord'. Saying 'men' to mean 'people' does call up a picture of males: but we can use 'Lord' almost as a proper name and let it quietly shed 'patriarchal' associations. It need not be sexist unless we make it so.

So I can be glad to use the prayer of Richard Baxter:

> *Keep me, O Lord, while I tarry on this earth, in a daily serious seeking after thee and in a believing affectionate walking with thee; that when thou comest, I may be found not hiding my talent, nor left asleep with my lamp unfurnished; but waiting and longing for my Lord, my glorious God, for ever and ever.*[17]

To pray that prayer you do not have to be the least bit of a mystic, but you do need some idea of what you think Jesus was like. He does not talk to us but we know quite a lot about how some of his contemporaries saw him. The picture may be unexpected: 'The Son of man came eating and drinking, and they say, "Behold a glutton and a drunkard, a friend of tax collectors and sinners!"'[18]

Lord Hailsham developed this idea in his autobiography, *The door wherein I went:*[19]

> *What exactly was Jesus like to meet? . . . Having asked this question, I looked at the Gospel again, and quite suddenly a new portrait seems to stare at me out of the pages. I had never previously thought of a laughing, joking Jesus, physically strong and active, fond of good company and a glass of wine, telling funny stories . . . applying nicknames to his friends, and holding his companions spellbound with his talk. And yet, it is a very odd thing that we do not think of him in these terms. Granted that we are told to think of him as having every perfection of human nature, do we not ordinarily regard a sense of humour and high spirits as among the most desirable attributes a man can have? . . . The tragedy of the Cross was not that they crucified a melancholy figure, full of moral precepts, ascetic and gloomy . . . What they crucified was a young man, vital, full of life and the joy of it, the Lord of life itself . . . someone so utterly attractive that people followed him for the sheer fun of it . . . The man of sorrows and acquainted with grief was in himself and before his passion utterly and divinely joyous.*

If we emphasise the delightfulness of Jesus Christ, are we presumptuous? One meaning of 'Lord' has always been that he is to be our judge, before whom we poor sinners can only beg for mercy. Nobody expressed this strand in our tradition more superbly than Verdi, in his picture of the Day of Wrath in the *Requiem*. As music, this is magnificent: as Christian theology, it will not do. The idea of wretched cringing subjects beseeching their Lord for pity, even when it does justice to what human beings deserve, is an inadequate picture of the mercy of God as shown in Jesus.

In the gospel there is toughness and there is even fear, but surely the most telling picture we have of Jesus as judge is of Jesus under arrest, forsaken and denied: 'And the Lord turned and looked at Peter. And Peter remembered the word of the Lord, how he had said to him, "Before the cock crows today, you will deny me three times". And he went out and wept bitterly.'[20]

To realise how we look in God's eyes *is* judgement: and can be the basis of restoration. Every reader of that story has known that Peter became the Rock on whom the Church was built. God's dramatic Day of Wrath is a shallow notion in comparison. It would be nice to think of this as a woman's understanding, learnt from the experience of dealing with beloved naughty children: but women cannot claim a monopoly of insight.

Jesus in the Gospels is gentle and tough, friendly and fierce, witty and serious; but always, from his birth to his rising from the tomb, he is unexpected. His contemporaries never had him taped and nor have we. Whatever God's second coming to judge the world may turn out to be like, it will not be what *we* expect, any more than God's coming as the carpenter at Nazareth was what people expected then. Surely God will always surprise us.

There is a poem by Edwin Muir[21] which captures this idea: whether we are looking for God, or think we have found God, or have even given up hope, in the end we are not going to find but be found.

The Question
Will you, sometime, who have sought so long and seek
Still in the slowly darkening hunting ground,
Catch sight some ordinary month or week
Of that strange quarry you scarcely thought you sought –
Yourself, the gatherer gathered, the finder found,
The buyer, who would buy all, in bounty bought –
And perch in pride on the princely hand, at home,
And there, the long hunt over, rest and roam?

Theology 96, pp437-444

Heaven

The chapter concludes with a passage from Looking Before and After *– the flourishing, fulfilment, delight and sacramental feasting of heaven.*

Heaven is play and maturity. It is body and spirit. It is love and fulfilment. We need not blur these contrasts, but hope to reconcile them.

For reconciling play and maturity, the image of re-birth helps. It suggests a kind of growing up into childhood, the innocence of a fresh start with the capability of a new stage. We have to be careful with the notion of innocence, as Christians have too often been thought to glorify immaturity and childishness. The innocence we need to fit us for eternal life is not naivety but the innocence which makes a contrast with blasé cynicism.

What children are innocent of is looking at everything with an eye to something else, whether economic or social. They live in the present, spontaneously and wholeheartedly. They know that happiness is right; and the happiness of children is literally heavenly. Yet we are not to imagine that children are all alike. There is not one characteristic 'child-likeness' to which we must all conform.

What we all have in common is that we cannot return to childhood by going backwards. To reach our new life we have to go on through death to rebirth. Death means letting go of everything, and for most of us that is a struggle. The best meaning of 'dying daily' is not sternly mortifying ourselves but making a start on the necessary offering up of what we are now: getting ahead, as it were, with something which will have to be done thoroughly in the end.

If we are acquainted with any saints, we may feel that they have begun their resurrection ahead of time, reconciling childhood and maturity. Their 'unselfishness' is not lack of interest in little things but a kind of straightforward appreciation of essentials. They give us a kind of preview of what human life could be if it were restored to us set free of the ugly muddle grown-up people have normally accumulated.

A Christian heaven must also be able to reconcile body and spirit. The physical universe is surely not a dead end, but somehow or other will turn out to have been raw material for the ultimate purpose of God. There are haunting suggestions in the Pauline epistles that nothing will be left out of the final reconciliation, since 'all things hold together' in Christ who is 'the firstborn of all creation' as well as 'the firstborn from the dead' (Colossians 1:15-20). The rebirth image is especially telling, for the picture of the whole creation 'groaning in travail together until now' seems so true as to be hardly a metaphor. Is it only wishful thinking to hope that one day all nature will indeed be 'set free from its bondage'? (Romans 8:8-24). These ideas have a robust tenacity which is not just starry-eyed. St Paul was no silly dreamer; and on the other hand there can be defeatist un-wishful thinking as obstinate as superstition.

Even physics takes its disciples well beyond sceptical common sense nowadays. If science is allowed to stretch our minds, theology is not to be ruled out just because it is wonderful. What we need for keeping our feet on the ground is a solid respect for real facts: our own embodiment, our dependence upon a physical context, the capacity of material things to serve as a vehicle for 'spirit'; the insistent awareness of many down-to-earth people that earth is not everything; the tradition we have inherited of a God who makes and saves. The notion of an ultimately sacramental universe in which not bread and wine only but the whole physical world will be consecrated as an 'outward and visible sign of an inward and spiritual grace' seems to give us a clue to reality rather than contradicting our experience.

The reconciliation of love and fulfilment is the most important because it is the reconciliation of each other. It ought to follow straight on from the unity of body and spirit. There would be no point in emphasising our embodiment or the sacramental character of the material world in which we are placed unless we were placed in it together and were to find our fulfilment by 'keeping in touch'. Whatever heaven is, it surely is not the flight of the alone to the Alone, if this world is in any way a preparation for it. If a person is a 'pattern of lovability', being a person has everything to do with relationships.

Heaven forbid that we should be carried away at this point by sentimentality. Realism tells us how far we are from heaven now. Fulfilment for ourselves and love of other people are still desperately at odds. Conflict, not Christian love, seems to be fundamental to our attempts to shape our lives. Human happiness is not just unequally spread but often positively based upon recalcitrant unfairness. We cannot pretend that people's interests are easily harmonised. Short cuts to heavenly peace are selfish or foolish or both.

What we have to encourage us cannot be short cuts, but foretastes. There are aspects of life as we know it that allow us to see that in principle fulfilment need not be 'mine' to be snatched from you, and love need not be 'yours' to be denied to me. Most of us can at least see what it is like to be truly pleased by someone else's pleasure or saddened by someone else's sadness. Human affections are not so corrupt that this equation has to be too difficult for them. Some people, lovers and parents for instance, can make a start with the sum already worked out for them.

An easy lesson in the heavenly mathematics is giving a present to a friend. Giving and taking just do not have to be distinct and opposite. The happiness of a gift is not a happiness handed over from one person to another, less for him, more for her, but a reciprocal happiness growing out of the giving. Even when the gift is what we nowadays call a sacrifice, an offering that hurts, the happiness for both giver and recipient which will be harvested in the end will have something to do with reciprocal gladness and nothing to do with 'quid pro quo'. A real gift, small or large, is indeed a means of grace, and the grace flows both ways if it can.

The best images of heaven are images of hospitality. The idea of the heavenly banquet where God is our Host recurs throughout the New Testament and appeals to us at many levels: nourishment, pleasure, the exercise of skills, fun, formality, reward, welcome, reunion, celebration, offering and gratitude. This image of heaven as a feast is sacramental through and through. It is not at all a legalistic image, but nor is it undemanding. We may be 'well-drest' (George Herbert, *Prayer is the Church's Banquet*) but we are not in uniform. Each of us is individually invited, and given the chance to enjoy each other's company. And we have to add: none of us has the right to walk in and demand service. The whole delight of the gathering is the limitless and marvellous generosity of the Host.

When we have encouraged ourselves with positive pictures to overcome our faint-heartedness it is time, not to dwell upon them but to put them carefully away in the back of our minds in case they should turn into idols. People who simply want to rebuild the agreeable life they know in heaven are, precisely, worldly. People who give themselves over to fantasies to compensate for the unhappy life they know are falsely 'other-worldly'. People who discount other people's earthly troubles and promise them heaven as a panacea or a placebo are putting themselves gravely under judgement. None of these are noticeably following the Lord who set his face to go to Jerusalem and found no short cut to by-pass the Cross. There is a great deal that we can rightly and hopefully tell ourselves and one another about resurrection; but always for Christians it must be triumph over death not escape from death.

Looking Before and After, pp145-149

SELECT BIBLIOGRAPHY

'Head and Members: the Priest and the Community he Serves', from ed. G R Dunstan, *The Sacred Ministry*, London: SPCK, 1970, pp400-408.

Marriage, London: Mowbray, 1990.

'Grievances' *Theology* 91 (1988) pp33-38.

'Temperance' from ed. A R Vidler, *Traditional Virtues Reassessed*, London: SPCK, 1969.

'Spirit and body', *Theology* 93 (1990) pp133-141.

'Christian flourishing' *Religious Studies* 5 (1969) pp163-171.

The Character of Christian Morality, London: Faith, 1965.

'Jesus Christ his only Son our Lord who shall come to judge', *Theology* 96 (1993) pp437-444.

Looking Before and After, London: Fount, 1988.

NOTES

1 These reflections are based upon a University Sermon preached in Cambridge on 1 May 1983, and printed by kind permission of the Select Preachers Syndicate.

2 Psalm 139: 21-2, *Book of Common Prayer* rendering.

3 *Centuries* 84.

4 *The History of the Decline and Fall of the Roman Empire*, chapter XXXVIII.

5 'After'.

6 This argument comes from an article called 'The Logical Paradox of Forgiveness', published by Dr Aurel Kolnai just before his death in *Proceedings of the Aristotelian Society* (1972-3), p99.

7 ibid, p97.

8 ibid, p105.

9 *Hymns Ancient and Modern*, 107.

10 *George Macdonald Anthology*, p103

11 Teilhard de Chardin, *Hymn of the Universe* London: Collins, 1965 p19

12 A Farrer, 'The Eucharist in 1 Corinthians' in *Eucharistic Theology Then and Now*, London: SPCK, 1968, p31.

13 Helen Gardner (ed), *The Faber Book of Religious Verse*, London: Faber, 1972, p26.

14 Alice Meynell (1847-1922). This poem is also in *The Faber Book of Religious Verse*, p292.

15 *Classics of Western Spirituality*, New York: Paulist Press 1978. Long text chapter 24, p221.

16 Philippians 2:5-11 (RSV).

17 Richard Baxter (1615-91). I found this years ago in a book lent to me. It appears, but modified from 'I' to 'we', in Frank Colquhoun *Parish Prayers*, London: Hodder and Stoughton 1967.

18 Matthew 11:19 (RSV).

19 *The door wherein I went*, London: Collins, 1975, p54.

20 Luke 22:61-2 (RSV).

21 *Collected Poems*, London: Faber, 1960, p122.

2

Janet Martin Soskice

GOD LOVES WOMEN

J anet Martin Soskice is a Canadian who now teaches theology in the
University of Cambridge. At one stage of her life she discovered that
the Bible was 'the most exciting thing she could read', and as it
happened, she was to study in Sheffield University's department of
Biblical Studies for a time, before continuing her study of theology and
philosophy in Oxford. Whilst finishing her doctorate, she met the artist
to whom she is now married. She became a Roman Catholic as an
adult, and found herself a teaching position at the Church of England
theological college, Ripon College, Cuddesdon, near Oxford. She
finished her first book there, reading the proofs whilst caring for her first
child, then only a fortnight old. She has lectured widely in Europe, the
USA, Australia and New Zealand. She was President of the Catholic
Theological Association of Great Britain 1992-94.

She represents a new generation of women involved in theology and
spirituality in various kinds of institutional contexts but as we see from
her work, we are far from having reached the point where everyone is
free from discomfort about having women teach and preach (from a
pulpit or not, at the eucharist or on some other occasion); and it is
certainly not the case that the widespread poverty and real suffering of
women is being addressed.

Women's problems

Sometimes I wish I had never heard of 'women', much less discovered that I was one. 'Feminist' seems destined to be a term of opprobrium. In the last century 'feminists' were people who thought women should be allowed to take university degrees. In the early part of this one they were people who thought women should have the vote. Now we call people who think women should be able to go to university and able to vote, sensible people. Success in the feminist field means that the changes campaigned for in the face of a sometimes violent opposition become accepted as 'just common sense', while the nomenclature 'feminist' is moved on to describe some other unspeakably radical group of activists in the female cause.

One reads, for example, in the Catholic press that 'feminists' are people who expect other people to look after their children while they go out to work. This definition would include most western European men. We can let that pass, except that it raises the interesting question of whether a man can be a feminist. The best argument in the negative which I have heard is that men cannot be feminists because men, except in very exceptional circumstances, do not have the experiences of a woman. The adequacy of this simple criterion was brought home to me recently as I stood in my college office at the photocopier, the secretarial staff busily employed about me. A student came to the hatch and called me from the copier to answer a question. It was clear he thought I was a secretary and why should he not? I was of an age with the rest of the women, dressed the same and so on. I simply gave him his answer and off he went. I am quite used to being taken for a secretary and in the past it has only bothered me to see how rude students can be with a secretary, and how much their manner changes when they discover that the would-be secretary is the Fellow in charge of the department from whose desks they seek a grace. But on this occasion I realised that what was relatively commonplace for me, being taken for my secretary, would never happen to my male colleagues.

Now the point of this anecdote is *not* that it is an ignominious tale, nor yet that it's a horrible thing to be taken for a secretary when one isn't one – it's not. Nor yet is one saying no one but women have such experiences – black and disabled people tell similar tales. The point is, as a female one is 'read' as a woman, with your society's expectations of what women do. If you are alive to it you will see it happening around you all the time. Yet, I suppose, there was a time when I had not heard of women or at least when I did not realise I was one. Let me explain by continuing in my somewhat anecdotal mode.

I have not always been interested in the topic of 'Women in the Church'. Throughout my postgraduate student days, splendidly isolated as a student of philosophy of religion at Oxford University, I was more interested in the place of laity in the Church. I would not have said, as I have heard some people say, that I had never experienced disadvantage through being female. This was clearly and empirically not the case. When I had applied to universities in the United States a number of the best did not take women, and when I came to Oxford, again, women were unable to apply to the wealthiest, most central colleges, the ones with housing and scholarships. Women postgraduates in theology could not be members of a college which had a Professor of Theology, and to which most of the other (male) theology students belonged, and so on. But this, and much else, one accepted as 'the way the cookie crumbled' – an unfortunate and unjust aspect of the system but no one's fault. The exclusivity of the men's colleges was represented by the liberal dons as an unfortunate but binding archaism which could not now be altered. (Much was the surprise of many, then, to see that when the men's colleges discovered it was to their academic advantage to take women, they managed to do so very quickly.)

I became more aware of the difficulties of women in the Church (or Churches) when teaching at an Anglican theological college. The experiences of my women students as well as my own, gave me pause for thought. We were all living, working and studying within a context formed by men and for men, but which, at many times, a woman's life fitted oddly and where women's achievements were undervalued. A candidate who had spent a couple of years working for a bank would be held to come with 'good life experience', whereas of someone who had raised a large family it was said; 'But she hasn't *done* anything'. A young unmarried man going into the curacy would have the ladies of the parish round (sometimes whether he liked it or not) offering to cook and even clean for him, whereas a woman curate not only was *not* cooked and cleaned for, but was expected to entertain the parishioners, and so on. This stream of little points of strain was constant, and cumulative.

Debates within the Anglican communion at that time about the ordination of women made it inevitable that we be interested in the history of theological discussion on the topic 'women'. Historical theology is, unsurprisingly, rife with accounts of women's mental and moral limitations, their 'natural' subordination, weakness of will and even (in the case of Richard Hooker) their 'imbecility'.[1] Literary, political and legal texts from the same historical periods give the same unfortunate picture, but nonetheless one couldn't help wishing theology had been a bit more generous than the other branches of human wisdom.

It made me aware of the exclusively 'male's eye view' I was getting and, to some extent, giving to my own students. For instance, I was at that time involved with an Oxford postgraduate degree in Christian sexual ethics. As I recall, none of the books on the reading list, for aspects both ancient and modern was written by a woman, and the topics for the papers very much reflected the interests of the male authors of the books. There was, for instance, a great deal on homosexuality and divorce, but nothing on abuse within marriage, or pornography, or the sex trade. Women, if they appeared in the texts, appeared as 'bodies with problems' – unspecified moral agents who might or might not take the pill, or have an abortion and so on. It was even evident that some of the classical texts, for instance Augustine's account in *The City of God* of what sexual relations might be had man (sic) not fallen, depended for their analysis of sexual morality rather heavily on male sexual and bodily experience. One could not help wondering what a woman would have said. So enters the so-called 'hermeneutics of suspicion'. What might women have written? It is not simply that women and men might (or might not) have different opinions about the same issues, women and men might see different things as issues in the first place.

On one occasion my students had a short placement at a chocolate bar factory. Most of the assembly-line workers were Asian women. The managers explained they had trouble with these workers, because if their children were ill they didn't come into work. No reference was made to the possibility of work place crèches. My own experience as a working mother with small children made me aware of the child-care difficulties many women faced. Television and 'women's page' newspaper articles had recently exposed the atrocious patch-up solutions that many poorer women (and shouldn't we say, men?) had resort to – ten children with an elderly aunt and only a television for stimulation and so on. The social cost of this early neglect of children can be, of course, dreadful.

About the same time, I met a bouncy young evangelical woman who was employed by an Institute founded in the last century to improve the workers' conditions. She explained that in the past they had campaigned largely for canteens and lavatories, but now that most workplaces had such amenities they were concentrating on trade union/management relations. 'What', I asked (being full of all this worrying data on child-care) 'about work-place crèches?' 'Oh', she said brightly, 'our boss thinks that's just a women's problem'.

The enormity of this answer did not strike me for some time. What a multitude of things shelter under the phrase, 'just a women's problem'. Is the neglect attendant on inadequate and unimaginative child-care facilities *just* a women's problem? More deeply, is that fact that so many fathers are absent or irresponsible just a women's problem? Poverty and especially child poverty in our country and world-wide, in one sense is a women's problem because it is women who are, quite literally, left holding the babies. But are women's problems not ones that need to be resolved by all of us? They certainly are problems from which we all, in the long run, will suffer.

It was at this stage I began to understand what was meant by 'patri-archy' (a term I still regard as ugly and unfortunate, but maybe that has to do with what it signifies). It does not mean that some men are nasty to women. It is not about 'men versus women'. It is about structures that have been created, over hundreds of years, in which men were the main determinants; structures that do not take women's lives into consideration. It is about structures under which not only women but children and men suffer. Furthermore, it is not just men who are sexist in this sense. It is perfectly possible for women to be blind, even wilfully blind, to all these issues, particularly if their own circumstances shield them.

As one worked and lived in the theological college, a college which was trying its utmost to be kind to women, one couldn't help, as a woman, being aware of working with texts, traditions and circumstances created by men with a male population in mind. A feeling somehow grew that in the texts of theology, my women students and I did not exist. Something important about us and our lives had not gone into forming this rich doctrinal, liturgical and pastoral mixture. Although there was much that one could learn and should learn from the great texts and tradition, somehow women's voices had not been heard, and we were all the losers for that.

On one particularly grim day I remember thinking, 'It doesn't matter, because God *loves* women!' and somehow, and to my surprise, this recog-nition made me weep with relief. Of course, I had never, consciously, doubted that God loved women. I had never doubted that God loved everyone. But somehow the barrage of ancient opinion, the structures into which one was perceived to fit oddly, the little niggling but perduring negativities, which one felt, in a place which fit the young male candidates like a glove, all conspired to make one feel that women were not really quite as good as men, that God didn't care about women *quite* as much as men, that women's sufferings (so many of them not even figuring on the ethics or pastoral courses) didn't matter *quite* as much as those of men, that what happened to women in the home didn't matter *quite* as much as what happened to men in the workplace. In short that somehow women didn't figure except as sources of gynaeco-logical problems in moral philosophy, or as people to make the tea.

There are so many variables to do with women in the Churches, but I can say one thing with absolute certainty – God loves women. And I think I can make another claim with a high degree of confidence and it is this, whether in theology or social theory, philosophy or politics, women's experiences have been left out and we are all the worse for it.

I was once asked to give a talk on the title 'Has the Church oppressed women?' Stumped by so global a topic, I did something I tell my students never to do, and turned to the Oxford English Dictionary. I was not disappointed. Four dense columns in the large OED on 'oppress' and its cognates, of which some highlights: to press injuriously upon or against; to subject to pressure with hurtful or overpowering affect; to press down by force; to crush, trample down, smother, crowd.

> *1382 Wyclif Mark iii 9: Jesus seith to his disciplis, that the litil boot shulde seue hym, for the cumpanye of peple, lest thei oppressiden hym . . .*

And later, chronicling some seventeenth century architectural disaster,

> *1642 R Carpenter: The upper part of a Church fell, and, the women sitting in the body of the Church, many of them were oppressed.*

Proof positive that the Church has oppressed women!

But through all this talk of smothering, crushing and squashing, we might discern another term, 'to silence'. It could be said that women have been silenced in the Churches – not just in the Churches but histor-ically there, as well as in other places and in modern times there, more than in most other places. Silenced, not in the simplistic sense of there being no women priests or few women theologians: nor yet in the sense that women don't speak out. There is a deeper kind of silencing which sometimes is referred to by its effect – 'voicelessness'. Cultural anthro-pologists speak of 'muted groups', groups who may speak but not in the dominant mode, whereas only the dominant mode of a group will be heard or listened to. The theory of mutedness does not require that the muted groups be physically silent – they may speak a great deal – but they have not access to the decision-making, to the public domain. They are of the group of 'indians' and not of 'chiefs': people from whose lives, insights and decisions are not meant to come.

The French philosopher, Michèle Le Doeuff, cites this passage from an anthropological account by Levi-Strauss,

> *The next day, all the villagers sailed away aboard some thirty canoes, leaving us behind, alone with the women and children in the abandoned houses.*[2]

As Le Doeuff notes, the women and children did not go away, yet for Levi-Strauss, *le village entier* (the entire community) had left. A small omission you may think, but here we have a major practitioner of a human science, speaking as though half the race didn't exist. What are we to make of the scientific status of this account?

Language and power are closely linked. Not just who speaks and who is heard, but how we speak betrays balances of power. One of my students pointed out that the commonplace philosophical example, 'Columbus was the man who discovered America' is scarcely obvious to someone who is descended from the Aztec Indians. It's not even true. But by the time young English or American children have learned the correct answer to the question 'Who discovered America?' they have learned to read world history from a particular perspective. Ours. But who is 'we'?

What might a woman's voice do in theology? Valerie Saiving Goldstein wrote an article in 1960, much in advance of interest in feminist theology, called, 'The human situation – a feminine view'.[3] Her suggestion was that soteriology was dependent on one's anthropology, and that the analysis of the human condition given by modern men theologians was very much from a man's point of view. She pointed out that Protestant theologians, like Reinhold Niebuhr and Anders Nygren, saw sin in terms of self-assertion, self-centredness and pride. But these, she said, are not necessarily the temptations of women. The sins of many women might better be suggested by terms like triviality and diffuseness, dependence on others for one's own self-definition and so on – what she calls an 'underdevelopment or negation of self'. What is interesting about theology written by women, whether feminist or not, is precisely this new visibility – the hearing of another voice.

Although in our society we are all well practised at this it might be helpful to point out two ways of ignoring women; first, we can fail to see them and second we can see them as women.

For the first, tragic examples can be found in the accounts of agricultural aid to African countries where aid packages, negotiated by male politicians and leaders took little cognisance of the fact that the vast majority of Africa's agriculturalists are women, frequently with disastrous results.

For the second we can again return to the chocolate bar factory. Identify problems specific to women as 'women's problems' and eliminate them from consideration. Speak of 'women' or even 'Catholic women' or even 'good Catholic mothers' and ignore the diversity of tasks, gifts and obligations concealed here. Assert, contrary to all evidence, that since most women don't work, we don't need to consider provision for working women. Pretend that every woman is 'someone's wife', and that being 'just a housewife' is a rather mindless and idle occupation. No wonder Michèle Le Doeuff says, 'We do not think that feminism is an operation by which 'woman' wants to be like 'man', we insist on the fact that here are *women*, quite different from each, and there are *men* as well. 'Women' is a mythical figure, a smokescreen which prevents people from seeing the actual situations of real women.'[4]

Thus it is possible both to ignore women, and to say that, because certain matters are 'women's problems', they are somehow beyond our ethical consideration, or perhaps beneath it. The philosopher Mary Midgley offers an explanation of why a woman's viewpoint could not matter:

> *From the ancient hierarchical point of view (unchanged from Aristotle to Kant and beyond) it could not matter because women themselves did not really matter. They were in effect an inferior kind of man, with no distinctive character of their own. They thus shared in the human condition to the extent that inferior men did, and needed no special comment.*[5]

This remark has a particular pertinence to the 'equal but different' line of thought which is now the official preferred line in the Catholic Church when considering the question of women in the Church. The phrase 'equal but different' allows of this unfortunate reading: women are *equal* to men insofar as they do not have different insights or visions to bring to the Church, or spiritual needs to be met, but they are *different* in ways that make them unable to contribute fully to the Church's ministerial, theological and evangelical life. And thus continues the double-think about women. The only resolution to all these interesting questions will come when women's voices are heard and their experience reflected in the whole of the Church's life.

It is still sometimes suggested that in a world that's full of suffering, women's issues should be a low priority. But who are the people who are suffering? In our own country families falling into poverty are disproportionately those single-parent families headed by women. The average wages for women are significantly less than those for men, and the childcare and domestic responsibilities greater. In many poorer countries women are disproportionately underfed and overworked, at times (still) even sold into slavery, both sexual and domestic. The western influence on these countries has not obviously improved the circumstances of women. In some parts of South East Asia the largest 'cash crop' is the sexual services of women. Pornography is booming.

And yet as Catholics we must say, 'God loves women'. One reason why, despite cowardly tendencies to trundle back to the ontological argument, or science and religion or some other safe topic, I feel a certain obligation to write on the topics of women and the Church, and women and ethics, is that one day I feel God might ask of me, 'You were there. You saw it. What have you done for these ones that I love, these women made in my own image?' What we must also ask ourselves as Christians and Catholics, and as women as well as men, is: has our Church made things any better or have we colluded in silencing the already half-voiced, and in making the problems of women, just women's problems? Bodies are being broken day after day on linked wheels of poverty, prostitution and domestic violence. How can we map these sufferings on the broken and risen body of Christ?

Priests and People, August – September 1992

Just women's problems?

I quote from a recent article in the New York Review of books by the eminent Indian economist, Amartya Sen, now at Harvard. He writes 'It is often said that women make up a majority of the world's population. They do not. This mistaken belief is based on generalising from the contemporary situation in Europe and North America, where the ratio of women to men is typically about 1.05 or 1.06, or higher. In South Asia, West Asia, and China, the ratio of women to men can be as low as 0.94 or even lower and it varies widely elsewhere in Asia, in Africa and in Latin America.'

Women outnumber men, he goes on to say, substantially in Europe, the United States and Japan, but 'the fate of women is quite different in most of Asia and North Africa'. In some places of course female infanticide is still practised but this is really not a significant factor and nor is death in childbirth. Rather it is the persistent failure to give girl children and women medical care similar to that which men get, the failure to give them comparable food to that which the men get, and failure to provide equal access to what social services there might be. Where there is anything, boy children and men get it first. The title of Sen's article is a chilling one, 'More Than 100 Million Women are Missing', because 100 million is the figure by which, if we project on the basis of European and North American figures, there is a shortfall of women in the world population. One hundred million. 'These numbers', Sen says, 'tell us, quietly, a terrible story of inequality and neglect leading to the excess mortality of women'.[6] A hundred million women missing. Sexism is not something that hurts women's feelings, sexism kills millions and millions and millions of girls and women each year. And yet the churches have been so slow to condemn sexism as a sin. Slower even than in declaring apartheid a heresy. Worse still, we are still told in many quarters that feminism is really not Christian, that it is anti-Christian, that it is a secular thing. It is even suggested that if you are a faithful Christian you won't have anything to learn from feminism, you would only teach the feminists perhaps. It's even said that feminism is just a middle class, white preoccupation that distracts us from the real moral needs of the world today. What world are people who make these remarks living in?

Over the years, I have learned a great deal from the debates about the ordination of women. I myself have never felt a calling to ordained ministry. What got me engaged was not so much the fact that women were refused ordination in various denominations, but the grounds on which it was argued they should be so refused, and in some churches, still are. Looking at the Catholic tradition, which of course embraces far more than just the Roman Catholic church, one sees that the question of the ordination of women has never seriously been raised in centuries preceding our own. The topic was hardly ever broached at all, a non starter, no more was female suffrage, or whatever. But at the very few points where it has been mentioned, the answer is invariable. Women can't be priests because they are subordinate to men and so could not signify the deity. Of course in recent documents, this argument is not used. Instead we have a new argument, and let's be clear, it is a new argument, it is not the traditional argument. The traditional argument is the one about subordination. The new argument is that women are equal but different, and different in such a way that they could not be priests. Women, in this new argument, still can't signify Christ. Then of course we have the well rehearsed argument about 'why not?' Jesus after all was a young man when he died yet an eighty year old priest is still judged able to signify Christ. Jesus was a Jew, yet a Chinese man can signify Christ. What then is so over-ridingly important about being a woman, that this feature out of all others makes some people un-Christlike in the one relevant sense? We are still told in some quarters that this is a matter of divine dispensation. This is the way God has ordered the world and God has ordered the symbolic reality. This is the way God has constructed both the order of creation and the order of redemption.[7] In this order women cannot be priests, but they can be mothers and nurturers. Their part indeed, in the symbolic order, is to be not-Christ. After all if everyone was Christlike then who would be the people who could be non-Christlike by contrast? The whole order of creation would be upset by ordaining a woman, we are told. It would be like, well like ordaining a pigeon or a bunch of bananas. (Such things and similar are said even in New Zealand!) In fact it might be better to ordain a pigeon since at least the Holy Spirit appeared as a bird at Christ's baptism. But the question can't be avoided. If women can't represent Christ, can Christ represent women? Is Christ only the saviour of men? Can a male saviour redeem women too?

Susan Brooks Thistlethwaite in her book, *Sex, Race and God*, relates this story of one of her students. The student, a woman, was raped while taking her garbage to the dump and as she lay bleeding there on the heap of garbage, wondering if her assailant would come back to murder her, and afraid to move, she had a vision of Jesus as a crucified woman who said to her from the cross, 'You don't have to be afraid, you don't have to be ashamed, I know what you are suffering'.[8] These kinds of visions, people never build shrines to. When we consider the global sufferings of women documented by Amartya Sen, their starvation, exploitation, and degradation; when we consider the specific cases like that of the prostitution and child prostitution trade in the Philippines, (just read that up if you haven't done so) then we must ask as a very real question 'Can Jesus be the Saviour for women?' Are their sufferings and their dyings not caught up and mapped on the cross? With questions like this, many women are moving beyond questions of institutional reform in the churches.

Many women are moving beyond asking the question of ordination to asking central questions about Christology and asking whether they can remain within the churches as they stand. Many women turn their gaze now to the churches and see them not as sources of good news and abundant life but rather as the validators of the oppression of women socially, politically, emotionally and symbolically. Sandra Schneiders, an American theologian and Roman Catholic religious sister, writes about this with some feeling. It is not simply that women are excluded from Holy Orders, she says they have been made invisible in language and imagery, the impositions society and family put upon them have been given divine sanction and their emergence into the public sphere has been loaded with guilt, especially if they are working mothers. Yet women do know Christ as their saviour. Perhaps it's a miracle of grace that they do. Schneiders says that women's 'experience as disciples of Jesus Christ makes them aware that what has been done to them in the name of God is contrary to the will of Christ for his followers.'[9]

Will the rediscovery, the repristinisation, of the human Jesus be enough for beleaguered feminists and, more importantly, for the sufferings of those girls and women who may never in their life read a word of theology? What does it mean for those, more than a hundred million of whose numbers are missing? The relations of biblical women to the human Jesus are very important, but I want also to know more about what our relations can be to the work of the risen Lord.

In *Faith, History and Society*, Johann Baptist Metz makes an interesting distinction between Christian hope and secular utopian vision. It is something like this: secular utopias envision a time which will be marvellous for those lucky enough to live then, but offer little solace to those whose lives have been a means to this glorious end. But Christian hope looks to a time, God's time, when all will be well; when every tear will be dried, when all the suffering of the world through all its ragged and jagged history will somehow be made whole. And this must mean, for me anyway, this Christian hope must mean that Hagar will find her home and that wholeness will return to Tamar and the unnamed concubine in the Book of Judges, to the child prostitute killed by one of her customers, to the rape victim, to the mother who sees her children starve to death. Unless I can believe in a risen Christ who somehow – and I don't know how – will redeem these sufferings, as well as promise a better future, I can have no hope. Even if things changed now, overnight, to be wondrously egalitarian and good for women all over the world, how can we forget, what kind of amnesia would let us forget two thousand, four thousand, six thousand years of pain and death? We must practice 'not forgetting', in Metz's phrase, anamnesia. This anamnesia, this painful memory, is only redeemed by Christian hope becuase it is only God who can promise healing for the past as well as to our future. This is even more so if we hope for the renewal of the earth. I'm not quite sure how recalling the human Jesus alone is going to give us a Jesus who renews the face of the earth.[10]

We can find traces of a feminist Christology in the Christological confessions of the women in the New Testament texts. These are confessions indeed whose significance has been grossly and to my mind incomprehensibly overlooked by historical theology, particularly if we reflect on how much attention has been paid to Peter's confession. Alongside Peter's confession we must put that of the Syrophoenician woman, the Samaritan woman, and of course supremely, Martha. I would like, in conclusion, to add Mary Magdalene, who met the risen Lord in the garden.

Christ and Context, pp117-122

Annunciation: Luke 1:26-38

Where then, does Janet Martin Soskice find her resources? First of all, in the incarnation of Christ. Here is one of her sermons and a further reflection.

The Feast of the Annunciation on 25 March is a wondrous and fruitful feast in the middle of the rather gloomy season of Lent.

Of course, the Annunciation isn't intended to be light relief from Lent. Its dating is determined in an almost bare-facedly biological way: 25 March is exactly nine months before 25 December. This points to one of the delightful things about the annunciation and about Marian theology in general – it's a strange mixture of the most exalted of Christian mysteries and the most human of human events, as I shall try to show.

In my investigations, I have discovered an interesting anomaly. The *Oxford University Diary*, that organ of rectitude, refers to this feast as 'the Annunciation of the Blessed Virgin Mary' – whereas the much less prestigious *Westminster Diocesan Year Book* calls it 'the Annunciation of the Lord'. Now, I know that the *Oxford Diary* is always right, or at least fastidiously correct, but in this case I'd plump for the *Westminster Diocesan Year Book*. For annunciation means announcement, and the announcement in question is not really the announcement of the Blessed Virgin Mary, but the announcement to the Blessed Virgin Mary, in fact, the announcement of our Lord to the Blessed Virgin Mary. Calling it 'the Annunciation of the Lord', seems to me to get the balance right because the feast, like all Marian feasts (and all Marian theology properly understood) is about the Lord. It is the feast of incarnation.

I started to think more seriously about the Annunciation after falling on some interesting remarks Thomas Aquinas makes about it. In a text no doubt familiar to you all, volume 51 of the *Summa Theologiae*, Aquinas says this:

> *Next we have to examine the announcement to the Blessed Virgin.*
> *Here are four points of inquiry:*
> 1 *Was it right for her to be told about who would be born of her?*
> 2 *Who ought to have told her?*
> 3 *In what manner?*
> 4 *Was the announcement well planned?*

These sound like inquires more appropriate to *Debrett's Book of Etiquette* than to a text of theology, but Aquinas has some interesting things to say, particularly about the *manner* in which the announcement was made to Mary. Of this he asks, 'Should the angel of the annunciation have appeared bodily (that is, visually) to the Virgin?' After all, as Augustine and the mystics tell us, physical visions are a low grade of religious experience. The mystics tell us that crude physical signs like these are usually given to those who are too weak to do without them and surely Mary wasn't one such. But, says Aquinas, in Mary's case it was entirely fitting that the angel appeared to her bodily, not because she was spiritually under-developed, but because a bodily revelation was consonant with the message itself – for the angel came to tell of the *incarnation* (the becoming flesh) of the *visible* God. The sensible nature of the appearance to Mary points to the actual appearance of the Son of God in the flesh. Mary was able to receive the Son of God in her womb as well as in her mind.

I am reminded of those early Italian paintings of the Annunciation, – the stylised ones where you see on the one side, Mary sitting in a pavilion surrounded by symbols of wisdom and purity (books and lilies and so on), and on the other side you see the Angel Gabriel with his hand raised in greeting. Between them, usually in gold lettering, you see actual Latin words written in, words which run from the angel's mouth to the Virgin's midriff. I had always imagined paintings like these were visual aids for illiterate church goers, as we're told stained glass windows were meant to be, and that the words were there so that everyone would know what occasion the painting depicted. But of course not! In the Annunciation the *Word became flesh,* and so of course, the painters have made *the words physically there* in the painting just as the word was physically there in the annunciation itself. The annunciation wasn't just a conceptual thing, but a very concrete one.

This understood, Luke's account of the annunciation is an imprimateur for painters and for all representative Christian art. God did not scorn to come in the flesh and because of this we can now represent him in earthly materials. (I believe the Orthodox Church's theology of icons draws explicitly on this incarnational line of thought.) Here again, is this odd mixture of the pretty mysterious and the close to earth.

Luke's account of the annunciation is an equally rich mixture of the literary, the typological, the putatively biographical – to my mind we should see it as a theological construction in which Luke not only alludes to Old Testament parallels, but weaves in the christological language and formulas of the post-resurrection church. So, Luke's infancy narratives, we are told, abound in echoes of Abraham and Sarah, of David's description of Gabriel, of the Samson story, of the promise to David, of the (other) annunciation – of birth patterns. Luke's actual format of the annunciation follows patterns seen in annunciations to Zechariah, to Abraham, to Moses and Gideon. Some have claimed that the portrayal of Mary here echoes back to female portrayals of Wisdom in the Old Testament, and have suggested that the angelic mode of greeting, 'Rejoice, highly favoured one', is intended to evoke the Old Testament female personification of Israel or Zion. Mary is thus depicted in the infancy narrative as a type of the new Israel, the church.

Some Roman Catholic interpretations have also understood that Luke, in the infancy narratives, alludes to a comparison between Mary and the Ark of the Covenant. In Luke 1:35, the angel says, 'The power of the Lord will *overshadow* you'. This same verb is used in the Greek version of the Old Testament when the cloud of God's glory *overshadows* the Tabernacle in the desert, and the winged cherubim *overshadow* the Ark of the Covenant. So just as the Ark bore the Old Covenant in the tablets of the Law, so Mary bears the New Covenant, the living Covenant, in Christ. Whether this parallel with the Ark of the Covenant was intended by Luke or not, 'Ark of the Covenant' is a traditional Marian title: Mystical Rose, Tower of David, Tower of Ivory, House of Gold, Ark of the Covenant, Gate of Heaven.

It has also been common for Roman Catholic theologians to understand Luke to be making this allusion in saying that 'when Elizabeth heard the greeting of Mary, the child leapt in her womb', for just as David danced before the old Ark (2 Samuel 6:14), so John the Baptist, yet unborn, leaps in his mother's womb before the living Covenant in Christ. (Not much credence should be given to the idea that Luke intended this allusion, but it is food for thought.)

It is more probable, however, that Luke deliberately weaves into the birth narratives christological formulas of the post-resurrection church. Here too, the mention of overshadowing in the annunciation is important for it echoes the overshadowing of Luke 9:34 when, at the transfiguration, 'a cloud came and overshadowed them' and 'a voice came out of the cloud, saying "This is my son my Chosen, listen to him"'. Furthermore, the language of the angel's promise, 'The Holy Spirit will come upon you, and the power of the Holy Spirit will overshadow you, and therefore the child to be born will be called holy, the Son of God' has overt parallels to the language used of Jesus' baptism: 'and the Holy Spirit descended upon him in bodily form, as a dove, and a voice came from heaven, "Thou art my beloved Son, with thee I am

well pleased"'. The significance of these parallels with baptism and transfiguration is that it would seem, for Luke, that the message of the
annunciation contains a basic post-resurrectional proclamation of the
Christian faith. Mary is being presented as the first one to hear the
gospel, hence her prominence in the Lucan infancy narrative.

I haven't spoken very much about the person Mary – just as though
she were some passive, shadowy figure whose only role was to act as a
vehicle for all the typological abstractions. You might think this feast of
incarnation isn't really about the person of Mary at all, but of course it
absolutely is.

It was *Mary*, not a woman, but *this* woman Mary – this *person* Mary,
who accepted Christ into her life in the most intimate way imaginable.
'Behold, I am the handmaid of the Lord; let it be to me according to
your word.' And this was not just a *passive* acceptance, but an active and
deliberate and free choice. The church has always recognised that it is
Mary's acceptance of God's will which is at the very heart of the theological importance of the Annunciation. As Augustine says, Mary is
better for having conceived Christ in faith than in flesh – for Mary would
have gained nothing from her physical and maternal nearness to Christ
if she had not first conceived Christ in her heart.

Mary is the first Christian, the first one to hear the gospel, the first
Christian disciple. She meets Luke's principle of ideal discipleship; that
is 'to hear the word of God and to do it' (Luke 8:21, 15). This gives the
key to the story, later in Luke, of the woman in the crowd who cries,
'Blessed is the womb that bore you, and the breasts that you sucked!'
But he said 'Blessed rather are those who hear the word of God and keep
it' (Luke 11:27-28). The Eastern Orthodox Church has always maintained that in this passage, far from slighting Mary, Jesus indicates
where her true glory lay – in her faithful response to God. Mary heard
the word of God and kept it, in her mind and in her body.

As the first Christian, the first Christian disciple, Mary is the pattern
for all Christians, for all human beings. For Christ becomes incarnate in
each of us. As Gerard Manley Hopkins says,

> . . . *the just man justices;*
> *Keeps grace: that keeps all his goings graces;*
> *Acts in God's eye what in God's eyes he is -*
> *Christ – for Christ plays in ten thousand places,*
> *Lovely in limbs, and lovely in eyes not his*
> *To the Father through the features of men's faces.*

If we look at Mary and see Christ this is not because Mary is unimportant. When we look at any human being (dead, stumbling, starving, sinning) we should see Christ – not just Christ so that Joe or Jane or Judith is cast away like a worthless husk, but in seeing Christ – the Joe or Jane or Judith that really *is*, for *to be* is to be in God.

Silence in Heaven, pp95-99

Incarnation and trinity

What I like about trinitarian theology and why I want to insist that it is not, despite many scholarly obituaries, dead, is that it seems to me a language of God Here Now. That's very simple. If it did a piece of work in the first Christian centuries, it is likely to have a piece of work to do today; not tell us about ourselves (we always want more on that topic) but to tell us about what God is, and what it is that God can be. The students of theology that I meet are, characteristically, sub-trinitarian even if they are good, even biblical Christians. They tend to believe in a Christ who is a demi-God or a semi-God, some kind of a divine messenger. God (in this account) is up there in the back of beyond and sends someone to tell us how to get right with him. But as trinitarian Christians we should insist that in the incarnation we meet true God. We do not meet a messenger boy. In Jesus we meet true God. The telling of trinitarian stories must be of continual importance for preserving this truth, and it's also partly what the doctrine of the trinity is about. Augustine, as a young man, was appalled by the barbarity of Christianity as compared with the more sophisticated Greco-Roman religions then on offer. He found especially distasteful all the stories in the Hebrew bible of those people with their horrible polytheism and immoral marital behaviour. But when he fully embraced Christianity (some time after he saw the intellectual persuasiveness of its neo-Platonic apologists), he seemed to see how important it was in the Jewish and Christian narratives that God has a human history. That is what the doctrine of the incarnation insists upon. And once Augustine believed God could have a human history, then the human history of the Jews, warts and all, became not simply a distraction to the story of 'God with us' but the very place where God is revealed. Augustine could then see that his own human history was also the place of God's divine disclosure: he could write the *Confessions*. By implication each life and every human history is a place where God is known: God here, now, past, present and to be. It seems to me that trinitarian formulations at their best protect this presence of God Here Now, with you, with me, with the grandest philosopher and the most modest slave girl of the second century. This legacy of God Here Now, in everyone's story, totally present, is a precious legacy. I'd like to hang on to it, and use the trinitarian language to do so.

The Christian Understanding of God Today, pp112-118

Creation and relation

So far we have read both Janet Martin Soskice's perspective on women's problems, and at some of the spiritual resources she finds in the Christian tradition for addressing them. Here is another statement of the value we should seek to recognise in one another, of the human dignity that is ours, from an essay on 'Creation and Relation'.

When we meet another person, however poor, lowly, diseased or dumb, we stand before something which holds the divine – we stand before someone who is mystery and must be reverenced as such, someone who, like Buber's God, is a 'You that in accordance with its nature cannot become an it'. Of course we can, and do, treat other people like 'its', as mere objects, but always to the loss of our own humanity. We do this in pornography, in harmful experiments on unwitting human victims, in indiscriminate killing in war. Ironically we can treat our neighbours as so many 'its' precisely in our eagerness to understand how they work.

God is mystery, and woman and man in God's image are mystery. The death of God will not, as Nietzsche thought, result in the glorification of man, but rather will take from women and men any claim they may have to be reverenced as participating in the divine economy. Without God and without the sanctity of the person made in the image of God, women and men will become not gods but mere objects to manipulate in a world of manipulable objects.

It is both salutary and confusing that the Genesis story should tell us that it is this same creature, made in the image of God, through whom sin and violence disrupt the created order. Adam and Eve disobey God, Cain slays Abel. In the story violence spreads from the human realm to that of the animals. In the garden the animals live peaceably with Adam and Eve and with each other. After the Flood, we are told, they dread them. The point of these stories is that sin keeps us not only from right relation to other people but from right relation to the whole created order. But the earth and all its life are not, after all, destroyed in the flood, for the God who creates is also the God who saves – a theme strong in both Testaments. The God who saves Noah and the animals can save his people Israel, and – so Christians assert – save humanity in Christ. A God who creates can save. 'Our help is in the name of the Lord', says the Psalmist, 'who made heaven and earth' (Psalm 124:8).

The prophet Isaiah prayed for a just king who, as God's regent over creation, would be a saviour to his people, who would bring order and banish chaos. This king would judge the poor with justice and strike down the ruthless; and then, when there was justice, there would be peace. Then, only then, says Isaiah, lapsing into visionary language, 'The wolf shall dwell with the lamb . . . and the calf and the lion and the fatling together, and a little child shall lead them' (Isaiah 11:6). This is a vision of Paradise, the New Creation, the Kingdom of God. We should not let the visionary nature of Isaiah's language distract us from the reality of the call.

Reverence for and right relation with God entail reverence for and right relation with other people who are made in the image of God, and further they involve right relation with the rest of the created order. The ethical imperative in this vision for the personal extends into the social and finally into the natural and cosmological.

On such a broad canvas religious writers from the biblical times onwards have painted a picture of God's creative and redeeming love. We might, I believe, in our discussions of the moral issues in science and religion, paint on a similarly broad canvas at least part of the time. Whatever we come up with must have regard, as St Augustine would have insisted, for the best science and for what we know of ourselves as creatures – of our biology, our psychology, our natural genesis. Yet we remain mysterious, for we stand in an odd position – fragments of the universe which are conscious of themselves as precisely that. The pop singer, Joni Mitchell, put it this way in a song written about twenty years ago:

> *We are stardust. Million-year-old carbon.*
> *We are golden. Caught in the devil's bargain*
> *And we've got to get ourselves back to the garden.*
> (Woodstock 1969).

She is basically right. Science agrees with Scripture in this – we are dust, million-year-old carbon. But we are dust that has come to know itself as dust, to know that dust can do right and commit wrongs. We are dust that sees the possibility, in God's grace, of glorifying God along with the rest of created order. Let us start from there.

Theology 94, pp31-39

SELECT BIBLIOGRAPHY

'Women's problems', *Priests and People*, August-September 1992.

'Just women's problems?' is an edited version of her 'Response' in *Christ and Context* eds H D Regan and A J Torrance, Edinburgh: T and T Clark, 1993, pp 117-122.

'Annunciation' is from *Silence in Heaven* eds H Walton and S Durber, London: SCM 1994, pp95-99.

'Incarnation and trinity' is from her essay, 'The Christian Rhetoric of God and Human Relational Experience', pp112-118 of ed. J M Byrne, *The Christian Understanding of God Today*, Dublin: Columba, 1993.

'Creation and relation' is from an essay of the same name, first published in *Theology* 94 (1991) pp31-39.

NOTES

1   See Bishop Stephen Sykes' entertaining article, 'Richard Hooker and the Ordination of Women to the Priesthood' in Janet Martin Soskice, ed. *After Eve: Women, Theology and the Christian Tradition*, London: Marshall Pickering, 1990.

2   Cited in 'Ants and Women, or Philosophy without Boundaries' in ed. A Phillips Griffiths, *Contemporary French Philosophy*, Cambridge: CUP, 1987.

3   In *Journal of Religion*, 40, 1960, pp100-12.

4   Le Doeuff, p49.

5   Mary Midgley, 'On Not Being Afraid of Natural Sex Differences', in Morwenna Griffiths and M Whitford, *Feminist Perspectives in Philosophy*, London: MacMillan.

6   *New York Review of Books*, 20 December, 1990, p61.

7   See for example the arguments in Manfred Hauke, *Women in the Priesthood? A Systematic Analysis in the light of the Order of Creation*, San Francisco: Ignatius Press, 1988, and see also my review of that book in *The Tablet*, 11 November, 1989.

8   *Sex, Race and God: Christian Feminism in Black and White*, London: Geoffrey Chapman, 1990, p93.

9   Sandra Schneiders, *Beyond Patching: Faith and Feminism in the Catholic Church*, Mahwah, N J: Paulist Press, 1991, pp32-4, p64.

10 This is not to say we can relax about environmental issues because God will clean up all our mess in the eschaton. As with our work for justice and peace, we strive as members of the risen Christ for the coming of the Kingdom which is already and not yet.

Margaret Spufford

CREATION

Margaret Spufford is an historian by profession, now holding the Research Professorship in Social and Local History at the Roehampton Institute, London. She began her career at the University of Keele, moved to Cambridge, and has occupied distinguished positions in places as diverse as the Netherlands and Japan. Outside the world of the professional historian, she is best known for a book called *Celebration* (1989) with which we are going to begin. It comes as something of a disturbing kind of surprise to discover that this book is about the problem of pain, and as such, has been the subject of debate in *The Independent* newspaper (in which some of her own work was to appear, re-published here) and resulted in a television documentary based on the book, which won for its producer an award for the best religious television of its year. Perhaps inevitably, she has accepted some invitations to write and speak on the experiences related in the book, and again, some of these reflections are published here, for the first time. For the last seven years she has worked on founding and managing a hostel for disabled or chronically sick students attending the colleges of Cambridge University or Anglia Polytechnic University. Not a memorial to her dearly loved daughter, nevertheless it arises from her experience of having tried creatively to foster her daughter's talents, whilst she and her husband and son lived and loved their way with Bridget during her own particular path through life. Margaret Spufford is a member of the Church of England, and is closely associated as an oblate with an Anglican Benedictine community.

Work

It is important to appreciate the kind of attention Margaret Spufford brings to a consideration of her and her daughter's experiences, by attending first to her understanding of her own work. She writes, in effect, in praise of accuracy, of truth-telling, of scrupulous care in description and honest evaluation of what has gone on, of what goes on. Practise truth in relation to what does not hurt, and we may be able to practise truth in relation to what most emphatically does.

I do not have the faintest idea why I am a historian. I work on the lives of people below the level of gentry in the sixteenth and seventeenth centuries, the latter being the first century you can really get at them with any ease. It is a very strange vocation indeed, to have fallen in love with these people, as it feels, to be working to re-create their lives from the mosaic fragments of evidence that remain. It is a matter of always sticking with scrupulous exactitude to the ascertainable facts.

I could never have been a historical novelist, much though I enjoy some of their work: to fill gaps with the imagined, or the fabricated, is impossible. I cannot even, because of this training, adopt Ignatian imaginative methods of re-enacting biblical events in prayer. Within this demanding factual framework, I am recreating with love, and respect for these preceding human beings, all that I can currently grasp that needs to be known, and can be known, of their lives. Vocation does not seem too strong a word for my passionate involvement in this work. But it is so very useless: I envy those, like doctors, who can feel they are ameliorating the human condition. When I was a student, I once thought of becoming a social worker, but decided sadly that I was probably better at the origins of King Athelstan's prayerbook, which I was then trying to unravel, so I had better stick to what I was.

Being a historian is an even odder vocation in a much longer perspective altogether. If you start, as a believer, thinking of the actuality of the Communion of Saints, you realise that you are trying to reconstruct bits of the lives of people who already know, a great deal better than you ever will, what their lives were really about. The whole thing becomes preposterous.

So I do not know where my vocation comes from, or how it was born, or why the drive to fulfil it has always been so strong. Like Mallory, who had to climb Everest because it was there, I try to put together jigsaw puzzle pictures of the 'unimportant' people of the past, compulsively, it seems, just because they *were*, and I need to find out about them. I am only sure of two things. The passion was not born as a 'displacement activity' for my physical limitations. When I married, I went into partnership with another working historian, and the arrangement has stuck. Secondly, the passion for empirically ascertainable fact has something to do with my mother. My parents were both very able scientists, and she, according to their academic records and to my father, the more able. She taught me during the War, before her stroke. I do not remember learning anything of religion at all from her: nor do I remember morality being plugged, although I suppose it was. I do remember, however, her saying to me, 'Never fiddle with the facts, dear. The pattern is this: you have an idea, and then you go away and find out if the facts support it. If they don't, you must discard it, and start again. Always change the idea, never the evidence.' I must have been about four at the time. I don't remember much else of her teaching, but I suspect it has been more influential than she, or I, realised.

Am I, I wonder, profoundly privileged, or profoundly handicapped, by being, as it were, an insider, in the tradition of the lives of the people I study? I admit to being very grateful for fire insurance. God knows, I owe enough to modern medicine. Without it, if I was not dead, I would be in a state of continuous pain I prefer not to consider, when I can help it. But even with it, I am in sufficient constant discomfort to feel that I can readily comprehend the problems of people in the seventeenth century with at least toothache. Like them, I know from experience about infant mortality. My problems are not essentially different from those of the people I work on, and with. As for ritual, it is at least as integral a part of my life as it was of theirs. My problem is not to comprehend, but to avoid over-identification, or mis-identification. What may be different is that I do not regard the evils which torment me as punishment from the hand of God, or signs of His wrath. I do, though, share their belief that these evils may be turned to His purposes. I do not feel distant from these predecessors, or remote from them. It may be that this common sharing of a world gives my work some quality of compassion which I would like it to have. Empathy is probably the historical virtue I most value, although I try to discipline it as strictly as possible within the bounds of the given facts, which are my canvas, and my stone, and my wood.

Of my motives for writing this story down, the account that rings most true would be that I would like it to make music.

I could be accused of self-justification, since I have not always agreed with the suggestions of modern medicine. I do not think this is right, although it does contain a truth, since I feel much more like someone engaged in a dialogue which has no 'right' answer, but in which both protagonists must speak and respect each other's opinions. But it seems a possibility. Last of all, there is the possibility of smug self-gratification of the crude 'Just look what I've done and where I started from!' kind. Is the whole thing some vast egotistical exercise? I am indeed amazed that out of the confusion of my own reality anything of value seems to have emerged, but if it has, it does not feel as if I were responsible, rather as if, despite the poor quality of the canvas, the Artist had managed to say something after all.

At first sight a book which is about physical or mental pain may seem very oddly titled *Celebration*. But it is written by a woman to whom, over the years, participation in the Eucharist has become the most important part of living, and being in silence before the reserved sacrament the most important part of prayer. Gradually, and with immense diffidence, I have come to see that my own participation in this offering of the Eucharist must involve the presentation of my own experience, for hallowing, along with 'the best bread that can conveniently be gotten', in the hope that it, too, can be redeemed and transformed. Becoming a Benedictine oblate fifteen years ago seemed just a logical extension of this procedure at the Offertory. The presentation at the Offertory is re-affirmed in the post-Communion prayer, which is so terrifying in its total implications. 'Here we offer and present to you, O Lord, ourselves, our souls and bodies, to be a reasonable, holy, and living sacrifice.' Much of the experience I have had to offer has been untidy and messy. A great deal of it has seemed to me to be purely evil, and as such, to make an extremely dubious offering, which at times was all I had. This private offering of mine has been deformed, and incomplete: I have been glad that if I was indeed part of the Body of Christ, the other members were bound to be making a better job of it. If I here concentrate on the evil, the pain, and the wrongness of creation as I have experienced it, I do so knowing that my initial emphasis is inevitably distorted.

I am also up against the barriers of language. It is much more possible for me to describe the experience of pain than it is for me to describe the ways it is capable of transformation. Perhaps we all find it easier to describe Good Friday than our own experience at Easter. It is probably impossible to convey that in the living-out they can sometimes, somehow, be one event. If I were a poet, or a musician, perhaps I would have the resources. But if Dante's *Purgatory* was more forcible than his *Paradise*, even this seems very unlikely. Even painters cannot, with the possible exception of Fra Angelico, paint Heaven. Hell, or the fear of it, comes more easily off the brush. Three and a half of the four walls of fourteenth century frescos by the significantly titled Master of the Triumph of Death in Pisa, are given over to Death, Judgement and Hell: only half a wall attempts Paradise, and that is strangely inept. I was reminded of that constrained and lame attempt in Pisa, when my husband and I were standing in front of a magnificent Flemish Last Judgement that had ended up in Danzig. The souls to our Lord's left in their descent to damnation were vivid enough: but the blessed to his right were curiously inert, smug at best. Our guide said suddenly, 'It's odd, isn't it, how the blessed always look as if they had been *stuffed*?' I was reminded of that conversation when I talked to a historian of the *Annales* school, who had not only observed the phenomenon, but of course, being French, quantified it. According to him, the overwhelming majority of 350 illustrations in the Office for the Dead in fifteenth century Books of Hours concentrated on pain and damnation: there was very little attempt to convey salvation or delight. He did tell me, though, that musicians could, and did, in settings for Easter week, make this attempt successfully. It is not an attempt I can make: here, indeed, I am deliberately focusing on the negative, and thus contributing a little to an unbalance I actually loathe. If I attempt to rectify the distortion in any way, there is a risk of travesty.

This book is therefore bound to be seriously defective at the point where it matters most. It may be good at describing brokenness, but I doubt whether it will ever begin to convey joy. Without this, the Offertory is indeed incomplete and the thanksgiving never moves into the *Sanctus*. Not only is this a theological incompleteness, but unless I can succeed in conveying the possibility of practical redemption of the most peculiar circumstances, even of bare survival as a family when it looked impossible, never mind the laughter that has so often accompanied it, the record can scarcely be of assistance to anyone else. And in the humblest possible way, I would like it to be. Survival through the various ills that beset us was so wildly improbable sometimes that to give help to anyone else similarly beset would be infinitely worthwhile. And all I can do is to tell a story: just one authentic story.

Celebration, pp62-65, 69-70, 20-23

Pain

As a seventeen year old, Margaret Spufford had a fall in which she hurt her back. There was another accident early in her marriage, the birth of her son, and three years later, the birth of her daughter, in and through more pain, and extensive acquaintance with orthopaedic clinics. At the age of thirty-two, she was told she had osteoporosis, a condition of fragile bones most commonly associated with old age.

I do not remember whether it was on the return from that visit to hospital or the next, that the worst thing ever so far to happen to me, myself, happened. Ambulance men are the most patient, and usually the most skilled, of all beings. This pair had a misadventure. As they carried me in through the door, one of them tripped on the step. As he recovered himself, he trod on his companion's foot. They stumbled. They dropped, and then caught, me. I can only have fallen a couple of inches, but the effect was terrifying. All my reflexes seemed to go beserk in the pain. I, who so much valued control, was completely out of control. I was screaming, not even able to stop in case my son could hear. My fingers were clenched in someone's hair, the world ran amok, and my husband, who was there, was utterly irrelevant through the pain. He could not reach me. Nor could anyone. 'She probably collapsed another vertebra or two', said the hospital on the telephone, apparently. 'Just keep her quiet'.

It was months before I dared tell even my husband, who was not likely to feel that I had suddenly been afflicted with religious mania, and knew I did not go in for pious or saccharine imagery, that quite extraordinarily at that moment of unreachability, I had suddenly been aware even as I screamed, of the presence of the Crucified. He did not cancel the moment, or assuage it, but was inside it.

Now the dance quickened. We thought we were stretched: now we learned that you always feel that too soon, and you can, in fact, nearly always take a bit more strain than you think is comfortable. The Lord may not permit you to be tempted above that you are able: but you usually underestimate your resources, or perhaps those He supplies.

The particular event which brought me face to face with some of the apparently irreconcilable bits of Christian doctrine, and taught me to live to some extent in the tension at the heart of a paradox, was this. When our daughter was a few months old, it became apparent that she was unwell. One of the experiences which we all have, I think, and which to me is one of the most important reflections of divine activity in our own lives, is the delight of creation. It does not matter if this delight comes through cooking a good meal, or carrying out an experiment that supports the original hypothesis; writing a sentence that both actually expresses exactly what we want to say, and balances; or creating a pot or a picture that works. There is satisfaction which is indescribable in making things, which maybe comes only after months of dreary slog. A minute piece of creation has 'come right', and there is nothing quite like the joy of the experience. Bearing a child substitutes for none of these things, but is greater than any, solely because on the parents then falls the vast responsibility of trying to see that this new human being grows up undistorted, warm, and able to receive and to give love.

Celebration, pp38, 46-47

Suffer the little children

Margaret Spufford's daughter was diagnosed as having a genetically-caused disease, from which she would die between the ages of seven and fourteen.

The time I spent in that ward in the Hospital for Sick Children was some of the most painful and formative in my life. The medicine and the support were magnificent. The problems lay in exposure to so many fundamental issues. Oddly, you only get any approach to Third World mortality in the most sophisticated wards of the most sophisticated hospitals of the First World, with, in this case, a national catchment area of the most intractable diseases. Children were dying, on the particular ward I was on, mainly of genetically-caused malfunctioning.

Now the existence of Belsen and its like, that is, of humanly-created evil, I could, as a historian, cope with intellectually. Genetic evil, creation malfunctioning from birth or from conception (as it was in my daughter's case), was more than I could account for or understand. These children suffered – and small children suffer very acutely, and worse because no explanation is possible to them – because they were *made wrong*. The evidence of divine activity in, and through, creation and the minute ways we share in it has always been particularly important to me. Now here I was, living week after week surrounded by the evidence of failed creation, the rejections of our heavenly Father, the pots on which the potter's hand did indeed seem to have slipped. I think the bottom came for me one day when I tried to comfort a tiny anguished child (words are useless, only touch will do), and as I reached to stroke his head a nurse said hastily, 'Don't touch him, his skull might fracture'. That same day a 'pious' friend called, and said enviously, 'Your faith must be such a comfort to you'. It was not. Belief in an omnipotent and all-loving Creator who is capable of producing results like those I was observing, produced for me at least as many problems as it solved.

So there was I, a Christian, committed to the doctrine of a loving, omnipotent Father, a Creator. And there was I, living in surroundings which persistently denied this omni-competence, amongst the 'failures' of His creation.

That was the worst problem at one level. At another, much more profound, came my discovery of what really mattered to me about our daughter. She was a much-wanted baby. When I took her to London, I did so in all eagerness to save her life, and all co-operation; it came as an enormous shock to discover about myself, in the days of intensive diagnostic tests that followed, that I had other, much less rational, instincts. I had never understood before why sows swallowed threatened piglets: now I discovered, as I held a baby who was increasingly only capable of screaming 'Mummy!', that my instinct to defend her threatened to override my instinct to protect her in the long-term, and therefore to get a diagnosis. The violence of my reaction to my child, constantly threatened by paediatricians incidentally hurting her in the need to get the result which both they and I wanted, was so strong that it took me totally by surprise. My experiences at night in the parental unit, listening to other parents shocked by the same response, showed me that my own reaction was not unusual. For half of one night I sat up with a father who had assaulted a houseman. The reason was simple: the child was dying of cancer and in great pain, and the houseman had a syringe of morphia, which he said it was not time to administer yet.

After a week or two of this, it did not matter to me whether our daughter had three left feet, or even, very much, whether she died now or later. What *did* matter was whether she became emotionally deformed by experiences which impaired her ability to love and to trust. Her emotional normality was all I cared about by then. We were long past wanting her to live at any cost, for possessive reasons, because we had so much wanted this child. What was intolerable was watching her learn fear.

There followed a year in hospital, with her husband looking after their four year old son. Finally they got Bridget home. The stress lay in the nature of the situation itself:

. . . nursing a child who would have died without constant and continuous medical interference, knowing with accurate foreknowledge that she was going to die in a few years, and transforming this situation to a 'normal', good, loving family life that felt as ordinary as possible, given the nursing restrictions. It is an almost impossibly taxing situation.

Some may think that man-made suffering is more evil and more incomprehensible than. . .

. . . the sort of genetic evil, fundamental malformation for which no human agency can be blamed, which I had now been brought to observe.

I can only speak of the physical world I have come to know, the world of innate defect, deficiency within creation, the world where the evolutionary process produces the whole and the strong: but also congenitally thin-walled blood vessels, defective bones, and malformed babies. If this is easier, and lesser, suffering, it is enough. It presents me with more material than I can contain, or perceive to be transformed, or even be transformable by any love. I was surrounded on the metabolic wards by the failures of creation, the drop-outs of natural selection. But the language of science, and of natural selection, and the language of theological belief in a loving, omnipotent Creator, have to be reconciled. Can they be? Here was the crux of my problem. These drop-outs were human babies, with all the needs of normal babies. I am never going to be able to forget the sound of those screams. Of all the Feasts of the Church, Holy Innocents is the most intolerable: of all sounds after the crying of children, the most terrible is the crying of Rachel weeping for her children, because they are not. Except when she is crying because they still are.

I cannot reconcile the images of tiny, deformed children with old men's eyes, in great pain (children who shrank from human contact because so often it represented more pain, the stab of a therapeutic needle which they could not recognise as therapeutic) with what I am bound to believe of a loving, omnipotent Father. I will not assent to all this pain as anything but a manifest evil. One of the commonest Christian heresies is surely to glorify suffering as somehow 'good'.

In three successive generations – my mother's, my own and my daughter's – I have known physical evil. Two of those three times it was caused by fundamental metabolic defects, and of those two times one was caused by an error in the genetic coding itself. I have searched for a theological answer. I do not believe there is one. Would, or can, any theologian produce any answer other than that we are here in the presence of a mystery, insoluble in human terms?

One of the most helpful things that was ever said to me was 'The definition of "Almighty" means that there is no evil out of which good cannot be brought'. This I have found, extremely painfully, to be true. The fundamentally awry can perhaps never be made whole in this life; yet like the twisted tree, or the child's courage and wisdom, it can take on a beauty of its own. And in this transformation, the constant presence of an enabling God seems to me vital. My image of a Creator in whose creation there are mistakes not logically comprehensible may be true, but it has to be extended into the image of a Creator who ceaselessly, patiently, works to transform and re-create what has gone amiss, above all in His own entry into this creation to amend and redeem it. Some of this re-creation and patient transformation of what has gone amiss I can myself bear witness to. But if those theologians who assert that God is in total control of His creation are right, I cannot worship Him. Integrity demands that I do hand in my ticket. For I still cannot cope with the endemic nature of pain. And integrity has to come higher than anything else at all, even God, or at least my present perception of Him.

Celebration, pp49-50, 60, 72-73, 80

God suffers with us

In the end, unless my image of a Creator had not been capable of transformation, by the very words of the Creed, into belief in the truth of a Creator who had himself entered into his creation to suffer with it, and to amend and redeem it, I too would have to quit . . . To the knowledge of the Incarnation, not to the image of an omnipotent Creator, I clung like a limpet. On those terrible children's wards I could neither have worshipped nor respected any God who had not Himself cried, 'My God, my God, why hast Thou forsaken Me?' Only because it was so, only because the Creator loved his creation enough to become helpless with it and suffer in it, totally overwhelmed by the pain of it, I found there was still hope. But without the Garden of Gethsemane, without the torture and the gallows, there would be no hope for any of us, overwhelmed in the present by pain. So the horror of Holy Week is the only hope of renewal of life for the derelict. For He whom we worship was made like His brethren in every respect. Because He himself has suffered, says the author of the letter to the Hebrews, He is able to help those who suffer now; but not, in my experience, by removing the suffering. The beauty of the twisted tree is still brought out *through* its contortion.

The centre of this pain, and also of this silence and light, lies in the Eucharist. Sometimes we are ill-served by familiarity. Even the language of the original events that we re-enact, Eucharist by Eucharist, has become so familiar to us that it has lost some of its force, partly through constant repetition. From the phraseology of picking up our cross, and following our Lord, we have to strip all the clothing of habit, take it back to its original meaning, and think of His torture and of His death on a gibbet. Sometimes I cannot understand our external placidity, as we stand there, faced now, afresh, with the agony of this death, and the flies on these wounds. The re-enactment is a burning-glass, focusing pain, drawing together all those screams I have heard, all those broken branches and bruised flowers, all those fossils in the Grand Canyon, all the fears I have for my own future of cumulative fracture. There is nothing, ultimately, nothing, that I can do of myself to transform all this pain. There have been times I have wanted to scream: times when yet another new bit of Bridget's body has given up, and I have not been able to bear to go at all. I do remember how once my own pain was transformed for me by pure gift, by the presence of the Crucified. Can I depend upon that presence? All I can do is to offer the pain. Sometimes the complete and stark accuracy with which the Eucharist embodies the totality of experience as I know it is in itself nearly unendurable. Like all total accuracy, it also brings relief. Then the Offertory is taken onwards, the action moves from Crucifixion to Transformation and Resurrection. Easter is less comprehensible than Good Friday, but I can at least, in the face of this silence and this glory, understand why Peter was reduced to chattering meaninglessly of building booths at the Transfiguration. Joy has to be silent. Or the only words are the *Sanctus*.

But it is because the celebration of the Eucharist and Christ's offering of Himself in it seems to comprehend all the realities of acute pain and death that I have not handed in my ticket. I have spoken openly here of suffering and of death, breaking my own taboos, because it seems to me that a faith which cannot comprehend these realities, and contain them within its central paradox of life through God's death, is not worth having. We have to learn to live in the tension which seems so much the crux of Christianity, in which present agony is also permeated with joy or the promise of joy. If we cannot, we are only subscribing to pious platitudes. So our own discovery that events which stretch us to the limit, and then beyond what we think we are capable of, these times of acute suffering can bring with them an insight into joy beyond our rational conception, is fundamental to our growth. I can at least bear witness to some of this kind of reality.

Celebration, pp83, 85-7

Riches

. . . when I eventually arrived at what became my abbey the Abbess asked me why I had taken so long to get there. 'Were you frightened of nuns?' she asked. 'No', I answered, 'I am a historian. I was frightened of God'. She seemed to understand perfectly.

My abbey has been very important to me. The density and opaqueness of contemplative silence is impossible to convey: in it there is room for movement and life of unexpected kinds. I never know what I go there for: the meaning comes out in the silence, and has never, so far, been one I knew of in advance. Of all the psalms, the eighty-fourth expresses it most accurately:

> *How lovely is your dwelling place,*
> *O Lord of hosts.*
> *My soul longs, yes, faints,*
> *for the courts of the Lord,*
> *my heart and flesh sing for joy to the living God.*

Despite, or because of, the sheer brutal hard work of presenting all the hard truths in my life to be transformed, and the terrifying meaning and all-inclusiveness of the post-communion prayer 'Here we offer and present to you, O Lord, ourselves, our souls and bodies, to be a reasonable, holy, living sacrifice', my oblation there is fundamental to me. I find depth of joy there that I do not often know elsewhere. It is for some reason easy for me to look at God and love Him: at my abbey, very, very easy. But although it has been made easy for me to look at Him, and I have loved Him for a long time, so long is the road to perfection in love, that only sometimes, very recently, have I begun to know that He looks back at me with any love. I need to learn much more.

I cannot remember when I started to pray the *Sanctus*. I do not know whether all those hospital clinics, at which it never seemed possible to work academically, all those gifts of unplanned time I resented so bitterly to start with, actually formed the habit. Or perhaps the habit transformed them. I do a lot of waiting, anyway: people who are not infrequently immobilised, or who have to rest a lot, do. I was aided perhaps by the view from my window. For seventeen years, our bedroom looked out westwards into the trees of an eighteenth century park. The form and structure of those trees, and the clear gold light that outlined them, meant a very great deal to me. I am tempted to say what is palpably untrue, that only the housebound really learn to appreciate landscape. 'The world is charged with the grandeur of God.' In some bad times, I lived on the shadow-tracery of leaves, reflected on my wall. At some point, my mind and attention began to be taught to use these periods of waiting to try to pray. At some point, I must have been grasped by some perception of the beauty of God. So my mind started to slip into the words of the *Sanctus* when it was not otherwise engaged, as, of course, it usually was, and is. I tried once to change this accustomed background mutter of 'Holy, holy, holy', into the words of the Jesus prayer, which seemed to be recommended. But it did not work, so I stopped trying. At some later point, I discovered St Teresa of Avila's *Way of Perfection*. I have still not got beyond the introductory chapters, and doubt whether I ever will. There seems no point in reading beyond what I can understand. However I do not comprehend how people can write, as one author I read recently did, 'There are times when the sort of prayer God gives us is the rather empty experience known as the prayer of quiet'. If this experience is empty, I cannot imagine riches.

When the discomfort has become so great that I can do nothing but lie down, and cannot think clearly, then I know my work has become prayer. While I am still sitting at my desk, I am still a historian. The confusing bit is the bit in between, when I am not sure whether I am still trying to think, or have become so uncomfortable that it is time to try to pray. This does seem a very churlish way to treat God: to attempt to focus on Him only when my attention is distracted by the discomfort is curiously unceremonious. His humility appears endless. However, the humility of other historians is not to be relied on in the same way. But using the apparently unavoidable pain as profitably as possible means continuing to do academic work 'upside down' as much as I can, and attempting to be aware of the presence of God.

It is very good to have something to try to do with the pain. While it still remains an unmitigated evil, I can yet regard it somehow as a means to an end. I cannot describe the process very well, but I have found it to be one of somehow *absorbing darkness* – a physical or mental suffering of my own, or worse, of someone else's – into my own person, my own body, or my own emotions. We have to allow ourselves to be open to pain. Yet all the while we must resist any temptation to assent to it being other than evil. If we are able to do this, to act, as it were, as blotting paper for pain, without handing it on in the form of bitterness or resentment or of hurt to others – then somehow in some incomprehensible miracle of grace, some at least of the darkness may be turned to

light. It can also be used as a reminder to focus on what is really important. Unlike impending execution, it does not concentrate the mind
wonderfully; indeed, pain scatters concentration for the most part. But
its emphatic attack on the body, its almost annihilating powers, can be
made helpful if they serve to scatter what is inessential in our feeling.

It may be tempting, in chronic pain, to give up on the body, to despair
of it; but the Word was made flesh. It seemed, and seems, important to
me that the incarnate Christ came to us, and into our world of
ramshackle bodies. Mine is so very ramshackle that sometimes it is
difficult to be patient with it, but I do try. I enjoy material things a lot,
which helps. It is only the *wrongness* I object to. I loathe and detest my
bone disease. I am often miserable, often shamefully discontented, often
isolated, often lonely. I fear pain, and the fear does not grow less. But
oddly, after twenty years, I can no longer wish that things were quite
otherwise, except for my husband's sake. Learning to live with the
disorder as creatively as possible has in the end formed the person I am.
I cannot, in the last resort, regret being the person I am, as historian, or
mother, or oblate. I think I can say, without any trace of masochism,
that the disease has indeed been a creative medium. I have tried to use
the pain of it to remind me to try to focus on what is really important.
And what is really important is adoration.

Celebration, pp88-89, 92-93

Communion

At the age of eight, Bridget had a transplant. The donor of her new kidney was her father.

That fortnight, and indeed the next week or two, was tough. In some ways I was most worried about our son. At eleven it is a lot to have one's sister perhaps dying, and one's father, however briefly, at risk on the same day. The new paediatric team was amazingly understanding when I said I wanted him on the ward with me during the actual kidney transplant. In my judgement, a highly intelligent and sensitive eleven-year-old was going to survive that sort of day better, if he could see what was happening, rather than do his own imagining, alone in a vacuum. Guy's said 'Yes' without externally turning a hair. The last thing anyone can actually want in an intensive care cubicle is an inquisitive eleven-year-old asking how the machinery works, particularly during a procedure which was then still fairly experimental. But they still allowed it. It helped me carry my elder normal child through the transplant quite enormously.

As for me – bizarrely, and, like all such developments, quite unplanned – I started to discover some reality in a bit of the doctrine of the Church that had previously been quite irrelevant. I walked around, those weeks, feeling as if I was imprisoned behind a very thick plate-glass wall. People were immensely kind: they mouthed words through the glass, just like fish, and just as meaningless. I responded, politely I hope, feeling totally unreal. My research supervisor, a short-tempered and deeply humane man with a gift of words, whom I had loved, had died some years before. Such was his care for me that he had come all the way to Great Ormond Street weekly for six months while Bridget was first in, to take me out to lunch to make sure I had a proper meal once a week. For five and a half of those months, he had never even mentioned his great love, Anglo-Saxon charters, to me. Quite correctly he gauged that I was unable to focus on scholarship. Now quite suddenly, inside the glass walls that cut me off from everyone, however kind, his presence was lent to me. It was utterly ordinary and familiar, as pithy-tempered, as ready to keep me up to the mark, and as kind, as ever. It was a very odd experience, and his company was withdrawn before the glass walls melted. But I felt that the Communion of Saints was a real concept, in a way that it had not been before.

Celebration, pp100-101

Love

Bridget was in fact to die just after her twenty-second birthday, after a second renal transplant. She herself had to make the final decision as she was over the age of eighteen when she had renal failure a second time. Her parents were both responsible for her care and completely powerless in this situation, loving and supporting her, but willing to let her die. Two years later, and she was back in hospital with more illness and distress. And soon, back in the care of her parents, she died.

Bridget herself made her contribution to understanding what had been going on, as her mother was to find.

On one occasion when she needed hospital treatment, when she was fifteen, Bridget was admitted to hospital and put in an isolation cubicle. The boy in the cubicle next door was very ill with a brain tumour and, a couple of nights later, he died. The venetian blinds only partially covered the window between the two cubicles; even if they had been complete, Bridget would still have had to face Simon's dying, for it was noisy. At this stage, she could not believe in a loving God.

Yet in her rage and distress, she still addressed the God she could not believe in on paper. A piece of blotted writing in an exercise book, in all its fifteen-year-old crudity and simplicity, turned up amongst Bridget's papers after her own death.

It ran, plus punctuation:

> *If 'you' exist, then why in blazes didn't you stick out a hand and help him fight his way through? It has to be a waste and if any fool starts throwing cliches like 'time will heal' or 'it was for the best', then I hope his parents react a) devastatedly b) in fury c) in a total feeling of 'why'? It can't help, nothing really can, but if heaven exists, then in the book of justice that ought to exist, to give a REASON for unreasonable, unexplainable situations, there will be a life with no medical record, his favourite interests, fabulous scenery and either a time-warp which allows his family to be there, or that means those here are also there with Simon – only more so. I'm very sorry. Bridget. (The girl in cubicle 1, who had a first-hand experience of dying which was not unpleasant, and is therefore sure that being dead is not nothing – though I'm fairly sure a 'good, fair God' doesn't exist at all.)*

All through Bridget's adolescence, I wrestled with her probing, angry searching, which mirrored my own, for coherent belief in an omnipotent God who was loving, cared for persons, and yet had made her, or allowed her to be made, so disastrously wrong.

It was only ever possible to begin to convey to Bridget a God who cared enough about her, and others, to immerse Himself in His own world and become helpless in, and share, its pain. It was the only argument that made sense at all. (For me, it is undoubtedly true that 'only a suffering God can help us'.) But, in the end, it was not argument that convinced her. She had her own experience of illumination, on Iona, through a combination of music and human love. When she was eighteen, and in hospital again, after this, I said to her, 'Is there anything I could have said about God's love that would have helped you? What should I have done?' And she replied, 'Nothing. There is no argument. You have to experience it'.

So again, we come back to the Incarnation. Maybe theology and intellectual argument are incapable of bringing solutions to the mystery of botched and suffering human beings, made wrong in a botched and suffering world. This mystery can only be shared, in patient love, which in the deepest and fullest sense, is compassionate, and reflects the love of God, impassible, unchanging, and yet so loving His world that He gives it power to affect Him, so that He died, as Simon died.

Lord have mercy

My daughter said:

'If there is a God, why did He make me like this?'
She is only ten, but has always been clear headed.
Even so, that is a big nail to hit square on the head at ten.
I suppose she doesn't know of all the hours, days, months
Her mother spent screaming inside, in one of those
Marvellous modern hospitals where the medicine really is good
And they even love the children, who mostly look like children
But not altogether, because somehow they came from the factory,
Warm womb, assembly line,
Chance's wheel, potter's hand,
Not quite right.
The blueprint slipped a bit.
So how did she hit her mother's nail so square?
We can forgive God Belsen, for we did it,
But how about blurred blueprints from an architect
   who is supposed to be top of the profession?
There isn't any answer to her question
I asked the theologians and the philosophers
Even the believing biochemist did not know
So I believe in one God, the Father Almighty,
Maker of heaven and earth, all things visible and invisible,
Whose hand sometimes slips a bit.
I do, too.
But if it wasn't for His Son, who came down from Heaven
And was incarnate by the Holy Ghost and shared
The whole bloody mess, and the pain of those children
I couldn't bear it, or Him, either.
Kyrie eleison.

A revelation of divine love

I have been perplexed in the last months about what to do about a vision. (I think that is the accurate word, but have taken great pains to avoid looking up 'visionary experience' and methods of describing it, to avoid blurring or changing what I saw, except in so far as the passage of time and recollection does that.)

On the one hand, a vision seems an intensely private thing. First, I want to avoid being thought of unsound mind, and to be babbling of visions could well be thought to be, and indeed is, synonymous with some medical states.

Second, and much more important, I have a much more real fear – the danger of other people, but most of all of myself, thinking that if I spoke of it, I might be made out to be in any way 'special' because of the extraordinary grace that was given. There is a major trap there. Somone wise said to me, 'It is so easy to smear the most important things with ego', and it is true. I fear it. I have been a little comforted since I remembered the number of times the Lord 'had compassion' on the wretched. If I can hold fast to that, and perceive this experience as his compassion, perhaps the temptation can be avoided.

These are reasons for silence. On the other hand, there are reasons for speech. The gift that was given me was so great that I feel a little the way the disciples on the road to Emmaus must have done, running back in the dark to say, 'We saw him! We saw him!' And a couple of times in the last year when people in great distress after a bereavement have spoken to me, I have felt the overpowering need to tell them, because I want to share the truth and joy of it. This was such a great gift, it does not seem to me it can only be private, but has to be for everyone else, because all the things I have said with my lips and my intellect over the years about the Resurrection I now 'know', in a quite different way, to be true, because I have seen the Lord, or rather, a flicker of his face. And now I, too, live from Easter backwards. How can I not tell people, or rather, how can people be let know, without the dangers of which I have written?

What happened is this. Our twenty-two year old daughter died one Sunday after the Ascension. I had been nursing her for a very long time. Because her death was expected – indeed, we had lived with the expectancy since she was one, and now we knew she needed, for mercy, to die – I thought the grief for her would be much lessened. The sheer size and immensity of what followed was a total surprise to me. It was like being a rag in a hurricane, or a bit of twig in a tidal wave. Someone said losing a child was like losing a limb. It wasn't. It was the loss of my womb and what had been created out of it, that person I had procreated, my life as a mother, and its fruit. I became limbs with no body, not a body without a limb.

My husband and I had arranged to go on an Ignatian retreat in September. I felt myself to be perhaps such a heavy burden for the retreat director that I rang her up to ask if she would like me to cancel. She said, 'Come'.

We were in silence except for the daily Eucharist at noon, and an interview with the director. She was compassionate and perceptive. But I was tormented by dreams. One night I had the most terrible nightmare I have ever had. I was seeking everywhere for our daughter, on earth, in the galaxies, in the universe. And she was not. And God was not, either. And there was nothing.

The next day all I could do was say the *De Profundis* over and over again. And that night, our daughter came to me in my dreams and hugged me. But I woke totally and completely clear that I had dreamed, and what I had experienced was nothing but a dream, born of my loss and my need.

That noon, at the Eucharist, I had an experience of a completely different quality and nature. It came to me as the Host was being passed round our circle, before it reached me. I saw nothing at all with my external eyes, and I have no idea how, or if, time was involved: if it was, I should guess the experience would have lasted a minute fraction of a second. Our daughter was suddenly in my arms, four-square, tactile, palpable, warm. She came there with the enthusiasm of a puppy, not in any need of me, but giving to me, and overflowing with affection. I could feel her: she practically landed on my chest with a 'thump'.

But behind her, to the right, stood the Lord. I could not see him properly at all, I just had the impression of a figure. What I did see for an instant, was not his face, but the expression on his face. I have always tried not to imagine him, but if I had, I could never have imagined this. He was looking down at her, this small creature of his with an intensity of love, delighting in her. And his face was alight with laughter. She always did make people laugh, when she was well. I have been told that the Gospels have puns in Aramaic, and never before understood what this tells us of him. But his amusement was integral, fundamental to what I saw, fundamental to him. I saw, lastly, that he had a quality of dynamism that was utterly beyond any experience or concept of a human being that I had ever had. (I would talk of him being 'like electricity', if it was not such a false analogy, being merely about power and force, when this was about humanity glorified, or about a human being with more vitality than I could ever have conceived.)

I am not sure if he looked at me. I thought afterwards there was a flicker of a glance that was not quite a rebuke, still amused, which I would have said, if there had been words, 'So you weren't sure I could look after her?' But I am not sure about that, as I am of the rest.

He was beautiful. I wish I could convey how beautiful. C S Lewis tied himself in an intellectual knot at the end of *A Grief Observed*. He worried about a possible tension between the Beatific Vision, the fruition of God, and reunion with his much-loved dead wife. He himself sensed an absurdity, and yet he still closed his book on a note of sadness. His wife, he wrote, 'said . . . "I am at peace with God." She smiled, but not at me.' And then he quoted Dante, when Beatrice finally left him in Paradise, 'and turned to the eternal fountain'. Lewis wrote as if there was a loss for himself, as his wife turned towards God; for Dante, as Beatrice turned away. In what I saw, there was no loss. I would have supposed that, to a distraught mother grieving as I was, a palpable hug from a warm and living daughter would be the focal point of all attention. It was not so. I held her, and my empty arms were full again, but I concentrated on him, as he looked down at her, in his beauty, and his amusement. There was no tension between the two sorts of love. Our joy in each other could only add to our adoration of him. It was very simple.

The experience has made a great difference to my life. I did not stop grieving, but the violence of grief went, for I knew all was truly well with her. I just miss her, dreadfully, sometimes. Much more than that, the whole focus and perspective of my life has shifted, and my attention moved onwards. Pain, both physical and emotional has been my un-friend for a very long time. The realisation of its sharing by the Crucified Lord has been its only redemption and hope. Indeed, the only similar visionary experience I have had, more than twenty years ago, came in a moment of such acute agony in an accident that I was actually screaming. Again, I saw nothing, externally; but internally I perceived that I was lying alongside the Cross. It lay on my right, parallel with me, so that one of the cross-bars nearly touched my hand. Again I 'saw' with my internal eyes only, a tiny fraction of him for a tiny fraction of time, if we were in time at all. I saw a little of his hand and foreshortened arm – above all, the shoulder muscles bunched up in agony. He was inside my pain, sharing it.

That knowledge made it possible to go on. Calvary is everywhere. But suddenly, I, who have survived so long by that image, found myself some months ago looking for something different. For a long time, a reproduction of the Christ Pantocrator at Daphne, that wonderful and terrible face that combines majesty, and the knowledge of the depth of pain, has hung on my wall. It served to remind me of what I had previously seen. But that image will not do any more: it will have to come down. It does not remind me of what I have now seen. There is no joy there, and no laughter, to complete the power and the suffering. Now I too live from Easter backwards, and I have searched art galleries for over a year, looking for Resurrections. There are so comparatively few. Calvary is indeed everywhere. Painters seem commonly to have stopped there, as if Good Friday was the end of the story. (I am reduced to wishing St Luke had not ostensibly spent quite so much time painting the Virgin.) The few Resurrections I have found quite often convey majesty, but I have not found a single one to act as a trigger to the memory of that expression I saw some months ago. Easter is unpainted.

What seems really important about what I saw, although I saw so very little, a flash of expression on his face, is that something is actually true, that all practising, or even nominal Christians know, or are taught, or believe, at different intellectual or emotional levels. The Lord is risen indeed, and is full of joy, as well as knowing all pain. The individual love he preached for all his creatures must be true too, from his delight in this one insignificant girl, who seemed to be risen from the dead. There is, I saw, no necessary conflict between love of him, and of those human beings very dear to us. All I can do is testify to the truth of these things, which we all 'know' already. I feel like a small child drawing the head of a 'pin-man' with thick chalk, when I need to convey a Turner. I can make nothing elaborate of this, only say as accurately as I can, in simplicity, what happened.

But in case it might be of use to my 'even-Christians' I have written down what I saw.

Theology 45, pp200-204

On joy

Joy is one of the gifts of the Holy Spirit: it is connected with two things for me, the vision of the Glory of God, and the perception of His love for us, which, for some of us is so unlikely that we spend most of our lives not perceiving it. Of these two, I intend to concentrate on the former. But visions of the glory of God are tricky things, as any reader of the books of Daniel and Revelation, and any seventeenth century historian, well knows.

You will remember that when Moses began to hunger for this vision, he said to God, 'I beseech thee, show me thy Glory,' and the Lord replied, 'Thou cannot see my face: for there shall no man see me and live.' But so great was Moses' craving, that the Lord hid him in a cranny of rock, and covered him with his hand while He himself passed by: but then He took away His hand, and Moses was vouchsafed the vision of the Lord's back. But that was not the end of that story. When, later, Moses came down from the mountain after talking to the Lord in His glory, and receiving the commandments from Him, Moses was transformed and the skin of his face shone, so the people of Israel were afraid. Even at second hand, the glory of the Lord was too much for them, so that Moses had to put a veil over his face.

Similarly, when the prophet Isaiah saw the Lord sitting upon His throne, high and lifted up, surrounded by the cry of praise of His seraphim singing, 'Holy, holy, holy is the Lord of hosts: the whole earth is full of his glory,' Isaiah's *first* response was not to delight but to say, 'Woe is me! because I am a man of unclean lips . . . (and) mine eyes have seen the King, the Lord of hosts.'

So the weight of the glory of God is too dazzling for our photophobic earthworms' eyes, and perhaps it is as well that only rarely are we vouchsafed glimmers of it.

But the second reason for the trickiness, even of these glimmers, is quite simply that we lack words for His beauty. The Word, we believe, was made flesh and dwelt among us: and so the Lord became man, and went around Galilee, healing, and preaching, and praying, and sometimes losing His temper – especially with those who thought they already knew the answers.

The apostles, those blessedly ordinary people, kept company with Him, and on one occasion at least, saw Him transfigured and shining and saw the Glory of God in human form. Yet they lived. But they were reduced to inanities because there *are* no words to convey the perception of Glory, or perhaps only the song the seraphim sing. Peter started to chatter of building little booths ('tabernacles' in the Authorised Version) in the face of this enormous perception of divine reality. For he knew not what to say: for they were sore afraid! But he *did* manage to say the one thing that really mattered: 'It is good for us to be here.'

The occasion of the Lord's transfiguration was enormously important. It was closely associated with His attempt to teach the disciples of His approaching Crucifixion and Resurrection: indeed, he forbade them to speak of his transfiguration until He had risen from the dead. And, entirely reasonably, they understood neither His teaching that He should be killed nor His teaching that He would rise again on the Third Day.

In St John's Gospel, the Crucifixion was explicitly associated with the Lord's glorification. 'The hour has come', he said, 'that the Son of man should be glorified . . . And I, if be lifted up from the earth, will draw all men unto me.' He also prayed, 'Father, glorify thy name.'

And here we enter the central mystery of the Lord, and the most inexplicable to us: that Crucifixion and Resurrection, Good Friday and Easter, were somehow one event. If the disciples did not understand, we may be comforted that we do not either. But it is vital to us, as we muddle our way through our painful lives, that we should receive the truth that Thomas received in the upper room. For then we might be able to receive the Lord's message, 'Peace be with you.'

Thomas refused to believe the Lord was risen unless, he said, 'I shall see in his hands the print of the nails, and thrust my hands into His side!' And the Lord, a week later, said to Thomas, 'Reach hither thy finger, and behold my hands; and reach hither thy hands, and thrust it into my side'. And Thomas's response to touching these wounds was 'My Lord, and my God.'

The resurrected body of the Lord was glorious not *in spite of* but *because of* the wounds, and the scars. And because the Lord God incarnate was made glorious through his acceptance of his wounds, *not* in spite of them, we may also have hope that we ourselves in our malformations and damage, may be redeemed, and become, in some small fashion, icons of glory. Blurred icons, indeed, but like Moses, or, if you prefer, like St Paul's translucent earthenware pots, we are intended ultimately to shine, as mirrors reflecting His glory, each uniquely in his or her own fashion.

It is not our business to know how, or when, or whether, we reflect His glory: but it is our business to co-operate in the process of trying to perceive it, for only by perceiving His glory and His beauty can we mirror Him. The 'how' of doing this I shall not try to go into; it is about seeing what is going on before our very eyes at the Eucharist and about learning to pray, which is also about being silent to listen, and to look.

St Teresa of Avila told her nuns, 'I am only asking you to *look* at Him. For who can prevent you turning the eyes of your soul . . . upon This Lord? . . . Can you not . . . look at the most beautiful thing imaginable?'

The Independent, 15 April 1992

The Lord's Prayer

Our Father

We are at once admitted to relationship with the infinite majesty who causes all things to be, without whom nothing would be. And what a relationship!

We know of our Lord that His relationship with His Father was the most important thing in His life: how and when he came to realise it, and whether gradually, we don't know. But there are markers we do know about. He discovered something when He was totally absorbed, in the Temple when He was twelve, and got left behind. 'Did you not know I must be about my Father's business?' The sense of relationship was already strong. It is there again at His baptism in the Jordan. The words He heard said by God, His Father, were 'Thou art my beloved Son, in whom I am well pleased'; and it was so overwhelming an experience that it sent Him into the desert to think it over and pray and define His ministry. The identity was re-stated towards the end of his ministry, at the Transfiguration: 'This is my Son, my Chosen; listen to him'. The disciples heard. It was from that experience of unity, which was the fundamental thing to Him that He prayed in agony in the garden of Gethsemane: and it was *because* that unity was the fundamental thing to Him that the ultimate dereliction of the Cross was its loss: all His life and mission became non-sense, He was mistaken, He was rootless, Fatherless, fallen into the abyss which is bottomless: 'My God, my God, why hast Thou forsaken me?'

So here is this fundamental fact of relationship and identity: and here is the astonishment of our vocation as Christian people. Through our baptism and our long, slow growth in Christian life, we become part of Christ, one with our Lord: again St John recorded that the Lord prayed at the Last Supper for all those who came to believe in Him 'that they may all be one; as thou, Father, art in me, and I in thee, and they also may be one in us'. I'm not going to try and wrestle with St Paul on the body of Christ: but the astonishing truth is that we, who are worthless except because He loves us, are so much loved that we too become sons and daughters of the Father: have you ever paused to consider, as you say 'Our Father' that our Lord is making himself our brother? So let us pause now, and think of that . . . we are in deep relationship . . .

Our Father,
Who art in heaven

The kingdom of heaven is within you. St Augustine wrote of seeking God everywhere, and eventually finding Him within himself. We don't have to rush about to find heaven, it is not 'only' an exterior state in the presence of the Beatific Vision after death, it is now, here, this instant if we will just be still and allow ourselves to be aware of God, present within ourselves. That practice of stillness takes time to learn.

It follows on, from allowing ourselves to be permeated with the knowledge of God present in us in this present moment, that everyone else is, too. Once one becomes aware of, absurdly, in one's human wretchedness, becoming a temple of the Holy Spirit, the major fight, I have found, becomes that to recognise the presence of God likewise, and equally, in all our fellow-men (and women). It is very difficult: one is frightened of them, shy, critical, finds some people downright objectionable: but it is no good, they also are the courts of the Lord, where the King in all his beauty is to be found, and we have to struggle, all our lives, I think, to make this elementary act of recognition.

Our Father, who art in heaven
Hallowed be thy name

In the year that King Uzziah died, the prophet Isaiah had a vision we all know:

> *I saw also the Lord sitting upon a throne, high and lifted up, and his train filled the temple. Above it stood the seraphims: each one had six wings: with twain he covered his face, and with twain he covered his feet, and with twain he did fly. And one cried unto another, and said, Holy, Holy, holy is the Lord of hosts: the whole earth is full of his glory. (Isaiah 6:1-3)*

And because these are the richest words that have ever been used to adore the beauty of God, we use them as a preface to the Prayer of Consecration at the Eucharist:

> *With Angels and Archangels, and with all the company of heaven, we laud and magnify thy glorious Name, evermore praising thee,*

*and saying Holy, holy, holy, Lord God of hosts, heaven and earth
are full of thy glory: Glory be to thee, O Lord most High. Amen.*

It always seems suitable to me at this point in the Lord's Prayer,
when we have been considering our brotherhood with Christ, and the
indwelling of God within us and our fellows, to move into these words
of pure worship 'Hallowed be Thy name' and go from there into the
Sanctus. 'Holy, holy, holy art Thou: the whole earth is full of Thy glory'.

And sometimes it seems suitable, and fitting to go on repeating, or
listening to, the words of the *Sanctus* for quite a long time, because
adoration is the appropriate response to the reflections we have been
having. So let us think the words of the *Sanctus* for a minute or two, and
then pause, before we move on.

*Holy, holy, holy Lord God of hosts, heaven and earth are full of
thy glory.*

Thy kingdom come,
Thy will be done on earth as it is in heaven

Kingdom is a difficult word, and full of associations I don't think our
Lord intended. The overtones of sceptres, crowns, thrones and
pomp aren't the right ones at all. The best suggestion ever made to me
was that the kingdom is the dance, the dance of God with man, for in
the royal dance of God, there are no outcasts (unless any choose to be
so). No-one is unable to dance. Our Lord sought out cripples, lepers,
women, tax-collectors, outcasts, to invite and enable them to join His
dance: and if every single one of us was dancing too, the kingdom would
be established.

And here we get to the tough bit. Tough two ways, at least, as well.
Pain and suffering are never, as such, the will of God: but in some way,
the perfect dance has been broken. The kingdom is *not* established.
'When the King came into His own, His own received Him not'. We all
know what happened in the second half of Holy Week: so if we are
indeed, joyously and incredibly, incorporate in Christ, sons with Him,
we may, God help us, share in His destiny which was in some way
redemptive. So we too may find ourselves saying 'Thy will be done' but
begging that that will is different from what we fear. The ultimate prayer
is 'Be it unto me according to Thy Word', that impossible prayer of

perfect consent and trust. It is sometimes too hard to say: why does no-one elaborate much on that equivalence between the prayer of the Virgin accepting a divine, apparently illegitimate pregnancy for which the penalty was stoning to death, and the prayer of her Son in Gethsemane, accepting his coming crucifixion?

But there is also a second way the will of God must be done on earth. We may reasonably suppose that in the kingdom in which God truly reigns among men, when the dance has *not* gone away, or is set right, we will all conform in a pattern of perfect harmony, chosen by all of us, in which there shall be no more weeping, and justice and compassion shall be everywhere: 'the earth shall be full of the knowledge of God, as the waters cover the sea'. And this state of affairs on earth is at present unimaginable. We saw what our Lord did in his lifetime: He summarised the practicalities Himself. When the imprisoned John the Baptist lost heart and sent to Jesus, saying 'Art thou he that should come? or look we for another?'. When the messengers arrived, they found Jesus healing 'many of their infirmities and plagues, and of evil spirits; and unto many that were blind, he gave sight'. And Jesus told the messengers 'Tell John what things you have seen and heard; how that the blind see, the lame walk, the lepers are cleansed, the deaf hear, the dead are raised, to the poor the gospel is preached'. This was the coming of the kingdom, according to His will.

Long before, Isaiah had fulminated against those who fasted for their own righteousness, and defined true fasting.

> *Is not this the fast that (is) chosen? To loose the bands of wickedness, to undo the heavy burdens, and to let the oppressed go free, and that you break every yoke? Is it not to deal thy bread to the hungry, and that thou bring the poor that are cast out to thy house? When thou seest the naked that thou cover him? . . . Then shall thy light break forth as the morning . . . the glory of the Lord shall be thy reward.* (Isaiah 58:6-8)

And *we* are commanded to preach the gospel to all the world! We are also told we are the branches of the vine which is Christ, and we are to bear fruit. But the thing about vines is that the trunk and the branches are none, indivisible. We are to *be* Him in the world; we *are* His hands and His feet. We are not only united with him in sonship, but activity. And this means we are to do what He did: we are to care about social justice, and about individuals. I don't know about liberation theology, about how to solve the problems of North and South, about how to stop governments spending ridiculous amounts on arms, I cannot myself heal the sick. But I do have a duty to be informed, and to take whatever puny actions I can: it may be a matter of writing letters to my MP, of joining Amnesty International or a relief agency. It may be listening to people in distress. It may be providing a lodging room for an anorexic who can find nowhere to go, because people are so frightened by her. And if I do that, I do it knowing that there will be no miracle, because I am *not* the Lord and natural law will not be suspended: she will probably die under my roof unhealed and it will be massively inconvenient – *but* that I am commanded to provide that roof, if my family situation is suitable. All we do is utterly inadequate, so inadequate it is ludicrous, yet we have to do it, so that the royal dance may be more as it was meant to be, so that the kingdom may come on earth, as it is in heaven.

Give us this day our daily bread

Now St Teresa of Avila glossed this by reflecting, in one of her most powerful passages, on the Eucharist, and our reception of the Lord in it. She dismissed prayer about what she called 'The bread of bodily necessaries and sustenance' as irrelevant – there was time enough to labour for daily bread outside the hours of prayer. 'Would the Lord ever have insisted upon our asking for food, or taught us to do so by His own example?' she wrote. And here, I think, she was wrong, and she herself grudgingly admits (*Way of Perfection*, chapter 37, p161) that those who 'still live on earth . . . may also ask for the bread which they need for their own maintenance and for that of their households'. Indeed, we are bidden to consider the lilies of the field and very unfair it is too, I have always thought, for unfortunately, we have a good deal more power of choice and decision, and hence responsibility, than any lily! Yet anxiety is corrosive, and it eats away at us: we have so *many* responsibilities. What am I to do about my job, my house, the bank manager's last letter, my profound anxieties for my children, and *their* decisions: how, on earth, am I to sort my *priorities* out, is probably key to the whole thing. And in the first part of reflection on this phrase of the Lord's Prayer, despite St Teresa, it seems to me good to go through the current list of these very practical anxieties, whatever they may be, for each of us. And if we can go through them calmly, and put them down at the Lord's feet, telling Him what is troubling us, and then be *still* – and *that bit is crucial*

– then we can try to leave them there as worries, the corrosive element is lost, or lessened, and often, mysteriously, we are given just that sense of priorities we lack.

But St Teresa was also right. She reflected on our daily bread as the Lord coming to us all the day that is our life, and told a story, in fact about herself, about a person 'who smiled to herself' when 'she heard people say they wished they had lived when Christ walked on this earth, for she knew we have Him as truly with us in the Most Holy Sacrament as people had Him then, and wonder(ed) what more they could possibly want . . . when (this person) communicated, . . . it was exactly as if she saw the Lord entering her house, with her own bodily eyes . . . and she went into her abode with Him. She imagined herself at His feet, and wept with the Magdalen exactly as if she had seen Him with her bodily eyes in the Pharisee's house . . . For we cannot suppose this is the work of our imagination . . .' This is something which is happening now; it is absolutely true; and we have no need to go and seek Him somewhere a long way off.

Now there is a trap here, for intellectuals. If we start worrying about *how* the Lord is truly present to us, and in us, in the consecrated elements, at this moment, we lose the whole point. That debate is for another time: and just how much of a trap it can be I will indicate by telling you that in 1577, a book was published discussing no less than 200 interpretations which had by then been placed on the text 'This is my body'! Queen Elizabeth was probably one of the most astute politicians who ever lived, but it may well be that we should do as she did, perhaps not only for political reasons, and imitate her response in verse and its deliberate ambiguity to the debate:

> *Christ was the Word that spake it;*
> *He took the bread and brake it:*
> *And what that Word did make it,*
> *That I believe, and take it.*

So let us not worry about the method and nature of Christ's presence in the consecrated bread and wine with which He feeds us: it is only necessary to know that this is His body and His blood, because He told us so.

I sometimes suspect that the fundamental difficulty of all people is to believe they are really loved. I can believe *you* are, yes, of course, and the people next door, despite their horrible dog, and the down-and-outs, even if they worry me . . . Everyone, in fact. But am *I*, me, myself? That is much more problematic. I suspect most of us spend our lives trying to believe it.

But here, in the Eucharist, if we can but look up and see, it is different. One of the Eucharistic prayers tells us 'He opened wide His arms for us on the Cross'. For all of us, for *me* personally, too. Take that analogy of our redemption further – take it to an embrace. When He feeds you in the Eucharist, this is His embrace.

And in the hour afterwards, it is very profitable, as St Teresa says, to stay quietly, aware of His love and company, looking at Him. Dame Julian of Norwich puts it like this – 'He is our clothing. In his love he wraps and holds us. He enfolds us for love, and he will never let us go . . . !'

At this time after receiving our daily bread, we are truly complete, there is nothing left to desire.

And forgive us our sins

After realising the size and enormity of our vocation, we realise how ludicrous we are, how short we fall, and we *need* to say 'Forgive us our sins'. And if we are anxious about this, it may help to remember the story our Lord told, of the Prodigal Father, overflowing with goodwill, running, tripping over his robe, perhaps, in his hurry to welcome home his dissolute son, who really was rotten, quite as rotten as we are . . . It is one of a series of comforting stories the Lord told, to assure us of His love and care for lost sheep, lost gold coins, lost people . . . through the way He acted them out in His own life, and demonstrated them, is even better than the stories. (We could think about that, the woman with the pot of ointment, Peter's feet being washed, the man up a tree . . ., for a minute or two.) But here we hit one of the few conditions. The prayer goes on:

As we forgive those that sin against us

We are able to forgive *because we have been forgiven*: we are able to love, *because we are loved*: we are able to give, *because we have been given to*: it is all that way round. First, we need to receive, in order to be able to give. (That is why it is so important to realise that we, even *I myself* are truly accepted and acceptable, truly loved – even *me*, in all my filth and my need. Only from this truth received can we go on. 'In this is love', St John says, 'not that we loved God, but that he (first?) loved us . . . Beloved, if God so loved us, we also ought to love one another.'

So *being* loved comes first. It is *not* more blessed to give than to receive: the ability to give depends on having received. But if, having received, we *fail* to give onwards, then God's anger is aroused. For He has loved and accepted us – like the king who forgave his servant ten thousand talents. But that King was justifiably angry when he heard that the servant, on his way out, had half-throttled, and then thrown into prison, a fellow servant who, in turn, owed *him* a hundred pence. And the king said 'Alright, pay *me* what you owe *me*'. This was a story the Lord told after Peter had asked him whether he, Peter, ought to forgive the brother who hurt him as many as seven times? And Jesus replied, as many as seventy times seven – that is, to infinity.

So we are to forgive, as we are forgiven. I don't know whether any of you have the problem I have, that usually there is no-one to forgive, because people are, on the whole, extremely nice to me! But sometimes, just the same, one does get hurt, sometimes badly, and it is extremely difficult to forgive the hurt. It usually helps to think about *why* and *how*, it has happened: sometimes I did something stupid, or unfeeling, and this is the reflex: sometimes I can't identify the cause in my own actions. And then it very often helps to consider why the person acted like that, what shadow out of her own past, maybe, made her respond like that? I may have to talk to a third wise party about it, if I still stick. And if I still stick, I think the damage is healed, very frequently, by praying for the needs of the person who has hurt one, not one's own needs, but hers. We can be of use to the person who has damaged us by holding them up in the presence of God, and asking for whatever they need, even though we probably don't know what that is . . . and then we should stop *worrying*. For God will forgive us, even our inability to forgive, if we ask Him.

Lead us not into temptation, but deliver us from evil

This I frankly don't understand. The Lord does not set booby-traps for His people. Yet it is quite true that we find ourselves not infrequently stretched, not only beyond what is comfortable, but beyond what seems possible for us to endure – as the Lord himself did. And we are to pray that, at these times, we may be supported and upheld, so that the 'impossible' becomes 'possible'! 'Out of the depths I cry to you, O Lord; Lord, hear my voice.' And the thing to do, at these times is to cry to Him for grace to endure – to make, in fact, an incessant racket, shrieking (internally) for help – and although we shall feel, and sometimes be, derelict, we are to remember the Lord, who, as we said at the beginning, is our *brother*, and was on the Cross, and we shall not be quite so alone. And when we are able, we are to trust that we shall be delivered. For truly, the grace of God never seems to fail us, though we become desperate. The valley of the shadow of death is an uncomfortable place, but you *can* walk in it . . .

For Thine is the kingdom, the power and the glory

Thine is the whole redeemed world, dancing in beauty and in joy, and Thine is the heavenly city where 'the river of the water of life flows from the throne of God and the Lord, with the tree of life on its banks whose leaves are for the leading of the nations, when night shall be no more, for the Lord God will be our light'.

For ever and ever. Amen.

SELECT BIBLIOGRAPHY

Celebration, London: Fount, 1991.

'A revelation of divine love', *Theology* 45 (1992) pp200-204.

'The Most Beautiful Thing Imaginable', *The Independent*, 15 April 1992, p27.

Other material in this section by Margaret Spufford is published here for the first time.

4

Carlo-Maria Martini

READING SACRED SCRIPTURE

C ardinal Martini is Archbishop of Milan, a diocese reputed to
have the greatest number of priests and laity in the world. Born
in Turin, he became a member of the Society of Jesus and has
been an ordained priest since 1952. He holds doctorates in Theology
and in Holy Scripture from the Gregorian University and the Pontifical
Biblical Institute in Rome, of both of which he has been Rector. He is
also President of the Council of Bishops' Conferences of Europe, and
plays a major role in ecumenical dialogues. He is reputed to speak eleven
languages!

Apart from his major administrative responsibilities in his own arch-
diocese and in Europe, one of the ways in which he exercises his pastoral
care for others is in giving retreats and addresses. Fortunately for the rest
of us, many of the reflections he offers on these occasions are now made
widely available both in their original language and in translation, so
that for about the last fifteen years especially his distinctive approach to
Scripture has become a resource for many.

His work represents a distinctive flowering of the tradition begun by
St Ignatius of Loyola, born in 1491, and founding the Company of Jesus
in 1540. Ignatius' *Spiritual Exercises* form the basis for many a retreat
undertaken by all sorts of people, and his own text has become a particular
resource within the living tradition of Christianity of continuing importance. (See Cardinal Martini's *Letting God Free Us* of 1993.) The *Exercises*
are scriptural in their orientation, and knowledge of this should in itself
help to dislodge from our minds any lingering assumptions we may have
about indifference to reading Scripture in Ignatius's age.

What is distinctive about the *Exercises* is that conversion and freedom
towards God require the exercise of the imagination, whatever else may

104

be required. Many a battle has been fought, and will still be fought about the limits of interpretation of scriptural texts, and those limits may be drawn differently depending on who is engaged with the text. For instance, a certain kind of scholar, searching for clues about what may be taken to be the primary original meaning of the text or texts in question, hoping to identify the intention of its author or authors, may assume that the text has only to do with 'what happened'. This may generate what will seem from another point of view to be an extraordinary preoccupation with the 'literal' sense, and with restriction of range and depth of possible meanings. Suppose now the scholar to be a preacher, or that her or his work is to be a resource for a preacher, irrespective of whether publication had a preacher's interests in mind, what then? What sense is to be made of the text? Simply a narrative of 'what happened'? For if the text is to be sung and prayed as well as preached, read in the context of worship, where imagination and affections as well as an analytic kind of intellect are to be integrated in the search for God, and where God may find us, the limits may be drawn very differently. Cardinal Martini helps us to explore Scripture with him and to find in it unexpected and refreshing dimensions, not least when we may have thought it to be all too familiar to us. We will read some of his work by following where possible the order of the Scriptural texts, and will inevitably learn a little of the Ignatian tradition of 'reading' as we go.

Ruth – in five scenes

Carlo-Maria Martini's David: Sinner and Believer *contains as one might expect an exploration of the successive stages in David's life, together with comparison between David and Jesus of Nazareth, interwoven with texts from the collection of Psalms. Psalm 63 (O God, thou art my God, I seek thee) and Psalm 51 (Have mercy on me, O God, according to your steadfast love) are particularly chosen to juxtapose with episodes from David's life; and the book also includes Homilies on Matthew 13:10-17; John 20: 1, 11-18 and Matthew 13:24-30, each of which may be read separately from the story of David. One of the most interesting features of this book, however, is the Cardinal's attempt to find the equivalent of an infancy story for David, not in the sense of a childhood chronicle, but rather something which would give us the roots of simplicity, humility and gentleness in the background from which David came. The biblical text to read here is the book of Ruth about David's great-grandmother, mentioned in Matthew's gospel as being an ancestress of Jesus (Matthew 1:5) and in Jewish tradition in any case, read especially at the feast of Pentecost. And the first thing to notice about Ruth is that she is a Moabitess, one of the 'enemy'.*

1   The first scene is sited in the countryside of Moab. A man of Bethlehem had been forced to emigrate with his wife Naomi and his two sons because of the famine that had broken out in Judaea. The man dies, his two sons marry two Moabite women, Orpah and Ruth. After a few years the two sons die too and the three women are left without a future.

Having heard that the Lord has given his people food once more, Naomi decides to go home and sets out with her two daughters-in-law on the return journey to Judaea. Prompted however by love for Orpah and Ruth, she says: 'Go, return each of you to her mother's house. May the Lord deal kindly with you, as you have dealt with the dead and with me. The Lord grant that you may find a home, each of you in the house of her husband!' Then she kissed them, and they lifted up their voices and wept. And they said to her, 'No, we will return with you to your people'. But Naomi said, 'Turn back, my daughters, why will you go with me? Have I yet sons in my womb that they may become your husbands? Turn back, my daughters, go your way, for I am too old to have a husband. If I should say I have hope, even if I should have a husband this night and should bear sons, would you therefore wait till they were grown? Would you therefore refrain from marrying? No, my daughters, for it is exceedingly bitter to me for your sake that the hand of the Lord has gone forth against me.' Then they lifted up their voices and wept again; and Orpah kissed her mother-in-law, but Ruth clung to her.

And she said, 'See, your sister-in-law has gone back to her people and to her gods; return after your sister-in-law.' But Ruth said, 'Entreat me not to leave you or to return from following you; for where you go I will go, and where you lodge I will lodge; your people shall be my people, and your God my God; where you die I will die, and there will I be buried. May the Lord do so to me and more also if even death parts me from you' (Ruth 1:8-17).

The passage is particularly beautiful and gets better as it goes on: there is Naomi's very humane love and Ruth's love, faithful unto death. Ruth's love leads her to a difficult choice: she chooses Naomi's people and her God. Probably she doesn't realise what such a choice will involve, although she is aware of not being able to belong to Israel, of not being able to marry again and have children. Hers is a totally unconditional love, open to faith. Not an explicit faith in God, but a certain awareness of him, responding to the love that God has put in her heart.

2   The account continues by showing that her choice of the God of Israel and of his people is followed by great devotion and service to another.

Very poor, the women have nothing to eat, but Ruth doesn't lean on her mother-in-law and say: go and look up your friends and ask them for something for us to eat. She goes out to work herself.

We are in Bethlehem at the time of the barley harvest, and Ruth the Moabitess turns to Naomi: 'Let me go to the field and glean among the ears of grain after him in whose sight I shall find favour'. And she said to her, 'Go, my daughter'. Ruth 'gleaned in the field until evening; then she beat out what she had gleaned, and it was about an ephah of barley' (Ruth 2:2,17).

The Moabitess asks for nothing; she submits to the laws of Israel; 'When you reap your harvest in your field, and have forgotten a sheaf in the field, you shall not go back to get it; it shall be for the sojourner, the fatherless, and the widow' (Deuteronomy 24:19). She lives humbly in a spirit of service and devotion to her mother-in-law.

3   Ruth's goodness and humility find their counterpart in the kindness and courtesy of Boaz, a man of faith and heart. Of faith because he gives the blessing prescribed in the Psalms: 'And behold, Boaz came from Bethlehem; and he said to the reapers, "The Lord be with you!"

And they answered, "The Lord bless you!"' (Ruth 2:4; cf Psalm 129:7-8). The entire episode takes place in an atmosphere of great faith and religious feeling.

Boaz then sees the young woman, asks who she is and is informed she is a Moabitess and so destined to remain on the margins of society. Next, Boaz approaches her: 'Listen, my daughter, do not go to glean in another field or leave this one, but keep close to my maidens' (Ruth 2:8). The conversation between Boaz and Ruth is rich in human feeling and deserves careful meditation, since it evokes those attitudes which are the fruit of the Spirit: 'love, joy, peace, patience, kindness, goodness, faithfulness, gentleness' (Galatians 5:22). The atmosphere is rather like that in the first two chapters of St Luke's gospel.

4   The fourth section of the book is about the love that dawns between Boaz and Ruth with the help of wise Naomi. Ruth makes herself look her best, perfumes herself, wraps herself in a cloak and, after dark, goes and lies down at Boaz's feet, where he sleeps among the heaps of barley. When the man wakes up comes encounter and recognition: 'May you be blessed by the Lord, my daughter; you have made this last kindness greater than the first, in that you have not gone after young men, whether poor or rich. And now, my daughter, do not fear, I will do for you all that you ask, for all my fellow townsmen know that you are a woman of worth' (Ruth 3:10-11).

5   The marriage contract is drawn up without a hitch. Boaz discharges the duty of meeting a male relative of Naomi's, who by law has right of redemption over the field belonging to Naomi's late husband and hence over Ruth too. The man renounces his right of redemption before witnesses. Boaz declares himself willing to take the man's place and the elders conclude it all by saying: 'May the Lord make the woman who is coming into your house, like Rachel and Leah, who together built up the house of Israel' (Ruth 4:11). This verse is all-important since it speaks of the wife of Jacob; Rachel, as you will know, was buried at Bethlehem where her tomb still stands. 'May you prosper in Ephrathah and be renowned in Bethlehem; and may your house be like the house of Perez, whom Tamar bore to Judah, because of the children that the Lord will give you by this young woman'.

So Boaz took Ruth and she became his wife; and he went in to her, and the Lord gave her conception, and she bore a son (Ruth 4:11-13). Thus Ruth begins to be part of that people whom she, prompted by a sense of faith, had chosen for love of Naomi, and is blessed by the God whom she did not know. Naomi called the boy Obed: 'he was the father of Jesse, the father of David'.

'Now these are the descendants of Perez: Perez was the father of Hezron, Hezron of Ram, Ram of Amminadab, Amminadab of Nahshon, Nahshon of Salmon, Salmon of Boaz, Boaz of Obed, Obed of Jesse, and Jesse of David' (Ruth 4:18-22).

So the book ends with its double emphasis on her descendant, David. Ruth the Moabitess who should have been shut out for ever from the Chosen People ('none of their descendants even to the tenth generation' cf Deuteronomy 23:3) becomes a participant in the assembly of the Lord, of the royal, messianic, Davidic line of Judah.

The message of Ruth

First of all, Ruth is a woman of great faith and great courage. She is the figure of faith in God and in the future of his people. She is a symbol of the free gift of self to God, and he in turn will never forsake whoever has made this offering. She represents the beginning of David's faith and has her place in that mysterious way of faith, described in the Letter to the Hebrews, which was to find its completion in Jesus.

If we want to compare her with a figure in the New Testament, Ruth is like the Canaanite woman, poor, belonging to a despised, heathen race, who is however praised by Jesus: '"Yes, Lord, yet even the dogs eat the crumbs that fall from their master's table." Then Jesus answered her, "O woman, great is your faith! Be it done for you, as you desire!"' (Matthew 15:27-28). Jesus had also bestowed praise on his mother Mary for having faith. But it strikes us that whereas Mary had responded to the angel: 'Let it be to me according to your word', here it's Jesus who has to yield to the faith of the Canaanitess: 'Be it done for you, as you desire!' The Canaanitess had no connection with the Chosen People, she didn't know the history and prophecies of Israel; she simply lets herself be guided by her heart, by the feelings she experiences under Jesus's gaze. In this she reminds us of the faith and courage of Ruth.

Ruth furthermore represents the opening of the heathen to the knowledge of the true God. The corresponding New Testament image for this is the centurion who asks for his sick servant to be healed. 'Lord, I am not worthy to have you come under my roof; but only say the word, and my servant will be healed.' When Jesus heard him, he marvelled, and said to those who followed him, "Truly, I say to you, not even in Israel have I found such faith. I tell you, many will come from east and west and sit at table with Abraham, Isaac, and Jacob in the kingdom of heaven, while the sons of the kingdom will be thrown into the outer darkness"' (Matthew 8:8, 10-12).

The figure of Ruth proclaims the universalism of salvation, which was to be foretold by the prophets; Ruth introduces it into the people of God, into the Davidic line that Jesus was to bring to perfection.

Reading the Book of Ruth in this sense, the roots of Jesus himself may be found in it.

We can relate the book of Ruth to certain other Old Testament texts, such as the book of Jonah and parts of the book of Isaiah, for instance Isaiah 19:18-25. On these passages Carlo-Maria Martini concludes:

This stupendous promise of messianic blessing, of reunion of all peoples in love of the Lord, has its roots in the Book of Ruth, is glimpsed at a few peak-moments of Israelite history, and is brought about at the end of the ages when Jesus Christ our Lord and Universal King delivers everything to the Father.

I invite you to reconsider the figure of Ruth also to help you contemplate how God comes to meet us in every circumstance of our lives, but comes to meet us as the One who loves each of us and who loves all of us, who wants to bless all human beings.

Let us pray for all the communities entrusted to us, for all the peoples of the Church and for those with whom we live, that the love and blessing of the Lord may come down on all mankind.

David: Sinner and Believer, pp162-168

Job, grief and lamentation

As we have seen in previous readings in this anthology, it is important not to treat the sufferings and griefs of others as trivial or unimportant, and important not to lie about them in the sense of thinking these happenings are intelligible when they are not. The book of Lamentations itself enables people to find expression for their grief and despair, and so too does the book of Job, on which Cardinal Martini has written especially in Perseverance in Trials.

A lamentation is a prayer that shakes up the soul, causing the pus to issue from the deepest wounds inflicted on us; it is therefore able also to free us interiorly. For the path followed by Job is one of liberation and purification, enabling him to see the face of God once again and to recover the sense of his own dignity and value.

I suggest four thoughts for your personal and practical meditation on Chapter 3 of Job.

1   We must learn to distinguish lamentation from complaint in our lives. Generally speaking, complaining is much more common because we tend to grumble at everything, while each of us complains of others; it is rare that one does not hear criticism of others in religious, social and political circles. We have lost the real meaning of lamentation, which means mourning before God. As a result, when the feelings of defiance, irritation, and anger that are aroused in the heart do not find their natural and proper outlet, people let them fly at anyone and anything around them, creating unhappiness in personal life and in families, communities, and groups. Only God, who is our Father, can put up with even the rebellions and cries of his children; it is because our God is so good and strong that we can quarrel with him. He accepts this confrontation, as he accepted it from Elijah, Jonah, Jeremiah, and Job. It is true that Jonah was rebuked when he asked to die, but meanwhile God allowed him to speak.

Releasing the flow of lamentation is the most effective way of shutting off the streams of complaint that make the world, society, and the concrete Church such sad places and that are utterly fruitless because, being utterances simply of human feeling, they do not get to the bottom of problems.

If we were to substitute profound lamentation in prayer for barren complaining that only opens new wounds, we would often find the solution of our problems and those of others or at least would find a more legitimate way of calling attention to suffering and hardship in the Church.

I must admit to having been in situations in which, in response to the question: 'Where in the Bible can I find something in tune with what I am now feeling?' I found myself reading the Lamentations of Jeremiah and experiencing peace. Instead of taking the path of criticism or various forms of revenge and resentment, I allowed the words of the prophet, intense though they be, to soften and thaw my heart.

The reason why the poor have greater powers of endurance than the rich may be that they have retained this profound, interior outlet, this wisdom about living. Those who have lost it can respond only with anger; they think they are masters of the universe, and if things do not go their way they avenge themselves on others.

2 A second thought. Job does not see the meaning of his experience and he refuses to accept it.

> *My sighing comes like my bread,*
> *and my groanings are poured out like water.*
> *Truly the thing that I fear comes upon me,*
> *and what I dread befalls.*
> *I am not at ease, nor am I quiet;*
> *I have no rest; but trouble comes.* (Job 3:24-26)

To use a contemporary term, Job's condition is that of one who has 'lost all motivation', one who can no longer find any reason to engage in the struggle.

When we find ourselves in this condition, it rings an alarm bell. When we examine ourselves at moments of uncertainty and exhaustion and we seem to have lost our motivation, we feel afraid, And when someone comes to us, perhaps even a young person only a few years married, and tells us he or she has lost their motivation, again we are frightened. There are two reasons for this: first and foremost, we realise that we can find ourselves in the same condition. Second, the term 'loss of motivation' seems to say that the condition is terminal; it seems to justify evasions: I no longer feel anything, I no longer have any desires; what fault is it of mine?

Job tells us, on the contrary, to face up to our condition so that it will lose something of its malevolent power. He urges us to look at the condition with courage, to think of it as not so terrible as to leave us no out. He prods us to ask ourselves what the condition means, especially since persons who find themselves lacking motivation have not changed much objectively, except that they are no longer able to understand action which is unselfish.

We saw in the Prologue of Job the wager made by God: he maintains that human beings are capable of acting out of unselfish love even when ordinary satisfactions are taken away. Those who find themselves lacking in motivation should in fact say to themselves: I have reached the point at which I can, for the first time in my life, begin to be a human being, because I no longer have the string of satisfactions which I had before.

Ninety-eight percent of our actions are the result of the ebb and flow of reciprocal satisfactions that sustain us; and it is right that it should be so. But the proof that disinterested, gratuitous love exists comes when we are completely stripped bare before God and his crucified love. This is the wager taken in the Book of Job a man who cries out, and with reason, that he has lost all motivation, that he desires death, that life no longer has any meaning, but who cries out before God and his friends. He continues to stir himself and to act; he continues to seek.

When motivation has been lost, freedom is purified: the freedom about which there could be some doubt, before the wager, as to its capacity for unselfish action. Job the man gradually reaches his true self.

When, therefore, we think we have reached a limit beyond which we cannot advance, we have in fact only reached the point at which our freedom can find its most authentic expression. Jesus manifested the self-lessness of his love not only when he performed miracles but also on the cross, for then two selfless loves came face to face and matched each other.

Let us learn from Job that our human dignity shows itself in loving God even when the lack of motivation has reached the extreme that is expressed in the words on which we have reflected.

If we find in ourselves any root of frustration, if we are frightened lest our actions have no meaning, and if we are afraid even to acknowledge this fact, we should try to say as much to God in the form of a lamentation.

3   We must accept ourselves as we are. When we speak of the poor, for example, we are always tormented that we cannot really share their situation. For, since we have in fact received a formation and an education, we will never be like the poor, no matter what may befall us.

How, then, are we to behave? Like the people back in 1968 who forced themselves to wear unkempt beards and go around dirty so that they might in some degree be like those who are deprived of everything?

That would be absurd. We should thank the Lord that we are who we are, and then ask ourselves what we can do, here and now, for the brothers and sisters who are different from us. We should ask ourselves what we can receive from them who in their turn will ask us the same questions. The important thing is that I should respond to God and that I should love others as much as I can. The desire to get out of myself is a form of Mephistophelean pretension.

Job helps us to tear down these castles in the air, to be able humbly to accept ourselves and to accept our brothers and sisters, because we are in this world to give ourselves to one another. The claim that we can enter into the skins of all so as to have a geometrically perfect solution proves in the end to be sensationally mistaken.

How often, for example, we think we can help the African peoples in their poverty and are completely mistaken, for we make gestures and adopt attitudes that are not accepted.

If, on the other hand, I set about to listen with love to these peoples, I find that I can receive a great deal from them; and even if I do not completely understand their outlook, I experience existential exchanges that allow me to say: Lord, I have done what I can in the following of your Son; now show me your mercy.

Such modesty of judgement, which inevitably requires intellectual sacrifices, is difficult and is acquired only with age and experience. When we are young we do not accept limits on our intellectual capacity to know everything, to know ourselves completely, and to assess others completely, in the light of ourselves.

4   Let us ask Jesus in the Garden of Olives: 'Lord, did you ever experience moments in which everything seemed to you to be bizarre, insipid, and meaningless, moments in which you had no desire to do anything and felt no spur of any kind to action? And how did you live through such moments?'

St Charles Borromeo tells us that he experienced frustration, a sense of uselessness and disgust. One day, when his cousin Frederick asked him how he acted at such moments, he showed him the little psalter which he always carried in his pocket. He fell back on the songs of lamentation in order to give voice to his own suffering and, at the same time, to recover his staying power and confidence in the presence of the mystery of the living God.

Let us pray that the Lord will give us too, the gift of being able to approach the purifying and restorative fountain of biblical lamentation.

Perseverance in Trials, pp45-50

From lamentation to praise

Cardinal Martini has a special gift in his ability to consider apparently unre-
lated texts of Scripture together. One section of his Perseverance in Trials *worth*
reading and re-reading has to do with the Song of Songs, like Job about an
unwearying search – in Job's case, for justice, and in the Song for the face and
presence of the beloved, and for the joy such a presence brings (p125). And we
noted in his reflections on the story of David that he relates some of the Psalms
especially to David's life. From his book on praying with the Psalms, What am
I that you care for me? *we can read Psalm 8 as though it sprang from a partic-*
ular period of David's life – and go on perhaps, to read in Cardinal Martini's
book his treatment of Psalm 150, under the heading of 'Everlasting Praise'.
Printed here is his illuminating exposition of Psalm 8 (O Lord, our Lord, how
majestic is thy name in all the earth!).

Psalm 8: David's experience

I don't know whether I shall be able to convey to you what I feel about
this psalm. It is not so much a simple hymn of praise as a canticle of
praise to God. It is a hymn of praise, and we have already seen how the
two attitudes of lamentation and praise are a rise and fall of humanity's
well-spring of prayer: praise for life, lament for the diminishing of life.

This time we have in front of us not simply an exclamation of praise
for the grandeur of creation, nor is it even simply a contemplation of the
greatness of humanity. Rather, this hymn finds its parallel in the *Canticle*
of the Sun and the *Canticle of the Creatures* sung by St Francis. But not
entirely. The *Canticle of the Sun* is a meditation by one who looks around
and sees God's work in the sun and moon and stars, praises him for
Brother Wind and Sister Water, Brother Fire and our Sister Mother
Earth, for those who forgive, for our Sister Death.

Instead it seems to me that the nucleus of this psalm, while it is still
a hymn of praise, is something else, and I want to try and express it by
reliving the psalm in certain biblical characters who probably lived it at
first hand.

It is a psalm which derives from meditation at night, a night in
Palestine, under a sky luminous with stars. But it is not simply poetical
contemplation of the night; it seems to me that it springs from amazement during a dramatic human event.

I picture myself the figure of David when still a warrior in the service of Saul, and there comes a time when he feels he is betrayed by the king, is trapped by his guards, and so he flees into the desert of Judaea. Into that desert which you may have seen, full of dark gorges, ravines, and precipices, David flees, and at that point night falls. So David stops; he feels alone; the enemy has lost track of him but still he is full of trepidation. Something irreparable has taken place. He has lost the king's trust, it seems that God has abandoned him, and he finds himself alone in the cold of the desert night.

It is at that moment that he raises his eyes and sees the sky above him, sees those marvellous stars which still amaze us when we gaze at them in the desert of Judaea, so clear and bright as to dazzle the eye. David starts to think: 'How great God is, how immense! And after all what a small thing it is that has happened to me. Yes, I made out I was important, I thought I was somebody, and now all my good fortune has gone to ruin. But what am I before this immense universe, before this infinity of God, before this boundless wealth with which the hand of God has decked the vault of the sky?'

While David is thus plunged in contemplation he gradually becomes calmer, forgets his anxieties and calamities. He loses himself in gazing at the works of God and then he thinks: 'But God loves me! After all, this whole universe is for me, God is mindful of me, God cannot deceive me, God comes to me!'

You see what is amazing about this psalm: a man aware of his poverty and his fragility, unexpectedly finds himself at the centre of the universe, in the loving presence of God.

The text says: 'What is man that thou art mindful of him, the son of man that thou dost care for him?' The Hebrew text has a word which signifies the visit of God: 'the son of man that you come to visit him'. With these two expressions: 'You are mindful of man; you visit him', the writer of the psalm has in mind the whole of salvation history: God mindful of his people. As our Lady says in the *Magnificat*: 'He has helped his servant Israel, mindful of his mercy', and as Zechariah says in the *Benedictus*: 'He has redeemed Israel, he has visited his people'. So David – and anyone praying this psalm – before the immensity of the works of God, which for a moment have taken him out of himself, sees himself greatly loved. He realises that in all this great universe he is an object of attentive love. He feels that the story of salvation is realised in him because God is mindful of his promises. God never abandons anyone, he visits each one, he fills our hearts in his own good time.

God's plan

David gradually passes from amazement to a clear understanding that really the world is his. To humankind has been given power over the works of God's hands: 'Thou hast put all things under his feet, all sheep and oxen, and also the beasts of the field, the birds of the air, and the fish of the sea' (Psalm 8:6-8). And then this man recovers his freedom. At first he felt a fugitive, a slave of circumstance; now, looking to God and with the certainty that God loves him, he has recovered his true status as a free man. He is able to influence history, and to grow in truth and justice.

So the psalm becomes a psalm of praise to God who in this immense, immeasurable universe so loves this little man that he has given him this great responsibility.

The man therefore feels himself much loved and much trusted by God: he has put history into his hands. The exclamation which begins and ends the psalm: 'O Lord, our God, how great is your name in all the earth' is not simply taking a contemplative, detached glance at creation, but is a profound experience of the man who feels himself loved and therefore finds again his rightful place in the cosmos and in history.

It seems to me that the nucleus of the psalm is this amazement expressed in the central question: 'What is man that thou art mindful of him?' Amazement shapes and orders the whole psalm: it is divided into two main parts centering on this question.

The first part speaks of the universe, the work of God, arriving finally at man, a little lost being. The second part proceeds from man much loved by God and once more considers the whole universe of which humanity is the keynote.

Here we have another example of the human-centred perspective that occurs throughout the psalms and a return to those three great concepts: God is creator, humanity is supremely loved, the universe is God's work entrusted to humanity. These are simple statements but they give us a whole framework for anthropology and human behaviour. None of us is alone! Each of us is the object of God's love. We are made the centre of a reality for which we are responsible by faith and love. That is the way I read the psalm: the experience of amazement at being so loved, at the centre of this vast complex universe which could appear so hostile, on which however we are tempted to lay destructive hands. If the vision we have of the universe were the only one that the human race had, then humanity could appear to us either as crushed by things or full of heroic drives, straining to subject the universe and be in control. Such an attempt can lead to a destructive use of the universe so that in fact it turns against humanity.

The perspective of the psalm, on the contrary, points to the universe, the work of God, as entrusted to humanity not for use against ourselves or against others, but to make of it a canticle to the glory of God.

The canticle of creatures

Looking at it in this light, we once again consider St Francis' vision in the *Canticle of the Sun*, and we find that it is not the canticle of a man contemplating the universe in peaceful tranquillity but that of an exhausted, blind, dying man who yet has the strength to recognise the greatness and goodness of God.

It seems to me then that we can try to understand the dramatic power of this psalm because it does not spring from contemplation alone but also from a living experience. So, to help you meditate on this psalm, I suggest three lines of thought to follow in reading it, which you might consider in depth in a moment of silence and which ought also to bring you to some practical conclusions. The first line to follow is an anthropological reading of the psalm, that is, with humanity at the centre; the second is Christological, and the third eucharistic.

Guidelines: myself and others

A person-centred reading suggests taking the psalm as a question: who am I? What am I at this point in my life? What am I, small and poor as I am? I am called upon to admit in prayer: 'Lord, I am nothing before you, but you are great and you are mindful of me!' So my poor self can express itself in praise and gratitude because God has done great things in me so I ought to begin by acknowledging the greatness of God's gifts to me.

Woe to us if we disparage ourselves or have a poor idea of ourselves. Each of us is great, made a little less than the angels. The Hebrew text says 'a little less than God'. Crowned with glory and honour: that is what I am. And so is every other person. Thus this reading points to the conclusion: honour all people. Do I really honour everyone? Do I truly honour old age? Is there in my behaviour towards an old person a sense of pity. Do I say that they are people who don't understand, or that I'm not interested in what they think? Do I keep the commandment: 'Honour your father and mother'?

Do I honour those whom God has made my neighbours? Or do I turn the soul, the life, the body of my neighbour into objects of my desire, greed, covetousness, egoism, sensuality?

Not to respect a person honoured by God is to assume a possessive attitude, snatching something for oneself. This is the person-centred reading: do I honour what God has given me, and do I honour the person next to me?

Guidelines: Christ

The Christological reading of this psalm, on the other hand, is suggested by certain passages in the New Testament. I am thinking in particular of the first chapter of the Letter to the Hebrews where we find the reference: 'I have made him a little less than the angels, crowned him with glory and honour', referring to Christ. Or again, chapter 15 of the First Letter to the Corinthians: 'I have placed all things under his feet'.

A Christological reading implies that in Christ the frail figure of every human being is given glory and honour by God and made Lord of life and history. Such a reading invites us to honour Christ, the Lord of life and history, the Son of God, who as man has been given all power over my life and my future.

The question which arises from this reading is: do I acknowledge Christ, Lord of life and history? How do I think of Christ the Lord of my life? Above all, do I accept my vocation from Christ, recognising Christ as the one who calls me to live my life according to his design? And then the prayer from this Christological reading is: 'Lord, what do you want of me? Lord of my life, what do you want me to do with my life, with my future? The Father has put the whole world in your command at your resurrection. I honour you, Lord of the world and of history, and by my life I desire to acknowledge your lordship over history. I wish to make my life conform to my vocation; and in my life and work I want to assert that you are Lord over everything.'

Guidelines: the Eucharist

There is also a eucharistic reading: who is this God who visits each one of us, poor as we are, who cares for us, is mindful of us? It is the eucharistic Christ, centre of the life of the Church. As we say: 'Lord, I am not worthy to receive you', we can say: 'Lord, what am I that you care for me, what am I that you should keep me company in our church? How can I repay your care for me?'

In this eucharistic reading we find Jesus the risen Lord of the world and the Church, in the Eucharist, centre, source and fountain of the life of the Church. All things are put under his dominion; everything comes from him into the life of the community.

What am I that you care for me?, pp42-47

From praise to sacrifice

Earlier in this book we read a sermon on the Annunciation by Janet Martin
Soskice. In his The Woman among her People *Cardinal Martini meditates*
on this text with a rather different focus, but one which is all of a piece with the
reflections we have so far read on Ruth and David, and with the Psalmist. He
wants us to say 'yes' to God as they did, expressing joyous, loving acceptance in
their and our very different lives. It is in the context of that acceptance that we
can begin to think about sacrifice, marked as it is by a fundamental choice for
God, and by the practice of discernment.

How does sacrifice enter into our daily life? By the 'right direction of heart', formerly called the good intention. This is a summary of Christian asceticism. The person who has invested his entire existence in the resolve to want to please God alone enters into Christ's sacrifice and thereby into the Father's kingdom. He shares in God's fullness and makes the realities that he sanctifies by the right direction of heart share in it too.

After Christ's sacrifice, Mary's 'yes' is clearly the image, beginning, consequence and summit of all human and Christian perfection. Mary's 'yes' comprises the orientation of her entire life to God and accepts in advance all Christ's choices from Bethlehem to the cross. The right direction of heart in its essential degree has another name: *fundamental option*. It is an option, however, which should be understood in a dynamic sense, for it is not sufficient to have made it only once. Rather, it is a vital tendency of love toward the good pleasure of God the Father, towards what pleases him, and it is a disposition that informs the whole life.

This option, renewed in prayer and above all at holy Mass, is like a living flame that imparts vigour and form to all moral choices, making them Christian choices.

It is important to live morality as a dynamism, a tending toward the good toward the better, a total dedication to the divine design in which man finds the fullness of sonship and true self-realisation. The absence of neglect of a dynamic concept of morality inevitably leads to shallowness and to scruples; it leads to all those forms of moralism that can be reduced to asking whether a thing is more or less allowed and how far one may go. All this certainly has some logical value and yet it has a depressing effect and is scarcely authentic for human life which as such is intensity, gift, vigour and largesse. It can lead to sullenness, sadness, indolence and discussions. In the community or group there arise quarrels over privileges, shirking of difficulties and sheer legalism.

Without the dynamic aspect of the fundamental option the view of the whole is lost, as well as the true significance of human existence which is living water continuously poured out in abundance from above and not stagnant water.

I believe that in many cases – for example, where either the faithful or their pastors stay away from the confessional – this can be explained by shallowness of moral dynamism. In truth, the sacrament of penance is meaningful and valuable in the measure in which it makes a person progress from bad to good and from good to better. All these reflections are suggested by Mary's 'yes'.

The person who is intent on this 'yes' is always seeking what pleases God in everything; in other words, he practises discernment.

In the Letter to the Romans, discernment comes immediately after sacrifice: 'to present your bodies as a living sacrifice . . . which is your spiritual worship' (Romans 12:1).

Discernment is quite different from the meticulous punctiliousness of the person who lives in legalistic shallowness or with the pretence of perfectionism. It is an impulse of love that knows how to distinguish between good and better, between what is helpful in itself and helpful now, between what generally works and what on the other hand needs to be fostered now. Discernment is fundamental to apostolic activity, in which it is necessary to choose the better and not to content oneself with doing good, with saying a good word or being a good person. Lack of will to discern the better often renders pastoral ministry monotonous and repetitive. Pious deeds are multiplied and traditional ceremonies repeated without correctly perceiving their meaning, but for the sake of complying with custom and making oneself irreprehensible before God.

Today's young people have a keen sense of dynamic search and should be formed in savouring the better and not merely the good. The fundamental option towards the perfect realisation of intimacy with the Father in the Son by the grace of the Holy Spirit is expressed in the religious vows which, on the wavelength of Mary's 'yes', must also be lived as a people and for all peoples. They must be lived now and 'at the hour of our death'.

Mary's words 'Let it be to me according to your word,' in Greek: 'katà to réma tu'. The same expression recurs, again in Luke's gospel, in the episode of the presentation of Jesus in the Temple, where Simeon says: 'Lord, now lettest thou thy servant depart in peace according to thy word' (Luke 2:29).

In the traditional translation – 'Now lettest' – it would seem that Simeon is making a request. Actually the Greek verb is in the indicative mood as in the above translation. Simeon is saying that the Lord has let him touch the summit of fullness. Indeed, his contemplation of the child, of the glory of this Son for all the nations, for all peoples, is already an anticipation of the fullness of the Christian community after the resurrection.

Simeon anticipates, as it were, the fullness that Mary in her divine maternity brings by virtue of her 'fiat'. And he says: 'Your Word, Lord, has filled me, and now I am with you forever. For me there is no longer either death or life; the entire past has been a preparation for this moment.'

Death is the fulfilment of life. It is those 'labour pains' in which the fullness of life is about to be manifested. In them our 'yes', joined to Mary's 'yes' at the foot of the cross, unites with Jesus' 'yes' to the Father: 'Father, into thy hands I commit my spirit' (Luke 23:46).

Every day we die in some way to things, to vanity, to worldliness, to carnal desires, to sensuality. If we live as a spiritual sacrifice in keeping with Paul's invitation – 'Do not be conformed to this world' (Romans 12:2) – we shall be dying every day and at the same pace growing into the fullness of true life.

May Mary, then, be near us on this journey whose culminating moment is death! We know that it is difficult to experience death this way; it is even humanly impossible for in each one of us there resides the fear, horror and hatred of death and of all that precedes or anticipates it, such as sickness, failure, loneliness and physical handicaps.

So, in prayer we ask for the gift of a new vision and a new heart with which to face 'the hour of our death' beginning with Mary's 'fiat' to Simeon's *Nunc dimittis* and finally to Jesus' words: 'Father, into thy hands I commit my spirit' (Luke 23:46).

The Woman among her People, pp104-108

Death and the revelation of love

Cardinal Martini's book Promise Fulfilled *is a set of meditations on the Passion narratives of the gospels. From the section on the first gospel we can follow him as he thinks about Judas, Pilate, and the centurion and his fellow-soldiers.*

Judas

Following Matthew's account, let us consider what flows from the fact that Judas is bent on exercising his personal freedom to the full, his own resentment, his own longing to achieve something great, disappointed as he is over what Jesus is not.

From it flows Judas' despair; when he sees how his own dream has come to nothing and an innocent man has been condemned to death, he realises that everything has gone wrong. As we read the account in Matthew 27 of Jesus' trial and death we must remember that he dies for Judas too (once again we observe the relationship God/humanity; God grants us freedom to act against himself, in Christ, and offers himself for this mistaken freedom). Judas will be to blame if he cannot grasp (as Peter on the other hand does grasp) that God was on his side.

So who exactly is Judas? Who is the traitor? Who is this deranged fellow who abuses his freedom to the point when he comes to see he has got everything completely wrong? I am; we all are. I am, whenever disappointed and embittered – rather than reflect on and identify the mistaken assumptions that have disappointed me – I make a false image of God for myself, and a false image of myself too. Rather than admit it, I cling to some mirage of revenge, of spite, and end up heaven knows where.

Who is Jesus in relation to me? He is each of my brothers and sisters who are victims of my spiteful actions, my acts of revenge, the wrong use of my freedom. Within us, around us and beside us, this tragic interplay between Jesus and Judas is going on all the time: this substantial misunderstanding that leads us, not wishing to look within, to lash out at others.

God no longer sends his Son to us directly (we think back to the parable of the murderous vine-dressers); he sends out brothers and sisters to us, he entrusts us one to another. With each of our brothers and sisters we can do as we please. We can make the worst use of our freedom. It is a fearful thought: the use of human freedom in our treatment of one another knows no limits; God entrusts each to us and us to each.

And the final scene of judgement runs like this: have you recognised one another? How have you made use of your mutual freedom? Have you welcomed me? Have you welcomed one another? Or have you made use of one another, as Judas made use of Jesus, as an object for revenge, for getting your own back, as a vent for your frustrated thirst to be someone important?

We have, of course, to think not merely on the family level but on the social and political level too: groups exacting revenge, acts of spite, personal interests, come into play in all political and social conflicts whether in national or international life, and act as the forces inciting this faction against that, prompting one group to impose its own will – ostensibly for humanitarian aims – but always to the detriment of others. Jesus' call is addressed to the nations, to each social group, to every class: what use have you made of your strength, of your power, of the trust placed in you by other people, by other groups?

Pilate

Who is Pilate? Pilate is the bureaucrat clinging to his post; for him, the most important thing is not to lose his job. Yet, as so often happens, he is caught between two fires: from above, orders, manoeuvrings, storms, work to be got done quickly; from below, worries, malcontents. Day after day, Pilate expends his energies in trying to maintain some kind of balance between these two fires: not to forfeit his career, not to offend anyone: not his own conscience, certainly not the emperor, nor the populace. For, all said and done, the emperor is a long way away, but Pilate actually has to live with these people.

So here we have the tragedy of a poor fellow, well educated, with a sense of dignity and basic decency, even though there are serious flaws. He seems to be someone with a mind of his own; at the same time, he wants to hang on to everything – his job, the emperor's favour, good relations with the Jewish authorities and the goodwill of the populace. Being cunning, he tries various expedients: when he gets that brainwave about Barabbas, he thinks he'll be able to get away with it, leaving everyone happy: the populace will be pleased because he'll be releasing a prisoner; the emperor will be pleased because he won't be getting any complaints; and his own conscience will be at peace because Barabbas deserved to be executed anyhow. But the expedient doesn't work and then Pilate seems positively naive as he faces an angry crowd, imagining he will be able to persuade them. This shows how out of touch he has got: his lack of political sagacity. He has forgotten how crowds normally react. Desperately, like a caged lion, he tries to extricate himself; he hopes to find some way out that will not be contrary to conscience, and thus to save himself as well as the prisoner who has not done anything wrong. Probably life hadn't prepared him for this sort of situation which, from being commonplace, has suddenly become troublesome and humiliating. He tries all solutions except the only right one, which would be to use his freedom and dignity.

A one-to-one conversation with Jesus can make us authentic, free of all those absurd fears which suddenly make us feel so ridiculous. Jesus dies to reveal the way-out to Pilate too. This is the liberating conversation Jesus wants to hold with each of us; the only solution for Pilate would have been to put himself on the same level as his brother and talk to him, for the person is more important than laws, career or bureaucracy.

Jesus teaches us that there is always, in every situation, the possibility of a sincere relationship with him, a relationship able to restore our authenticity. He teaches us that a momentary pause can always be made, even in the most intricate, most absurd, most ridiculous of situations, in which to discover its deeper significance, to grasp the true relationship with persons, to attach importance to the person rather than to things and structures.

We stand before Jesus who reveals God's vulnerability to us, allows himself to be treated as we choose, because he wishes each of us to recognise him. We are Pilate who has a façade, a respectability, a label, that has to be preserved at all costs.

Let us ask ourselves what there is in us of Pilate, what prevents us from being free, what our fears are, what our labels, what the costumes and masks we wear in public and would not care to jeopardise; let us try to detect all our absurdities, our capacity for neglecting and trampling on others for the sake of keeping up appearances, maintaining the façade, or the important job, or people's good opinion with regard to our respectability, our reputation or good name.

'Talk to me', says the Lord, 'and set yourselves free, know that at any moment you can be bounced into trampling on your neighbour to defend a world you have constructed for yourself, into putting yourself in a hopeless situation from which there are no ways out'.

By entrusting himself to us, with all his vulnerability, God reveals his will to us, to illuminate us as to what we are and what we can be if we recognise him in his Truth.

Lord, you have manifested your Son to us in the poverty of a man; reveal to us what we are. Grant that the blood from your wounds will not have been shed in vain for us and that by your wounds we may be healed; that by virtue of this blood we may each find the freedom destined for us. Amen.

The centurion

After Jesus has yielded up his spirit, the curtain of the Temple is torn in two, the earth shakes, the rocks split, the tombs of the dead burst open, their corpses are seen to walk abroad, and the centurion is filled with awe. In general, biblical commentators are puzzled by this description in the gospels. To me, it seems however that the description is an attempt to express the inexpressible.

True, at Christ's death there is only silence; but a silence with cosmic and human resonances, which can be picked up in faith.

Let us confine ourselves to considering what happens to the centurion and the guards.

When the centurion and those who were with him, keeping watch over Jesus, saw the earthquake and what took place, they were filled with awe, and said, 'Truly this was the Son of God!' (Matthew 27:54)

Here we have the first proclamation of Jesus and the first display of the effects of the paradox of God on human experience. At the least suitable moment, humanly speaking, when Jesus' death had taken place in all its bitterness and most people had watched while indifferent or in a hurry, the centurion and guards, who are outsiders, cannot hold out against the language of events and exclaim, 'In spite of everything, this Jesus was Someone, possibly the Son of God'.

How did they acquire such insight? Here appears the paradox of God, who revealed himself in the way most contrary to what we should have expected. What the passers-by, the men in the street, and the priests had not grasped, the soldiers did. We may imagine that among them was one who had insulted Jesus earlier and then, standing very near him, had begun to understand God's patience, his mode of being and acting.

Those who watched from a distance didn't grasp the meaning of the scene, while those who saw Jesus from close-to could not rid themselves of the impression that God was in the Crucified, even though everything implied the contrary. Hence the centurion and the guards are ready, and when the outward signs jolt their imagination and their strong sense of the Godhead, the step is completed: Jesus really was Somebody, he really was beloved by God.

Let us ask the Lord not to let us reflect on him merely from a distance (who are you? why did you behave like this? was it really necessary? why should we have to do the same?) but to let us go up close to you, like the soldiers, in spite of themselves, in such that all our mental questionings dissolve in contact with the Truth.

If we have the courage to break out of the circle of people mindlessly shouting at a distance, and speak to him, and enter into the mystery of his heart, then there will be a new revelation for us too and the veil of the Temple will be rent in twain, for this is the old-time knowledge of God, of a great and powerful God overcoming the enemy, crushing the foe. The mysterious God who used to be hidden by a veil preserving at once his intangibility, his absolute otherness, his inaccessibility, has now made himself weak, poor, vulnerable in Jesus and can enter every human heart to become a living experience.

Experience be it of Christ, be it of human sufferings which we dread, which we prefer to look at from a distance, from which we shield ourselves with conventional phrases and to which we shall eventually have the courage to draw near, however bitter, incomprehensible or absurd they seem to be.

Grant, Lord, by the intercession of Mary your Mother, that we may stand with the soldiers under the cross; and put on our lips the words with which the Church bids us ask to be stationed close to the Crucified: Holy Mother, grant that the wounds of the Lord may be imprinted in my heart.

Promise Fulfilled, pp52-53, 56-57, 58-59, 70-72

SELECT BIBLIOGRAPHY

David, Sinner and Believer, Slough: St Paul Publications, 1990.

Perseverance in Trials: Reflections on Job, Collegeville, Minnesota: Liturgical Press, 1992.

What am I that you care for me? Praying with the Psalms, Slough: St Paul Publications, 1990.

The Woman among her People, Slough: St Paul Publications, 1989.

Promise Fulfilled: Meditations, Slough: St Paul Publications, 1994.

Brendan Byrne, '"To see with the eyes of the imagination . . .": Scripture in the Exercises and Recent Interpretation' *The Way Supplement* (1991) pp3-19.

Christopher Rowland, 'The Revaluation of All Values: Reflections on the Spiritual Exercises' *The Way Supplement* (1994) pp84-91.

5

Jacques Pohier

GOD IS GOD SO GOD IS NOT EVERYTHING

In Jacques Pohier's *God in Fragments* of 1985 we have a book made out of the lived experience of a French Dominican who found himself, in his late fifties, leaving his Order, out of the priesthood, seeking God. He has to break with his image of himself as a Dominican and to break a certain image of God. Those who are not Dominicans, or even those who are, reading this book, can with difficulty regard it *only* as autobiography, since what he says about Christ and about God and about our relationships with one another have enough resonance with our own predicaments to be recognisable, even though how he became the sort of person he was, saying what he did, was the result of whole-hearted commitment to a particular vocation, lived in a particular country at a particular time in culture and history, a particularity which may not be ours. And if we want another example of an 'experience-based' spirituality and theology, this book of his must be high on the list, born as it is of a profound personal crisis. His proposed possible solutions to some questions of belief may not be the best ones, but the way he has brought his experience and his faith into interaction with one another, through his crisis, may at least encourage some of us to comparable honesty. The 'bones' of his career are simply stated: born in 1926 (and with parents in their eighties when he told them that he was leaving his Order) he had joined the Dominicans in 1949. He worked in Canada as well as in France, at the great study-house of Le Saulchoir, near Paris, and became well known as a moral theologian. This was precisely the area in which he found himself in conflict with the authorities of his church, when he publicly supported the legalisation of abortion. Then he

131

wrote a book, *Quand je dis Dieu (When I say God)* which provoked much controversy on its publication in 1977; and as a result of long negotiations, found himself in 1979 forbidden to preach (at the heart of his vocation as a Dominican) as well as to preside at the eucharist, or to teach theology. *Dieu fractures* (published as *God in Fragments* in English) of 1985 records his experiences and reflections on what was happening to him between July 1981 and April 1984.

Decomposition

I disliked the word, and recoiled from it or avoided it. So for a long time a variety of factors joined forces in me and prevented me from accepting it even in my mind. It was like seeing those bubbles which sometimes break the surface of a pond and silently indicate that the depths conceal something unknown and vaguely disturbing.

But the word would not go away. Eventually it broke through by itself, infrequently to begin with, and then more often. Its repeated appearances did not produce bubbling on the surface of the water; one might say, rather, that the ephemeral point at which the first bubble had burst met up with increasingly distant points, as if what had emerged in this way could no longer be located at a specific spot but had extended so as to cover almost the whole surface of the pool.

Today I am defeated. I can no longer shield myself, as I have tried to do so far – calmly or desperately, depending on the day – by isolating myself in areas which have not yet been disturbed: there are none left.

Strictly speaking, I did not decide to write these pages: they are not the result of a desire to write. They are the traces of what is rising from the pool. They have overcome my last defences. They are invading me. Will I at least be able to read what is written in them? May they even make sense, contain a message, a call? I have no other way of deciphering these writings than to let them write themselves. However, regardless of whether or not they can be interpreted, I can no longer stop them writing themselves; I have been stripped of this last protection. Will I be submerged, drowned? Or will I feel that I have finally given birth, to a stillborn or a live child?

Decomposition. The more often the word has been borne in on me, the more impossible it has become for me to keep it to myself: I have been unable to keep it to myself, forced to try it out on those nearest to me. It has pained them and made them afraid. My own pain and fear have then been redoubled. As a protection, I took the precaution of making it quite specific: decomposition, not in the biological sense of rotting away, but as an indication of the way in which one has to dismantle the various elements of an inlaid surface in order to put them together again in a new order, since the old world has gone. It was a 'proper' process, marking the passage from one order to another, the interim disorder thus acquiring the double merit of both being provisional and preparing for the emergence of a new order. So there was no need to be afraid: I was still alive, I was not lost. Just astray.

It is a good thing that I took this precaution, for myself and for those close to me. Otherwise we would have been too afraid. We would have done everything possible to stifle what was expressing itself in me, in us, around us – the groans, the cries that indicated that this old order has become an order of death and that we have to die to it in order not to die from it. And no doubt, no matter what, we would have turned a blind eye to it and claimed that this decomposition was not decay.

Today I no longer have the strength to take the precaution, or rather, the strength that I exerted then is no longer enough. The other force is winning. I am condemned to look it in the face. Decomposition towards death or decomposition towards life? At the moment I do not know: all I know is that this force is stronger than I am.

It is so strong that today it is perhaps even my life. It is myself. I can no longer not say it, not write it. I have done everything possible not to be reduced to writing, to saying this. But today I am beaten. I must write this decomposition. To end a sorry existence if it leads to death. To stop living so badly if it contains life.

There. I've written it. Decomposition.

God in Fragments, pp3-4

134

No longer being able to preach

For example, I would listen to sermons. If the sermon was bad, I was cross to think that I was being prevented from doing it better (and to judge from what others thought of my sermons, that was not always an illusion). If the sermon was good, if it did not, as so often, waste the word of God and the unsuspected capacity which people have for listening to it and finding happiness in it, then I certainly rejoiced at the word which I had received, at the goodness of the God who had spoken it to me, and at the happiness of the congregation celebrating it. But I felt mortally wounded at no longer being able to do the same thing myself. My community had an underground garage built immediately under the church: coming out of one Sunday mass, I fled into its darkness and isolation in order to weep, to cry out there, to shout, 'But why, why? . . . They're mad!'

The preacher that day had been someone who for long years had been my *père-maître* (the person responsible for the spiritual training of religious), then my spiritual adviser and then my friend. Some days before his sermon, this man – one of the two or three to whom I owe my best understanding of God and the gospel – had asked me for advice about it. 'What would you say?' He took notes, as I had done thirty years earlier during his lectures on spirituality: that in itself had shattered me, for this trust turned the world upside down, by reversing the master-pupil relationship. When the Sunday came, in his own inimitable fashion he gave a quite remarkable sermon. My ideas reappeared, transformed, alongside others; at one point he even said, 'A few days ago I was talking with a brother from this community and I pass on what he said to me all the more readily because he is no longer able to speak in public.' And while, as on every Sunday, after mass some regular members of the congregation were sharing their delight with the less shy among the religious (the preacher was certainly one of these), there I was in the garage, smelling the oil and the dust, and sobbing, 'But why? They're mad to stop me preaching. They ought at least to know that I would do no harm to God, that I would do no harm to believers. On the contrary, I would do them good, make them want to believe, make them have joy in believing, make them delight in God. They're mad, it's not possible.' And I shouted out 'It's not possible' at the top of my voice.

Perhaps there is something ridiculous or hysterical about this scene, but you can understand it. Others can understand it. I understood it myself, and at first sight there was nothing else to understand. However, it was on that occasion that I became detached enough for an unforeseen question to pop up. Not 'Why am I suffering so much?', but 'Why am I suffering in this way?' Something was wrong, less in the violence of this suffering than in its nature and the reasons for it. My vocation as a Friar Preacher, my passion – there's no other word – for preaching, my genuine gift for it, were good reasons for this suffering, but they were too good not to be suspect.

The question which then emerged into consciousness was so unforeseen and affected me so radically that I quickly lost interest in the rearguard actions in which part of me was still with those of my brothers who persisted in a friendly way in their efforts to gain permission for me to preach again. Bizarre though it might seem – I had a more important and more urgent problem to settle. What was behind the nature of the suffering that I felt at no longer being able to preach? What had I invested in preaching, what had I made it into, that being deprived of it should wound me in this way? It was more important to answer this question than to be able to preach again as soon as possible. It was also necessary for me to see the question more clearly if I was to be able to answer it. The difficulty it had in making an appearance, its slow and laborious progress, was helped on by the way in which it served as a sounding board for the tribulations of another ban which was inflicted on me.

Not being able to preside at the eucharist made him experience the difference between what he believed – that it is the community which acts in the celebration and the importance he had come to attach to the fact of presiding. Not being able to engage in 'official academic teaching' was less painful than not being able to teach something in connection with his faith, not least because apart from enjoying teaching, it had been an important way in which he had come to develop and focus his own ideas.

. . . when it is a question of God, Jesus Christ and their Spirit, here more than anywhere else it is the case that what we can know is sought, discovered and verified by a common quest among believers (and among non-believers too). This common quest may just as well involve silence, doubt or forgetting as celebration, the word, prayer, ideas . . . and theology. And by forbidding me even the non-academic forms of teaching, the authorities robbed me of the best way of keeping my own understanding of the faith alive and verifying it.

Blocked. I was blocked. No way out. No precedents. No directions. No other prayer than to repeat, come what may, 'Your kingdom come. Let me not be an obstacle to it, let me not be a scandal, let me be useful, if that can still be the case.' But for all that, I did not see any more clearly, and when the word 'decomposition' appeared in my conversations with myself, at first I took no heed of it. When it began to force itself on me, I told myself that I would rot where I was. If I could not be cheerful, that was a natural consequence: since everything was blocked and yet I still kept on living, life was transformed into pus, into decomposition. Besides, that is what happens to life, whether animal, vegetable or spiritual, when its old forms are no longer possible and there are no new ones. That is what happened to me: I began to rot.

I was so tired that this discovery was almost a relief. At a pinch, I caused myself some amusement by recalling the dung-heaps on the farms of my childhood, and I told myself that this dung-heap might be of some use for a future of which I knew absolutely nothing, since dung is very useful for making things germinate and grow. I told myself that at my age many men and women are at the end of the most important stage of their lives, in their family, their job and their resources, and that many of them have not had the good fortune to succeed; I was fortunate enough to have had a good deal of success in my life. What more could I ask? Could I perhaps even go on to provide some dung for tomorrow's crops? The psalms had taught me something like this: some sow in tears and others reap in joy. It was my turn to weep. As I sowed?

Great suffering seldom produces much clarity. So I needed time to discover that not only was decomposition the only possible outcome, but it was the course I had to follow. Since I did not understand enough about what was composed within me around the functions of preaching, presiding at the eucharist, and teaching, it was necessary for it to decompose, for me to let it decompose. Since I did not understand enough about what was composed around functions elaborated by the apparatus of the church and the latent desires of those who were anxious to submit themselves to it, that had to decompose, in me and around me. Whether it was a matter of my person in my own specific relationship to these functions, or the social significance of these functions, since the forces involved were obscure and powerful, escaping as they did my consciousness and my power, I therefore had to allow these contradictory forces to come up against each other within me, beyond my consciousness and my power; I had to let these drifting continents clash and shatter. The old order had to decompose.

I felt that I was on the way. I felt that there was a way. I really believed it. But I was wrong about what would happen, though perhaps my inexperience might excuse the mistake. When I discovered that this decomposition was the only solution for dismantling the old order – both of my person and of its functions – I immediately thought that this was a 'proper' process, since it was an intermediate stage between two orders and the means by which a new world could arise from the ruins of the old. So I thought that things would happen properly.

I had still to discover that there is no decomposition without decay. One cannot control the decomposition, one cannot dictate its ways, which are unknown, and the phenomena which allow them to be identified afterwards are never very savoury nor reassuring. From then on it became vital to resist as little as possible. Not to be too afraid, not to be too disgusted, not to be too disturbed if others became too disturbed. Not to concede one thing in order to preserve something else better. Not to become attached to something, although it had always been the source of life. That was difficult, even impossible, beyond a certain limit: one fights against resistance, one forcibly tries to keep something, for oneself or for others. One wants to keep one's dignity, one cannot allow things to go so far. Be a man, have faith in God!

Now if decomposition was salvation, all that had to go. Particularly everything around which my personality as a Friar Preacher was organised, particularly that way I had of investing myself in preaching, in presiding at the eucharist, in teaching. That, myself in that form, I myself had to be decomposed. That was all I knew, except for having an almost suicidal conviction that life can sometimes win (not all moulds make penicillin, but in the end, sometimes . . .). I had a kind of almost suicidal conviction that God can raise up life from death. But that is deep down, vague, out there, almost beyond the borders of consciousness, will or desire. All the rest of the field is occupied by decomposition. As I write these pages, I wonder whether the fact of writing them is not itself a distraction, a resistance, a false diversion, a false respite; for writing, even on decomposition, is still composing. I just don't know. I can only say again the prayer that I have learned, for I have had to invent this version of 'Your kingdom come', which previously I would never have dreamed of: 'My God, my friends, if that is the way, help me not to shun decomposition, do not leave me to my resistances and my evasions. My God, help me to decompose myself: you see that otherwise we shall never get anywhere.'

Having spent thirty or so years of my life in the Dominican Order, having received so much from it and wanting so much to serve it and make it fruitful, having lived with people and remarkable groups which have brought me to life, with all that in my bones so that it has become an intrinsic part of my identity, I still find that it costs me great effort and tears, bravery in the face of panic, passion which is nevertheless coupled with hesitation and evasion, to dare to say of this institutional decomposition what I dared to say about the decomposition of my personal identity as one who preached, presided at the eucharist and taught theology: 'My God, my friends, if that is the way, help us not to shun decomposition, do not leave us to our resistances and our evasions. My God, may your kingdom come. Help us to experience our own decomposition; you can see that otherwise we and you will never get anywhere.'

God in Fragments pp6-7, 11-12, 16-18, 35-36

On Jesus Christ and his resurrection

One major problem he needed to face was this: 'are there ways of believing in the resurrection of Jesus Christ and in that of human beings which are other than the products – in a more or less subtle form – of the fear of death and denial of that fear?'

In fact, if Jesus Christ is risen, that is to say, if death does not have the same type of effect on him as it has on us, his resurrection tips him – if I may dare put it that way – over into the transcendence of God, leaving our historical and empirical world. It is the very premise of his resurrection, namely that he is something of God that we are not, and that God, after raising him, frees him from our historical and empirical world. I had long interpreted the resurrection rather along these lines, as inaugurating the absence of Jesus Christ from our empirical world, while at Pentecost the Spirit inaugurates his presence in a way quite different from the presence of a risen form which can be discovered historically and empirically in our world, or from any traces of it. However, the more I discovered a possible meaning for the resurrection of Jesus Christ, the more, paradoxically, this resurrection set up a distance between Christ and us which is just as great, since it is the same, as that between God and us, by tipping Jesus over into the transcendence of God. So the two questions had to be raised in the same terms: can one say God, and can one say Jesus Christ?

It was enough for me to return to the earlier stages of my personal faith, or to the way in which Christian faith in the resurrection is lived out, to see that very often the various forms of Christianity understood it in a totally different way. Instead of seeing the resurrection of Christ, as I do, as something which opens up greatly the distance between what Jesus Christ is and what one can say about him, because in the resurrection God makes him Lord, these seem to see it, rather, as the most direct guarantee possible for their scriptures, their sacraments, their institutions and their powers. And so we arrive at the staggering paradox that an authority can itself declare its actions infallible in a historical, empirical and contingent world, taking as its authority the fact that it is a direct successor to the witnesses of this resurrection which has in fact been transformed into the empirical basis of an absolute empirical immediacy. What opens up a distance becomes that which abolishes it. Everything goes on as if the most important thing about the resurrection of Christ were that it gave us a direct and adequate hold over God, in

140

other words, as though it tipped the Risen One down into our world, rather than tipping him up into the transcendence of God.

God in Fragments, pp51

The Word made flesh

For the Christians of my generation, and beyond question especially for priests and religious, one theme related to Christ has been very important in our prayer, our spirituality and our apostolic life: the perfection of Jesus Christ, the way in which all the potentialities of the encounter between God and human beings are recapitulated in him, the way in which he possesses to the full all the perfections of the Christian life, not only because he was God in person but because with all his potentialities as true man he had committed himself to the realisation of the plans of his Father. So Jesus Christ was both perfect man and the perfect form of encounter between human beings and God. I had long lived on the basis of that conviction, and I had seen many people around me doing the same thing; it was an important thing which led to other important things. Moreover, it was only in a very fragmentary and spasmodic way that I could entertain a question which, put more brutally, would have seemed to me to be too blasphemous to accept.

How indeed could such perfection fit with what we can learn of the historical Jesus? What would that person have thought of the exaltation of himself and his God? And did the fact that he was raised from a death which was the most extraordinary sign of his rejection of this type of power for God and for his envoy authorise the restoration of this kind of power, as if the post-Easter conditions of the faith abolished what seemed to have been a key point in the life of Jesus and his manifestation of God?

One way of conceiving Jesus as perfect man also seemed to me to dilute and absorb the specific character and consistency of human life in what Jesus Christ was thought to be fully, once for all. Because he was the Word made flesh, did Jesus Christ realise the potentialities of Christian perfection as they were realised, for example, by Thomas Aquinas, Thomas More or Teresa of Avila? Indeed he was the Word made flesh, but he was made flesh as a Galilean, and not as a Greek, a Roman, a Frenchman or a Chinese; he was only a prophet and not the father of a family, a peasant, an intellectual, a politician, a monk or a bishop; he was a man and not a woman. I reminded myself of something very obvious which one may nevertheless have powerful reasons for hiding from oneself or reducing to trivial banality. Jesus Christ had not by himself been all the perfection of human life: he had had the perfections corresponding to his individual condition and his vocation, and not others. His own perfection did not devalue the others any more than it replaced them, but for all that it did not find itself devalued. For his perfection did not consist in having all perfections, nor was his mission not to accomplish everything. What was true of his human perfection was equally so – if one can speak of Jesus Christ in this way – of his Christian perfections. Jesus devoted himself wholly to the realisation of his vocation and his mission, and for him that was to bear the name which is above every name and before which every knee bows. But he is the firstborn of a multitude of brothers and sisters and not an all-embracing totality of which each of these brothers and sisters would only be a part, destined to be absorbed into the whole. Jesus did not have all the Christian perfections, but this does not devalue the other Christian perfections which were not his. It is even necessary to reject the view, however widespread, that the perfections which he did not have are only the development of the potentialities that one could find in those which he did have: this would be to make the same mistake as over God the creator. Jesus Christ is the principle and the initiator of the Christian life; he is not its totality.

God in Fragments, pp53-56

The renunciation of God

With these and many other questions, Pohier approached Easter 1981, with of course, Psalm 22 to pray: 'My God, my God, why hast thou forsaken me?' A Dominican thoroughly familiar with the way in which his community would have kept Holy Week was now convinced that 'we should do something different, something that we have not yet invented.'

Meanwhile, I was there, between two worlds, between two ages, I still had this text and this psalm, this celebration *à deux* reduced to a bare minimum, with this inner feeling of decomposition and incorrigible nostalgia. A strange Good Friday. The Saturday was even harder: nothing. No celebration, many memories, especially of a somewhat fantastic episode helping my brother Cardonnel to celebrate a paschal mass at Plogoff in a country setting with the background of the nuclear power station, and deep down this certainty that it was wrong to go back, impossible to go forward, and unbearable to stay still, I went for a walk, at least content that nature had made me in such a way that I did not inflict the burdens which sometimes overwhelmed me on those around me – except for very, very intimate friends.

And then, all at once, something made itself felt: gently, almost crudely. Inconvenient, unacceptable, revolting a minute later, and suddenly there, tranquil and soothing in spite of its content. I had just understood something. I had to renounce God. Renounce God . . . Incredible! All the more incredible since it was not a matter of no longer believing in God, no longer bothering myself with him, for the moment or once and for all. What I had to do was to renounce the God on whom I thought I had a hold, of whom I thought I could speak, whom I thought I could celebrate, to whom I was dedicated. I had to let God go, liberate him, break the ties by which I wanted to hold him because I was too afraid. I had to let him be himself, let him go, so that he would return as he wanted, when he wanted, in the way he wanted. I had to renounce God. If someone had told me this some moments earlier, I would not even have understood. Some moments later it was clear, simple, evident. It was also tranquil and soothing. Decomposition had to go to the point of renouncing God. I knew all at once that it really had been Easter. I don't know very clearly what death and resurrection are. But I do know that it was a good Easter. A transition. A deliverance. It called on me to renounce God. I shall try.

Faith (he wrote) has always been partly bound up with death, sexuality and guilt, and has run into trouble with them:

God is a God who comes, and who comes from elsewhere than man: he comes from God. But he comes among us, in us, and in what we experience of him; what we say of him is taken, fashioned, conformed, deformed, annexed, humiliated, subjugated, served, exalted and magnified by all that takes place in us and among us under the signs of death, sexuality, guilt, power and the power-relationships between rich and poor.

But our experience of death, sexuality and guilt is changing.

The old alliances and the way in which the old experiences embodied God must decompose so that new alliances become possible, until they themselves have to disappear in another century.

Because I had the good fortune – yes, it really is good fortune, provided that one does not die of it – to experience the decomposition of these old alliances between God and death, between God and sexuality, between God and guilt, I want to indicate here how they take God prisoner and alienate human beings, distort faith in God, turn God from human beings, put human beings off God, themselves and one another. I want to destroy these figures which become idols of God and humanity, which transform God and human beings into idols. Destroy them for what God? I do not know. For what human beings? I do not know. For what new alliances? I do not know. But we have to begin by leaving the kingdom of death. And to do that we have to try to identify the faces of the idols, call them by their names. So that we can go over to the other side. So that human beings are not held back from going to stay there, since that is now where their life lies. So that God can come, if there is a God and if he is a God who comes. To establish whatever new alliance there may be, if there is one.

God in Fragments, pp68-69, 76-77

To be where God can come

Pohier had come to believe that the claim to eternal life which people made when they said that without it, for instance, their love made no sense, was less an expression of the fear of death than of 'the mixtures of hopes and doubts, strengths and weaknesses, confidences and terrors which are the flesh and blood of our lives.'

It appeared equally clearly that faith in the resurrection and the desire for an eternal life were not so much the desire to live fully in the presence of God, which would be enough to fulfil all human desire for ever, as a way of coping with the changes and chances of present-day life. If the comparison were not too frivolous to use in connection with the matter in question, one might use as an illustration the game of billiards, where the cushions are a decisive element in the game to the degree that one uses them for ricochets in order to get at the ball aimed at. Often faith in the resurrection would seem to be less a mystical aspiration to live eternally with God than something off which to ricochet in order to attain the goal a person seeks in his or her present historical existence; that the fight for justice sees itself assured of success with no possibility of failure, that love, work, every human enterprise thus finds itself grounded in an unshakable way.

I do not claim that the fact that God is God and that he wants to be a God-with-us does not confer an extra meaning on our human life: I believe (*credo*), I hope, I love to exactly the opposite effect. Nor do I claim that if we keep making the experience of our condition more profound we shall be led to discover God and the meaning that we can be given by the fact that he is God and that he wants to be God with us. God is not born of human flesh and blood; he is born from elsewhere and he comes from elsewhere: from God. I only claim – but in this 'only' I now believe that all my life as a human being and a believer is at stake – that in order to be better at receiving what comes from elsewhere, in order to be where God can come, we must exist humanly in our condition, discover the significance of our human existence independently of any reference to God, since it makes sense without reference to God. That is the whole achievement of the modern experience of unbelief. To be where we are, in our space and time, we must first explore them, inhabit them, independently of any reference to what would abolish this space and time.

Did this mean that he was contemptuous of human beings, of their suffering and wretchedness, of their successes and their happinesses, of God and his justice?

Still, one voice stood out from the rest in the midst of the outcry. It was that of Nadille, Nadille who was dying of cancer and whose marvellous blonde hair had already fallen out. Nadille said to me, 'Jacques, I do not understand how someone who speaks so well of God cannot believe in the resurrection: you must be wrong somewhere, but I'm blowed if you are wrong about God, and it is with your God that I want to die.' Yes, someone who knew the death that awaited her, someone whose death was going to be a terrible waste even more for those close to her than for herself, someone who believed in the resurrection and who knew that I did not, said to me at the doors of death, 'Jacques, it is with your God that I want to die.'

I have spent months, years, being tossed around by these accusations and expressions of approval, telling myself that the God by whom I wanted to live and bring life made sense, that Christ and the Spirit in whom I believed made sense, asking myself if I truly had contempt for human unhappiness, if I was spoiling human happiness, if I was insulting divine Justice. I have come as close as I could to some quite terrifying forms of unhappinesss, at the risk of being scarred by them, in order to test myself and to see if it was really true that I scorned them, so that the excess of their suffering might burn away the contempt for them that there had been in my faith. I have also come as close as I could to happiness, at the risk of scarring it if there had been anything in my faith which might have endangered it. I have come as close as I could to God, asked him to come close to me; I have asked believers, men and women, to bring me to God, to apply their faith to mine so that any contempt there might be in it for the justice of God could be burned away – as by the coal on Isaiah's lips.

Have I done well or badly? I have got no further over the resurrection of human beings. But I have learned something about suffering, about happiness, about God. And above all, I have learned more about the way in which faith in the resurrection of human beings, in its most current form, organises relationships between God and the happiness or misfortune of human beings. For we are talking about an organisation, a system. Some of its features have made it impracticable for me from now on and suggest to me that we must look for another.

God in Fragments, pp90-94

A Holy Week, or
'Is sin important like that?'

This happened exactly ten years ago. Our Dominican faculty of theology at Le Saulchoir was in its last days, but the teaching body still had some style and the teachers met regularly for a working week which we called the 'internal week'. During that time we spent at least half of every weekday working together on a theme and invited several other Dominican theologians or philosophers to enrich our reflections. Some of the great names of theology or French religious study came, and the youngest and least known were by no means inferior. The theme discussed on this occasion (spring 1973) was in fact guilt: I had been asked to give a theological paper which came after a psychoanalytical paper given by one of our number, who was at that time interested in the practice of psychoanalysis, something to which he has since devoted himself more exclusively. At that time I had already been teaching for more than fifteen years; I had had several articles and two books published in which I had brought together theological theory and psychoanalytic theory to study the problem of sin, guilt and so on. So people expected that I would give quite a theoretical paper, and that is what I planned to do. However, quite a different approach forced itself on me in an unexpected and irresistible way. I had just spent Holy Week in a village in south Finistère to which I had been going for almost ten years. I would work there gently, rest, perform whatever ministries the rector asked of me on Sunday or during the week, confidently and without any fuss. To deal with my topic I simply told this eminent gathering about three new 'perceptions' which had forced themselves on me during these recent celebrations and which had made me ask: 'Is sin as important as that?', or rather, 'Is sin important like that?'; in other words, 'Is that how sin matters to God and to humanity?'

Maundy Thursday

I followed the liturgical order of the celebrations and began with what had occurred to me on Maundy Thursday. I had been asked to preach, and I had prepared a sermon on the theme of a God who shares himself with human beings. In fact I have never seen Maundy Thursday so much as a commemoration of the eucharist and its ministers, the priests, though that is the way in which a certain Catholic mentality sees it; for me it is the feast of that of which the eucharist and the priesthood are only the instruments and the symbols: it symbolises the fact that God wants to share himself as really (and the presence is real primarily in this sense) and as simply as we human beings share the bread and the wine. The life that God comes to inaugurate among us is a life of sharing and service, like that of Jesus, as is evidenced by the story of Jesus' washing of his disciples' feet which is included in the liturgy for this day. These are the themes over which I never cease to marvel: for several days, I was steeped in them, turning them over in my mind all day, letting them 'simmer on the hob' as I used to do when I was preparing a sermon. I never wrote anything down in advance (how I used to love that way of doing things!) and in the seconds before this celebration on Maundy Thursday I concentrated and relaxed as athletes do before a race. At the beginning of the celebration I never had any trouble in saying, 'Look, we have the good fortune to be gathered together for a splendid festival and what we are going to celebrate we shall celebrate *in the name of the Father, and of the Son, and of the Holy Spirit.*' That in effect is how mass began from then on. And the vigorous response came back, 'Amen'. I kept to the classical liturgy after Vatican II, observing the wish which the celebrant then expressed because it is the wish not only of the whole community but also of God himself, and the least one can do when one invites and receives people in someone's name is to introduce that someone and to give the reasons for the invitation. That is what I did, making my comment in this spirit and then pronouncing the phrase provided for by the ritual: *'The grace of our Lord Jesus Christ and the love of God and the fellowship of the Holy Spirit be with you always.'* And they would reply very politely, according to the liturgy, *'And also with you'.* It was a lively yet tranquil Breton parish, where the liturgy of Vatican II had been well received and was performed well, largely because people had taken the trouble to explain it to the fishermen, the farmers, the workers and the small businessmen, who could now pray as well in French as in Breton or in Latin. So it was not a matter of making unexpected innovations, and at that time I had no reason to want to innovate at this point of the liturgy. Then I immediately went on to what the liturgy provides for after what I have just recalled: *'Let us prepare for the celebration of the eucharist recognising that we are sinners',* and I intoned one of the penitential formulas provided.

It was then that I suddenly felt that something was wrong, that what I was doing was not right, that it did not fit. Why? I had just welcomed the participants in the name of God, given them God's welcome and introduced God and his wishes to them. Now that we were introducing ourselves in turn, what did we find to say to God, what did we think we had to say to him before anything else? We had to talk about our sin, the fact that we were sinners! No doubt the fact that it was Maundy Thursday and the themes that I had prepared for my sermon emphasised this impression, but reflecting on it later in the day I told myself that the whole thing was wrong. That is not the way in which you behave when friends invite you to a party; indeed to behave in such a way would be impolite, out of place. When friends invite you and welcome you, you say, 'What a splendid meal', or even 'I'm hungry', or 'What I like about you is . . .' Or you talk about them, ask how they are; or you talk about yourself, tell them what a pleasure it is to be with them, how delighted you are about the occasion for the invitation, in short express your pleasure. So why, when God invites us to his meal, do we feel it necessary and find it normal to begin by telling him that we are sinners? Why is it that the way to 'prepare ourselves for the celebration of the eucharist', is to acknowledge that we are sinners and not first of all to tell God that we are happy to be there, that we are happy because of him, because he is who he is? Why not begin by singing the *Gloria*? Would that not be a better way of preparing for the eucharist, leaving the confession of our sins until later? It is not a matter of removing sin and confession altogether; it is simply a matter of their place, the importance attached to this confession. So I asked myself: 'Is sin as important as that?', or rather, 'Is that the way in which sin is important?'

I immediately told myself by way of objection that according to a fine old expression the eucharist is the table of sinners, and I recalled that Jesus had been censured for having shared meals with them. But the point is that never in the gospel is Jesus said to have required sinners first and before all else to recognise their own sin, so that he could then listen to them or accept an invitation from them. Besides, what does the fact that the eucharist is the table of sinners tell us about God? Many of the penitential formulas which follow the exhortation 'Let us prepare to celebrate the eucharist by recognising that we are sinners' repeat the phrase, 'Lord have mercy'. Granted, our human life is often miserable and wretched, not to say intolerable enough for us to deserve pity. But what are we saying about God when we think that this must be the first word that we address to him when we celebrate the eucharist? Is God someone whose way of being interested in us and reason for this interest are such that the first thing we must say to him, the best way of greeting him, of responding to his salvation, the best way of interesting him in us is, 'We are sinners, have mercy on us'? Is God going to be a better God, is he going to be more God because the first thing that we have invited him to do has been to pardon us for our sins? It is enough to imagine the situation with anyone other than God to see that we would not behave in this way with anyone who invited us to his table, even if this person had some offence to forgive us.

So I discovered that it was out of place to treat God in this way, out of place to encourage this way of meeting on the basis of our condition as sinners, out of place in relation to God, ourselves and sin: indeed sin was important, but not in this way. The fact that God pardons us was important, but not in this way. What was it that happened to upset the apple cart, distort faces, spoil relationships? What was it that found fulfilment in this shift of emphasis? I did not say more to my colleagues of ten years ago, because I did not say more to myself: I was just becoming aware of the question. I simply stressed the phrase 'out of place', which I used in its two current senses of a change of place and impoliteness, because my colleague – who had spoken before me about guilt in the psychological sense – had used the same term in its psycho-analytical meaning of displacement. But I did not press it further because I could not see more clearly myself; I preferred to describe other experiences which had come up on subsequent days and which reinforced this impression of the sense of the importance of sin being out of place.

Good Friday

The day after Maundy Thursday is Good Friday. Of all the offices of Holy Week, the great office of the veneration of the cross on the Friday afternoon is the one which has always seemed to me to be the most sombre and the most solemn; besides, it is one of the earliest monuments of the Roman liturgy, and some of its hymns are among the masterpieces of Gregorian chant. It was my good fortune from the first year of my life as a Dominican that the novice master, a man of the gospel to whom I owe a great deal, put all my Good Fridays to come in a remarkably different light from that which had cast shadows on the

Good Fridays of my Christian childhood, although this was a day of almost complete fasting and total silence (the offices apart), marked out by weariness after a nocturnal vigil. He said to us: 'My brothers, you must not confuse meditation and sadness: today it is wrong to be sad, since it is the festival of man's salvation through Jesus Christ; it is the festival of Christ the saviour, the festival of a victorious death.' I was to take that up much later in my own way when I preached on Good Friday: 'It's a good thing for a man to die for God; it's a good thing for a God to die for man.' In fact the liturgy was not sad but glorious, including the long procession of the veneration of the cross, an Eastern inspiration, in which each of us approached the cross, prostrated ourselves before it three times and then kissed it, during the singing of a splendid hymn, *Crux fidelis*, which I can always remember.

After two introductory biblical readings, the first high point of this liturgy is the reading of the text of the passion according to the Gospel of John. As the community's cantor, I have sung or read this passion in Latin or in French about twenty-five times. Being neither a real bass nor a real tenor, but able to sing higher than most basses and lower than most tenors, I would vary which of the parts that I sang; sometimes I would have the part of the narrator which is better suited to a baritone; sometimes that of the crowd, which is better suited to a tenor; and sometimes that of Christ, which is better suited to a bass. While singing the other parts, or singing that of Christ, I was able to note something that is not perhaps so obvious if one is not actually involved. The Christ says virtually nothing; he undergoes his passion silently, almost as if he were dumb; the din of the crowd or the long hesitations of Pilate have a far more prominent place. I had noticed this for a long time, and in the days when we were reading the Gospel as though it gave us direct access to the personality of Jesus and his behaviour, I had meditated on this attitude of Jesus long enough to be amazed at it. The reading of the passion was followed by a series of prayers, the 'great catholic prayers', addressed to God for all conditions of human beings and for all their needs (hence the name catholic, in the original sense of the word: that which concerns everyone, including those whom this liturgy called the 'perfidious Jews', until Pope John XXIII suppressed this designation), each of these prayers being preceded by a long admonition from the deacon which almost doubled its length. Then came the central ceremony, that of the veneration of the cross. We all took our shoes off and walked in bare feet towards the cross, stopping three times to prostrate ourselves; the veneration began with a prayer known as the 'reproaches'

(Latin *improperia*). Two officiants held the cross in their hand and presented it to us, singing a long entreaty placed in the mouth of God and punctuated by a refrain, 'O my people, what have I done? How have I grieved you? Tell me.' The couplets which came between the refrain made God enumerate one or other of the benefits which he had heaped on his people (that is to say, all of us, not just the Jews), and each time the reminder was followed by the description of ill-treatment or insults which human beings had inflicted on Jesus of Nazareth: 'For love of you, I smote the Egyptians . . . and you scoured me before delivering me up . . . I opened the waters of the river before you. And with a spear-thrust you opened my heart. I gave you living water which sprang from the rock, and you gave me gall and vinegar to drink . . . I raised you above the others by my omnipotence; and you raised me up on the tree of the cross.' 'O my people, what have I done for you . . . O my people, what have I done for you!' I sang, directed or heard this dialogue dozens of times; it was the best part of the office not only musically but also dramatically. Dozens of times I prayed this dialogue in which everything possible was done to evoke both compassion towards Christ and consternation at the way in which we treated him through our lives as a result of our sin (for it was more a matter of blaming ourselves for all this rather than the 'perfidious Jews'; we were the ones who were perfidious, in the etymological sense of the word, the ones who betrayed the faith).

That Good Friday, as on the day before, suddenly, hearing these reproaches once more, I had the vivid impression that something was wrong, that something was out of place, was displaced. I discovered for the first time that these reproaches put in the mouth of God were not at all like what we had heard half an hour earlier in those few words which the evangelist had put on the lips of Jesus, not to mention the silence which he had made him observe. Certainly, I no longer read the Gospels as if they gave me direct access to the person of Jesus, his behaviour and his psychology. But the fact remains that the first Christians, whose worship and faith underlie the writing of the Gospels, wanted to celebrate the Christ in this way, because that was the way in which they perceived him; the fact remains that Jesus of Nazareth existed and behaved in such a way that these first Christians could not just invent any way of celebrating him. The passion narratives are certainly the most 'historical' and at all events the earliest part of the Gospels: if Jesus had suffered and died uttering a flood of words and constantly interrupting each and every one, the passion narratives would not be like the ones that we possess.

Each reading of the passion had confirmed this impression for me: Jesus had been silent; he had not complained by constantly saying, 'O my people, what have I done to you?'; he had not made a catalogue of all his good deeds in order to overwhelm us with shame by cataloguing all our misdeeds. He did not humiliate us; he was himself humiliated, and in a far different way from that which we associate with him. Certainly, he had complained, but as a man who was suffering, not as a man giving a lesson or listing what his debtors owe him: 'I hunger . . . Why do you strike me? . . . If possible, let this cup pass from me . . . My God, why have you forsaken me? . . . It is finished . . .' So where did these reproaches come from? Raising the question compelled me to return to the rest of the Gospel. Nowhere did I see Jesus behaving in this way towards sinners, nowhere did I see him presenting God in this way because human beings are sinners. Never did I see Jesus utterly complacent over sin, but he never moaned, never (if you will pardon the familiarity, which I need to stress what I want to say), never said, 'Why have you done that to me after all I did for you? Aren't you ashamed?' If Jesus had never used the language which the reproaches attributed to him, if he had never presented his God as using this language, who was speaking? Who was allowing himself to attribute to Christ, to God, a language alien to that which the Gospels recall? Who displaced this divine language, who was so out of place as to displace God?

Reflecting on this displacement, I noted – as I did with the 'Let us prepare to celebrate the eucharist by recognising that we are sinners' – that in attributing to God and to Christ this language and this attitude, this moaning aimed at obtaining a distressed acknowledgement of guilt, we were treating God as we would not dare to treat a human being, and attributing to him attitudes which we would not like anyone to have towards us or which we would be ashamed of if we had wronged anyone or they had wronged us. Of course we sometimes say or are told, 'What do you think you're up to, how could you have done that to me after all I've done for you, I must be fond of you to forgive you after doing all that to me', or, 'I must have been awful to have treated you like that after all you've done for me, you must be fond of me and be an extraordinary person to pardon me when I am so unworthy'. Yes, we sometimes talk like that and even mean it: it makes a good scene, like those in novels, the theatre or the cinema. But we are well aware that when we talk like this we are not showing our best side, and we hope that the best side of other people will be rather different. We feel that when we find real forgiveness possible it is more profound and more silent. It gropes for

154

words and gestures; in such cases it is enough to have found something – which emerges tentatively and with difficulty and from deep within us – for the other and ourselves to hang on to. We know that, like charity according to 1 Corinthians 13, real forgiveness does not take account of evil, that it does not reckon up good and bad in order to calculate debts and credits. Real forgiveness does not give lessons, it is too concerned to remain, almost unable to believe it, on the threshold of the renewed encounter, to get used to the fact that the other person is there again, that the separation is over, that the relationship is restored, however bruised. So who is introducing God in another guise? Who is interested in making us have such a scene by reproaching God, a scene as out of place given all we know of God as it is out of place given the little we know about genuine forgiveness? Again, I did not say more to my colleagues of ten years ago, because I had no more answers to the questions which were only just emerging and which not only filled me with trepidation but also provoked considerable resistance in me. But there again, I stressed the phrase 'out of place', the idea and the mechanism of displacement, since my colleague had spoken of displacements in connection with guilt. And again, I preferred to go on to a similar experience which had raised analogous questions for me.

Holy Saturday

After Good Friday it was Holy Saturday. The Christians of this village in South Finistère were good Christians; so they made their confessions before their Easter communion (that was ten years ago; since then, even in this area, the practice of confession has diminished a lot). There were four of us priests to hear confessions: I was the only one unable to speak Breton, but that was hardly a problem since the Bretons preferred to make their confession to me in French rather than spend a long time queueing at another confessional. I may perhaps have occasion later to describe my personal practice at confession as a pentitent, but I have no difficulty, as a minister, indeed quite the opposite, in hearing the confession of believers who seem full of good faith, provided that this good faith is not too contaminated by bad conscience – in which case I try to invite them to make another kind of approach. So I heard confessions for several hours that Holy Saturday, as I had done in many other circumstances, with the mixture of attention, respect, monotony and weariness that this ministry involves.

Then suddenly, as on the previous day, and the day before that, I began to see what was happening in a different way. These men and these women, these old people, adults and children made their confessions very well, as they had learned to, and their whole heart was in it. As required, they began by saying, 'My father, bless me, for I have sinned'. But I noted for the first time – though it had certainly happened before – that immediately after that they went on to what they had to say next without even waiting for me to give the blessing that they had just asked of me. As I began to notice that, I decided to vary the words of the blessing in one way or another or to give a brief commentary on it. Those to whom I was giving it did not even notice, or if they did, they stopped on being interrupted, as if I had not respected the rules of the game, as if I had departed from my role: I was not there to speak to them, or at any rate to speak to them like that at that moment. I am not stressing this point as a criticism of them or of those who had trained them, but to indicate how and why my astonishment grew. It is precisely because these Christians made their confessions well and their clergy had trained them well that the incongruity of my interventions appeared all the more clearly, and I was led to ask myself what was out of place in blessing people when they asked you, or rather what was out of place in what they were asking of me without actually asking me for it.

The hours went by. My disquiet increased to such an extent that I stopped hearing confessions for a while – as the call of nature sometimes demands. In fact I was beginning to be disturbed, asking myself what I and the penitents were doing. Sometimes, on the basis of what I thought I could perceive of them from what they said to me and what I could read in their faces through the grille of the confessional, I would risk talking to them, after they had confessed their sins to me and asked absolution of me, 'If I thought them worthy'. I did not talk first of all about their sin or about the penance that they were waiting to be given, but about Easter. Just Easter. After all, it was Holy Saturday; they had come to confess because of Easter; it was not improper for me to talk to them about Easter. However, they were completely nonplussed. When they had finished and done their part, I sometimes said, quite simply, 'Well, so tomorrow's Easter'. Amazed silence. I said again, 'Have you come to make your confession because tomorrow is Easter?' Embarrassed and affirmative reply after several moments of astonishment. So I went on: 'How do you feel about Easter?' Silence. Embarrassment. Panic. I must stress that I do not hold this reaction against those with whom I was speaking or those who had trained them. Besides, most of them worked hard and had taken the trouble to add a long wait on to their end of their day in order to make their confession, and if the priest had to add to that . . . But I would stress that precisely because they were good Christians and made their confessions well, my interventions seemed even more out of place, or it became even more evident that it was out of place to talk to them about anything that was not directly related to their sin, its forgiveness and their penance.

After the embarrassed silence of one woman following my question, 'So, tomorrow is Easter. What does that mean for you?', what she had said earlier prompted me to add – and this was clearly not in order to get back on the right wavelength – 'Do you have television?' A period of silence, then this time a clear and calm answer, 'Yes, of course'. So I said, 'Well, you will have seen reporters interviewing people in the street, asking their impressions. Suppose for a moment that when you came out of church someone from radio or television stopped you and asked you, microphone in hand, "Madame, tomorrow is Easter, what do you think about that?"'. Silence. I was afraid I had gone too far; it seemed unfair to ask this woman a question like that, but at the same time I was looking for a way in which Easter, the God of Easter, could be involved. Then, slowly, this woman began to talk. In her own words. Not naturally, because it is not natural to talk about such things. But truly, and simply. About God, about herself, about Easter. Very briefly: people are not very chatty in that part of the world. But truly. I was embarrassed. I could have wept.

I went out for a few moments. I walked in the large square behind the apse of the church while my three colleagues continued to hear confessions until I had pulled myself together. And I asked myself, 'What is all this din rising up to God today from all the churches in the world? What is all this talk? What are people talking about? Is it what they ought to be talking about today? If a din has to rise up from the churches today in this silence of Holy Saturday, between the death of Good Friday and the dawn of Sunday, should it be this din? Is sin as important as that? Or rather, is that how sin is important? What is it that displaces the importance of sin, that displaces God, that displaces man, in such a way that even people of such good will have to think so badly of themselves, bring up misunderstandings, incidents or quarrels in order to take their place in the blessing they want from you, to take their place at Easter, with the God of Easter they come to celebrate? Couldn't people stop all this noise for a moment, to prepare themselves, in the silence of Holy Saturday, for the dawning of Easter, for the rustling in the garden, the journey of the women, Peter's heart pounding, the running of the younger man, the tears, the false doubts, the trembling joys . . . What is it that changes God and human beings, what is it that displaces them so much that they are displaced from a place that is theirs by right?'

There too, I did not pursue the matter further with my colleagues of ten years ago, for the good reason that I myself had not gone further during the few weeks which separated my telling of it from this Holy Saturday. I was still too embarrassed by the resistances which asking such questions aroused in me, the way in which they disturbed me; these questions seemed to go against a current the power of which I had not hitherto experienced. I do not know what effect my account had on these Dominican theologians and philosophers; none of them said a word about it, apart from one person who spoke one phrase as we were leaving. Since they were expecting me to give a theoretical theological and psychoanalytical account, I suppose that several of them would have thought that I had not had time to prepare a serious paper. That happens to me, as it does to everyone, and perhaps to me more than most. So they might have thought that I had got round the problem by giving them lived experience, a first-person account; they might have thought that all right for a less posh audience, but not good enough for them. As far as I was concerned, while I was doubtless wrong to entitle this account 'Is sin important in that way?' without any further explanation, it marks the first elements in what was still a very embryonic awareness of the way in which the displacements of guilt ravage faith, our views of God and our practices as believers, and of the monstrously parasitic way in which individual and social systems of guilt feed on the best of Christian faith and pervert it.

God in Fragments, pp202-212

Jesus' attitude to sinners and sin

It could certainly not be said of the Jesus of the Gospels, and the God whom according to these Gospels, Jesus proclaimed, that Jesus neglected sin, or treated it with 'false indulgence or complicity'. He could sometimes be more demanding than his critics, and there are 'Woes' attributed to him as well as Beatitudes. For Pohier, it is crucial to recognise that:

. . . everything suggests that Jesus sought to make his contemporaries understand that sin did not have the kind of importance that they attributed to it, and that he himself and his God attached a different importance to it from that which they were supposed to attach to it. One could be the emissary of God and eat with sinners; one could be the emissary of God and keep company with publicans, prostitutes, Samaritans or those whose infirmities and misfortunes were supposed to have something to do with sin: the lepers, the deaf, the blind, the lame, the paralysed, or even the second-class citizens among the people of God – the women and children.

So everything suggests that Jesus had sought to tame, calm, sort out all the complications felt by the sinner with his view of himself as a sinner before God: he did not deny sin or neglect it, but rather, even before forgiving it he sought to disentangle the bonds through which the sinners were caught up in their sin, to open up a gap in the wall that the believer thought had to be built to testify to his exclusion. Everything suggests that Jesus said: 'You do not need to be afraid of being a sinner like that; look at me, I am not afraid of you because you are sinners. You don't die from being a sinner, you die if you think you are going to die from it; let me come, let me eat with you, and then we'll see. But that's not the first problem to settle; we must not begin there; you and I have other things to do; we have to be together. I want to dine with you this evening'. After that, he evidently had to make up a parable to explain to the others what he was about, since, in a bizarre way, those men and women who were directly involved (Zacchaeus, the woman taken in adultery, and so on) knew straight away and did not ask for an explanation. So when it came to the Jesus whom the Gospels showed me there were complications: there was no question of dismissing sin without leaving Jesus and his following (in the sense of being a disciple of Jesus, the imitation of Jesus Christ), but at the same time there was no question – this was more difficult but more decisive – of attaching the kind of importance to sin that the Jesus of the Gospels had constantly fought against because it deformed the image of his God and that of humanity.

The Jesus whose features other Christian communities had constructed by remembering what he had been and celebrating what he would be from now on down the centuries was in fact dead, he had been assassinated, he had not avoided death and had accepted it as his destiny when it proved to be necessary. But one of the main reasons for his being put to death by the religious authorities of the period was precisely that he said and did things in connection with sin, the nature of the sinner and the relationship between God and the sinner which abolished the religious structures human beings had made in connection with sin. That is why he is our saviour, the servant of God and man, the revealer of God and of what we are. He shifted the foundations of these constructions, just as he destroyed the foundations of the temple and of its priests. It was this shift that they had at all costs to prevent: this man had to die for the general good, for the good that all people thought they could find in what this Jesus had displaced.

As I have done so often in preaching, celebrating, teaching and writing, I must recall once again the mass of men and women whose encounter with Jesus the Gospels have remembered and celebrated: Zacchaeus, the Samaritan woman, the Syro-Phoenician woman, Matthew, Peter, Mary Magdalene, the woman taken in adultery, the paralysed man, the lame, the blind, and so on. Certainly we are told that some of them, when they saw him, cried out, 'Son of David, have mercy on me'. What else does one say to an emissary of God when that is what you think he wants to hear from you? But when Jesus takes the initiative in the encounter, or in the majority of the encounters in which his various conversation partners take the initiative, he never asks the other person to recognise that he or she is a sinner so that they may claim the right to speak with him, to become the object of his attention. Jesus never presents himself as occupying a position which he only holds to the degree that people confess their sin to him and ask him for forgiveness. So, to take up the words of the *Miserere* again, this is not the way in which he proved to be right, nor is it the attitude that he wanted to have towards human beings. He had other and better things to do; he had other and better things to bring out in others; he was in more of a hurry: 'Zacchaeus, I want to eat with you this evening'. Afterwards, and only afterwards, and precisely because it had not been asked of him in the first place, Zacchaeus understood. And he redistributed the fortune that he had so greedily acquired.

God in Fragments, pp217-218, 221, 242

God is God so God is not Everything

On Genesis 2:18ff

You will remember the text: the Lord created earth and heaven, then Adam whom he formed with the dust taken from the earth, and into whose nostrils he breathed the breath of life: 'And man became a living being'. Then the Lord planted a garden, took man and established him in this garden, Eden, to cultivate and keep it. He gave him every tree but forbade him to eat of the tree of the knowledge of good and evil. And the text continues: 'Then the Lord God said, "It is not good that the man should be alone; I will make him a helper fit for him"'. So the Lord created all the animals and the man gave them names, but 'For the man there was not found a helper fit for him'. So the Lord put Adam to sleep, took one of his ribs, made it into a woman and brought it to the man. Then the man said, 'This at last is bone of my bones and flesh of my flesh. She shall be called woman because she was taken out of man. Therefore a man leaves his father and his mother and cleaves to his wife, and they become one flesh. And the man and his wife were both naked, and were not ashamed.'

I have read, reread, studied and preached this text, and have learned from the commentaries the background to it and the perspective it adopts. But it took me many years to see that at one point the text moves in a direction which it would not have taken had it been written by authors who shared what was then my conception of the religious life and the conception of God that it implies. What does God say after creating Adam? 'It is not good for man to be alone.' But Adam was not alone. He was with God. He was very much with God, not even alienated from him by sin, not even distracted from him by all these other animal and human creatures which did not yet exist. Here was the encounter with God, the one that I sought, the one that I had been taught to seek, the one that we had been told would be eternal bliss. And what was it that made God feel that Adam could not remain alone? If we had written it, the text would have been like this: 'And Adam got bored with being on the earth and only being with God. And God said to Adam, "Since you are not yet perfect enough to see that I am Everything for you and that you too should find complete fulfilment in the simple fact of being with me, and since I am a God who takes pity on your weakness as a poor human being and I do not want you not to have understood already that I must be enough for you since I am Everything, for the moment I am going to give you a helper who will make life less boring. You will go your way together. Obviously this is a digression; but I am good, I shall make this digression a way of learning, by no means devoid of charm, even if it is dangerous. When you get to that point, you will at last be ready for true life, life face to face; you will have learned that I am enough for you and that I am Everything for you. When you human beings get that far you will not take either husband or wife, since you will be as angels"'. But that is not how the text was written. However, that is how it should have been written if God wanted to be Everything for man or if the religious life – with its vow of chastity – were best suited to the nature of God and human nature, if God's dream had been enough for human beings, if the life of human beings had to be shaped by the fact that their God was enough for them.

Familiarisation with the other creation story, that of six days followed by the seventh, confirms both the orientation of the other story and the questions that arise from it. On the sixth day, after everything else had been put in place, creation was given its crown in the creation of man: 'Let us make man in our image, according to our likeness . . . God created man in his image, in the image of God he created him; male and female he created them. God blessed them and said to them, "Be fruitful and multiply, fill the earth and have dominion over it . . ." God saw all that he had made. And behold it was very good'. Commentators had taught me that one of the original features of this text as compared with the majority of ancient cosmogonies with which it shares common features is that the creation of two different sexes is the outcome of the positive will of God and not – as in so many other cosmogonies or creation myths – an accident which happened to a creature who initially was unique, monosexual or asexual.

Creation is 'a matter of God establishing the creature in the difference between them', and being God consists, among other things, 'in having instituted sexuality and given it to me'. Some people may prefer to express their relationship to God in such a way that they choose not to have a sexual life, but their choice is not to be presented as if it is endorsed by the nature of God and the nature of sexuality.

God in Fragments, pp272-274, 277

Breaking the rock

I am going to try. I do not know whether I shall succeed. I do not know whether I shall survive. I have no choice. I am well aware that other men and women, in other circumstances, could and should do otherwise.

I am going to break the ordering of my life. If I am not broken from top to bottom, what will come out of this? What will be born of this death, what life will this death produce and raise up?

If I am going to go further forward in the exploration of this good news that God is not Everything but that he is God, I must put down my pen, lay it on the table – probably for a long time – and break the order of my life.

I'm going to try.

God in Fragments, pp313-314

SELECT BIBLIOGRAPHY

God in Fragments, London: SCM, 1985.

F Kerr OP, 'Pohier's Apologia' *New Blackfriars* 66 (1985), pp216-224.

R Butterworth SJ, 'Pohier's Liberation of God', *The Month* (1986), pp191-197.

6

Kenneth Leech

A PASSION FOR JUSTICE

Kenneth Leech has had an extraordinary career, both by the way he has been involved in some of the most intractable and important social and political issues of our urban life, and in the manner in which he has written about them. From his home in Lancashire he took himself off to London to work as a student in the Cable Street district of London, taking in degrees in Modern History in London and Theology at Oxford universities. At the latter he also trained for the priesthood of the Church of England, and back in London, first in a parish in Hoxton, then in Soho, he became heavily involved with problems of drug abuse among young people, and opened centres for the care of heroin addicts and the first all-night centre for homeless young people. He gained experience at St Augustine's College, Canterbury of the training of candidates for the ordained ministry, whilst involving himself in prison and borstal chaplaincies. Once associated with Bethnal Green as Rector of St Matthew's, he actively opposed racism, developed his work on social-theological theology, and began to write on spirituality and spiritual direction. Included here is material from two books from this first phase of writing, namely, *Pastoral Care and the Drug Scene* (1970) and *True Prayer* (1980). His writings on the drug scene have always expressed his extraordinary capacity to think perceptively and constructively about the spirituality of those for whom drugs are part of life. His writings on spirituality as such have with equal consistency sought both to draw on the tradition, both scriptural and experiential, of those who have been committed to prayer and worship, and to think very hard about what it all could amount to in today's world.

164

It was therefore not altogether unsurprising that whilst Race Relations Field Officer for the Church of England's Board for Social Responsibility, and then Director of the Runnymede Trust (an educational venture concerned with race and racism) he began to travel and lecture widely both in Britain and the United States, honing his understanding of the relationship between contemplation and action, prayer and politics. He is currently M B Reckitt Urban Fellow, Community Theologian at St Botolph's Church and Crypt in Aldgate, London. So he has returned to base himself once again in the area which has been the focus of so much of his ministry. Major publications have included *True God: An Exploration in Spiritual Theology* (1985) from which there are extracts included here on the activity of the Holy Spirit; and *Struggle in Babylon: Racism in the Cities and Churches of Britain* (1988) – together with the drug scene, a most important focus of his life and writing. *The Eye of the Storm: Spiritual Resources for the Pursuit of Justice* (1992) examines the link between spirituality and human liberation, and is the last of his major books used here. His latest book is called *We Preach Christ Crucified* (1994).

The priest and the drug scene

G iven that a priest is concerned with the reconciliation of all things in Christ, a priest needs certain qualities generally, and not just in the drug scene. These include naturalness (grace perfects nature, and does not destroy it); humility and willingness to learn; being free of a 'parsonical' approach and manner; a ridiculously well-developed sense of humour; and a capacity to build up trust and confidence. At root, so many of the agonies and frustrations have deeply spiritual roots, and here the priest who is quiet and compassionate may find developing a new style of pastoral care, caring for the souls of people who would never come near a church, but whose hearts God is drawing, and whose anguish Christ shares.

The priest who ministers in the drug scene will experience a terrible sense of sacramental aloneness as he articulates the prayers of those who cannot pray and feeds on the body of Christ for those who cannot share it with him. He will lean very heavily on the group of fellow-Christians whom he has gathered around him. But a very large part of his ministry will be spent with those for whom the inner reality of his life in grace will mean nothing. Yet his ministry is set within the sacramental life of the body of Christ.

The sacramental world exists at the heart of the drug scene as it does anywhere else. Here, in the mystery of baptism, the Christian soul turns his back on the powers of darkness and is plunged into the waters of liberation and cleansing. Here, in the Sacrifice of the Mass, the soul loses itself in the cosmic offering of the Son of Man and shares in his life. This is the heart of the Christian experience of life in God, and it may be the priest's joy to guide some souls out of slavery into the liberation of the sons of God, to initiate them into the mystery of Christ's dying and rising. But in reality, whenever the sacrifice is shared, those who share Christ's suffering in the world also share his life and are drawn in to the fellowship of his body.

The priest acts too as confessor and spiritual director. He will certainly find that he hears more 'informal confessions' in the bars of pubs, clubs, and coffee bars, in prison cells, court waiting-rooms, and streets than in the confessional. It is difficult to know in such cases where the seal of the confessional should be upheld. It seems best to treat any conversation which is explicitly of a confidential nature as if it were under the seal, even though technically this is not so. The priest's responsibility here is very great, for from the moment that he reveals any fact which has been told to him in confidence his ministry ceases to be trustworthy and secure. Young people in particular will not feel that they can rely on him. In principle it is wise, even before speaking to doctors, psychiatrists, and probation officers, to ask the person's permission first. It hardly needs to be emphasised that anything told in the confessional must never be revealed, however grave or terrible it may be.

Two types of problem which will face a priest in his role of confessor must be referred to briefly. The first is that, in the drug field as in the whole field of mental illness, the priest will find himself in contact with people for whom 'sin' and 'guilt' are often confused, and where it is hard to draw a meaningful distinction between voluntary and involuntary behaviour. The priest, as confessor, is concerned solely with the absolution of *actual* sins consciously committed. He is not there to diagnose the movements of the unconscious, nor is he trained to do so. It is probably best, in cases where actual sin is uncertain, to err on the side of leniency, but there are some souls who need fairly strict guidance and direction if they are to make any progress at all.

The second problem concerns the moral status of drug-taking. There is no sin about drug-taking as such. The ingestion of a chemical substance into the body, itself a series of chemical substances, is in itself neither good nor bad. The Christian must be very careful not to fall into the Manichean heresy of regarding the body as evil and looking with disapproval on the physical components of the world. Nothing which goes into the body can defile a man (Matthew 15:11ff): this is a basic biblical principle. The taking of drugs under strict medical control does not concern the priest. The point at which moral questions arise lies in the field of non-therapeutic drug use. What attitude should the priest take here?

First, if the person concerned is an addict, whatever the cause of his addiction might be, he must be treated as a sick person. Whatever may be the rights and wrongs of his becoming an addict, at this moment in time his dependence on drugs is a physiological and psychological fact and must be accepted. Secondly, the priest must try to lead the person to view his drug-taking responsibly. He needs therefore to point to the Christian teaching that the body is the temple of the Holy Spirit (1 Corinthians 6:19) and is formed in the image of God. If the person has come to the point of confession, one can assume a degree of Christian commitment. The priest has no authority or right to direct a non-

Christian, although he may advise him if the advice is sought: but his commission is to feed the flock of Christ within his body. Christian drug-takers will need very careful spiritual guidance. It should not be difficult, in principle, to advise those whose drug use has reached the point of chronic abuse with harmful effects such as may be described elsewhere. The difficulties may arise, generally in the case of cannabis, where the young Christian genuinely sees nothing sinful in his use of the drug for pleasure. In such cases, the priest may *advise* him, as a personal opinion, that it is unwise to continue, and may feel the need to avert a forthcoming casualty: he has no right, as a priest, to treat such drug use as *per se* sinful. If the person sincerely, after prayer and reflection, is convinced that he is right, he must not be refused absolution any more than the drinker, the cigarette-smoker, or the taker of snuff.

There remain two aspects of sacramental activity which should be mentioned. First, the laying-on-of-hands and anointing. This sacrament is applicable to drug dependence as to any other illness and the caution and judgement applied elsewhere should be used in this sphere also. The danger of 'mechanical' or even 'magical' concepts must be avoided. But clearly there is an important place for the use of anointing within the framework of a healing ministry. The addict who is a Christian will, of course, be guided through prayer and sacrament, and anointing will take place in this context. The addict who is not a Christian but who expresses faith in God of some kind can also be anointed and this may indeed have a profound spiritual impact upon him.

Secondly, the ministry of exorcism or the binding of evil powers. This ministry needs to be studied very carefully indeed before any action is taken, and there is clear danger of irresponsible use of these spiritual powers. Briefly, the theology of exorcism is based on the New Testament teaching about the existence of non-human evil forces and the triumph of Christ over them. It is important to remember that exorcism of persons was a normal routine action for all candidates for baptism and has been an element in baptismal rites since the time of Hippolytus. The emphasis is on the liberation of creation and individuals within it from disorder and distortion. The act of exorcism consists of the recital of a formula, accompanied by some action such as the sprinkling of holy water, the sign of the cross, or (as in the Paschal blessing of the font) a deep directed breath. The more specific exorcism applied to a case of demonic possession can only be performed by a priest under the express authority of the bishop, and it should not take place except after long medical and psychological investigation. The short exorcism, however, which is of 'every unclean spirit', could certainly be used in cases where the influence of uncertain evil forces was perceived. It is dangerous to assume that addicted persons or any other sick individuals are necessarily 'possessed': it is evident, on the other hand, that, like the rest of us, they share the consequences of evil in the world, and it would seem right to accompany prayer and sacramental acts with a prayer for their liberation from the influence of any adverse power.

The priest in the drug scene acts as one mediator of the life of Christ in his body the Church. He is present both to heal and, by prayer and sacrament, to draw the scene within the love of Christ. It is a scene characterised at many points by loneliness and desolation, but so is the spiritual way itself.

The Priest and the Drug Scene, pp120, 124-127

On the Beatitudes

In True Prayer, *ten years later, (and only one of a stream of publications) there is a key chapter on 'Prayer and Penitence', from which this section is taken. At the heart of our relationship with God must be an appropriate sense of penitence, that is, 'a commitment to examine one's own inner motives and intention, and, bringing them into consciousness as far as we can, to acknowledge them to God', and this turning to God in trust has to do quite fundamentally with the reception of forgiveness, which 'brings about a new chain of relationships by introducing a new and unpredictable factor into the situation'. Whether or not confession is part of one's religious practice, we all need assistance of tried and reliable kinds in self-examination. Thinking through the Beatitudes is one way of going about it.*

One way of self-examination which many find helpful is to use the Beatitudes in Matthew 5. The Beatitudes were addressed to the disciples of Jesus who came to him on the mountain away from the crowds (Matthew 5:1). They are not general hopes addressed hopefully to the world at large, and still less are they utopian idealist sentiments with no demand for the human being now. They are an invitation to the life of the Kingdom of God, a life which brings with it unspeakable joy and ecstasy, but which will entail suffering and struggle.

Blessed are the poor in spirit. How do we practise detachment? Are we seeking simplicity, avoiding waste and the accumulation of unnecessary possessions? What does austerity mean in modern circumstances? How do we rid ourselves of encumbrances, superfluities, things which serve simply for effect, and so on? Do we have a place for silence in our lives? Or are our lives over-crowded with unnecessary words? What about poverty of the mind, the refusal to acquire useless information, preferring instead the *ascesis* of intellect which pursues one end with dedication? Poverty of mind is more necessary than poverty of the body, for the amount of mental baggage we acquire is enormous. In seeking poverty of spirit, we seek to be free of compulsions to acquire and possess, free therefore to receive what life has to give us.

Blessed are the meek. Are we humble? What about arrogance and conceit in our lives? Do we try to understand and therefore respect others? So much of what seems to be religious conviction goes hand in hand with a violent spirit: we defend our positions with arrogance, aggression, violence, and we seek to crush our opponents, to smash them, despising them in the process. Are we seeking to become non-violent and gentle in spirit? How often does our commitment to principle lead to contempt for people?

Christian meekness is not weakness or lack of principle. It is a strong virtue and requires great inner spiritual strength. Are we seeking to build these inner resources of meekness?

Blessed are the peacemakers. Are we *making* peace, positively making it? What are we contributing in our district to human unity, to the removal of divisions and barriers? Do we possess inner peace, stillness of soul, serenity? Is there a movement towards peace and harmony (*shalom*) within my personality, in the relationship of body and mind, the integration of the personality? Inner peace is vital in the peacemaker: only the non-violent of spirit, as Gandhi stressed, can live the non-violent life. As he once told Nehru, 'If you have a sword in your heart, it is better that you bring it out and use it.' Peace of soul is intimately bound up with physical stillness and quiet. What about detachment from anxiety, not attempting to suppress or get rid of anxieties, which would be fruitless, but seeking to become detached from them? What about peace of mind, the quest for inner mental calm? We can only make peace if we are on the way to attaining peace.

Blessed are those who hunger and thirst for justice. Justice and peace stand and fall together. Only false peace can abide with injustice. So we need to cultivate that sensitivity which cannot rest while injustice abounds, that holy restlessness which refuses to be at ease while others suffer. Christian concern for justice must go beyond the 'eye for an eye' morality of the Pharisees. In the New Testament love and justice are not opposed: love is the culmination of justice, justice the practical expression of love. How do the demands of justice in society and in political structures enter into our self-examination?

Blessed are the pure in heart. 'Purity of heart is to will one thing' wrote Kierkegaard, perceiving the essential simplicity and directness of this demand. Are we aiming at utter sincerity, seeking to avoid compromise and duplicity? Do we perpetuate deceitfulness, sophisticated and subtle forms of lying which undermine purity? Purity goes beyond the area of sexuality with which it is often identified. It involves a passion for the authentic, the genuine, abandoning the promiscuity of not discriminating between truth and falsehood. Do we try to see through the unreal to the real, to retain our integrity and identity and not allow ourselves to be swallowed up in affairs and causes? Harry Williams defined chastity as 'the capacity so to sift my experience as to be enlarged and enriched by it instead of being diminished or destroyed'. Inner purity is seeking a direction, an orientation, seeing God.

True Prayer, pp136-138

On the Seven Deadly Sins

Hieronymus Bosch in his painting *The Seven Deadly Sins* shows the envious man being torn apart by dogs, the lustful man being eaten by wild beasts, the slothful man being beaten, the angry man being castrated, and so on. In other words, the greatest harm done by sin is to ourselves through a death-dealing kind of possessiveness. These sins need a close, prayerful look.

First, *Pride*. Do we cling to our false identity, our image, our purported superiority to others? Gregory the Great put pride at the head of the list of sins, for pride is a form of idolatry, self-adoration, self-love. We become the centre of the universe. But pride, as Reinhold Niebuhr showed, can be a corporate sin, 'collective pride', national self-deification. How does pride affect us? In lust for power and control of others? In making ourselves into little gods? In allowing ourselves to be conned by the pretentious and proud claims of social and political groups?

Secondly, *Anger*. Do we distinguish normal healthy anger from sinful destructive anger? Do we feel that the expression of anger is beneath us, and so allow all our repressed anger to boil up inside, festering, eating away into our personality? Repressed anger is really poisonous. It can turn inwards into depression, or it can appear in twisted forms such as envy, bitterness, cruel sarcasm, and so on. Anger which is so repressed becomes buried very deep within us so that we cease to be able to recognise it and so to confess it. We need to learn from our anger about ourselves, to suspect our capacity for 'righteous indignation' and moral outrage, to question our motives. Jesus related anger to murder (Matthew 5:22), and we need to realise how injurious and harmful is our anger, our rudeness, our contempt for others. The real remedy against anger is to learn how to use our aggression to the glory of God – to imitate the wrath of the Lamb, that burning zeal for righteousness which was purified by gentleness and love.

Thirdly, *Envy*. Are we guilty of the sin of the eyes, the sin of competition which is encouraged and propagated by advertising techniques? Envy begins with the erection of a false image of others, which is then sought after. So we lose respect for ourselves and for the other whom we envy rather than love. How concerned are we with status and position? Do we have a true self-love, the only remedy for false self-love?

Fourthly, *Lust*. Again, it is essential that we distinguish sexual desire from its distortions, or true lust from sinful lust. It is the *sinful* lusts of the flesh that we renounce. Do we despise our sexuality? Are we afraid of our desires? Do we allow our own sexual fears to lead us to fail in compassion and understanding of others? Do we treat others as mere material for the satisfaction of our sexual hunger? Monica Furlong has well defined lust as 'the condition in which love becomes swallowed in hunger'. Yet hunger is not sinful, nor is it wrong to satisfy that hunger. Lust is sexual hunger which is out of control, hunger which dominates the person. Opposed to such uncontrolled lust is the virtue of chastity. Are we seeking chastity and so seeking to escape the slavery of a lustful, self-destructive way of life?

Fifthly, *Gluttony*, a sin closely linked to lust. Just as a true assessment of the seriousness of lust depends upon a high view of sexuality, so in order to appreciate the evil of gluttony we need to hold food and the body in high regard. Gluttony arises when we seek to use food and drink not as sources of pleasure but as drugs, anaesthetics, ways of escape from reality. Compulsive greed is the enemy of real pleasure. Do we really appreciate food and drink, seeing all food and all drink as sacramental? Are we sensitive to the needs of the hungry and the poor as we eat and drink, and do we take this into account in our practice of fasting? Do we treat our bodies as machines into which we can pump any number of noxious substances?

Sixthly, *Sloth*, the sin of *acedia*, which is much more than laziness. It describes the inability to act when one knows that it is necessary and right. Sloth is not merely time-wasting or inactivity. In fact, over-activity and obsession with time is one of the greatest threats to our inner lives, and a degree of sanctified laziness is something we need to learn. Sloth is not simply inactivity, but more the inability to rouse oneself from the midst of death, from compulsions, from the tyranny of habit; it is a paralysis of the spirit. Are we slothful in this sense, paralysed in our situation, refusing to act when justice demands? Are we indifferent to wrong and suffering, more concerned for peace and quiet? Sloth is the ultimate sin of omission, the state of doing nothing which allows evil to triumph. So we are right to confess that we have sinned 'in the good we have not done'.

Finally, *Avarice*, the sin of greed. The New Testament word is *pleonexia* and it means excess, the state of wanting more and more, 'ruthless greed' (Mark 7:22, New English Bible). Against this vice, the New Testament places the virtue of *epieikes*, translated as moderation. But this has nothing to do with the political vice which masquerades under the name of 'moderate' as opposed to 'extremist': in fact, moderation is an extreme demand for simplicity of life and for justice, *against* avarice and oppression. So St Paul defended his ministry by saying that he had injured no one, spoiled no one, and taken no more than his fair share (2 Corinthians 7:2). In our society, avarice is often disguised under other names, as in *Pilgrim's Progress* where the covetous man was called Mr Prudent-Thrifty: so today we are likely to be addressed by 'enlightened self-interest' or 'private enterprise' or 'the virtue of competition'. Are we allowing ourselves to be seduced by the spirit of the age under its various names – through advertising, through the prevailing secular morality of accumulation of goods, through the false view of man which values him for what he has rather than what he is? Are we worshippers of Mammon rather than Christ? Bertrand Russell once said that 'it is preoccupation with possession more than anything else that prevents men from living freely and nobly'. Are we seeking to create a more equal and less broken society, or are we content to acquiesce in the midst of wealth and squalor – sloth living upon accumulated avarice?

Again, these questions are not exhaustive, of course, but are merely suggestions for beginning self-examination through the Seven Deadly Sins. In no way are they out of date: indeed the American psychiatrist Karl Menninger has suggested some new ones to add to the list. There are many other approaches which can be used. New Testament passages such as 1 Corinthians 13 or Galatians 5 can be used effectively. So can the much-despised lists of sins provided one does not become obsessed with minutiae or confuse sinfulness with quantity of acts committed. The purpose of self-examination is the identification of the trouble at the root of our beings, the stripping bare of the spirit, and the tackling of falsehood. It therefore involves wrestling and conflict, not a mechanical formalism. Indeed, formalism and settling into a groove can itself lead us into sin and block off the channels of grace. In all our self-examination it is essential that we begin by asking the Holy Spirit to show us the root difficulty which lies behind each action, to enable us to see beyond the sin to the cause of it. Not only that, but to see beyond it to the cure, to the grace of God, and to allow gratitude and joy in the experience of forgiveness to be the basis of our continuing sorrow. Sorrow and joy go hand in hand for the Christian is *peccator simul justus,* a sinner who is yet justified.

True Prayer, pp139-142

Spirituality for today and tomorrow

We turn now to Kenneth Leech trying to work to a 'prescription' he writes for himself, and to extracts from his major book, True God *of 1985. Of all the great images explored in that book, it is arguable that the chapter called 'God of Water and Fire' is crucial, since it seriously as well as in a most lively way tries to illuminate both past tradition about the Spirit and also present experience of charismatic renewal.*

Contemporary experience poses some issues to the tradition of spirituality and spiritual direction which we have inherited.

First, it is clear that the increased awareness of the political dimensions of spirituality does represent a real maturing of Christian consciousness, and one to which the spiritual tradition of the past gave inadequate attention. Today's soul friends, comments Peter Selby, must be also friends of the soul of the world – or its enemies. It is therefore essential for spiritual directors to consider where they stand in relation to the political structures of the world, where they stand in 'the system'. Selby goes on to speak of the 'radicalising experience of pastoral care' and of the need to see the 'heightening of dissatisfaction' with the present realities of evil in the world as a necessary aim of the pastoral task.[1] We need to see how spiritual direction is part of the wider process of 'integral liberation'. In the present climate, as one American school of spirituality puts it, 'we cannot do spiritual direction without a major emphasis on justice issues'.[2]

Secondly, questions need to be asked about the role of the solitary in the work of spiritual guidance. In the early Church, many spiritual guides were desert solitaries. Today when, in Daniélou's memorable words, 'St Antony is coming back from his desert',[3] we may find that many directors will be drawn from the ranks of those in the thick of social and political struggle.

Thirdly, a major issue for the contemporary ministry of spiritual direction concerns the place of doubt. Unlike the past, many of those seeking guidance today are on the margins of the Church. Many of them are deeply troubled with intellectual, moral and spiritual doubts, yet within the overall framework of faith. They need someone 'who is still in touch with the emptiness as well as the glory, the doubt as well as the certainty'.[4] If Carolyn Osiek is correct that most spiritual directors tend to be feeling types rather than thinkers, clearly there is a need today for directors who can help those struggling with the dark night of the intellect,[5] those who realise that to know God is not only to be free to question everything, but to be bound to do so.[6]

Fourthly, contemporary insights, particularly those from within feminism, must raise serious questions about the dangers of manipulation and disabling of people by spiritual élites, vanguards, and those with hidden agendas. Sheila Rowbotham defines a vanguard as 'a small band of fanatical know-alls, trotting about, raising other people up to their level of consciousness, the very notion of which is necessarily élitist and invulnerable'.[7] She had Leninists in mind, but the words have relevance to religious groups who set themselves up as élites with superior knowledge. If I am correct to see much evidence of a new kind of gnosticism around in the west today, the warning is of special importance.

Fifthly, it is clear that, as the shift away from clericalism increases, and as the role of the laity in spiritual guidance is affirmed, we are seeing more people not only seeking direction from, but also confessing their sins to, their fellow lay people. This must compel catholic Christians to face more seriously than they have the issue of lay absolution. Guidance needs to be given on this which is more than a mere reassertion of the clerical role, and which takes serious account of the facts of lay direction.

Finally, as the constantinian era ends, it is not surprising that the need for spiritual direction has been recovered. Spiritual direction itself grew up as a by-product of desert monasticism, and so today as the era of the 'flight to the desert' gives way to a new era in which Christians are once again in the position of minority groups in non-Christian states, there needs to be an interrogation of the tradition in the quest for spiritual resources for this new situation which now confronts us, as well as a courageous awareness that we are part of the tradition and will help to shape its future.

Interrogating the Tradition, pp18-19

Holy Spirit experienced as profound liberation

There is the sense of great love. It is through the Holy Spirit that the love of God is inflamed within us. God's love has been poured into our hearts through the Holy Spirit (Romans 5:5). Love is seen as the greatest of the spiritual gifts (1 Corinthians 13). To know the love of Christ is to be filled with God's fullness (Ephesians 3:19). St John, in the First Epistle, writes of love as the nature of God. Mutual love is the sign of the resurrection (1 John 3:14), the person who loves is born of God and knows God (1 John 4:7). Moreover, the gift of the Spirit is the proof that God dwells within us (1 John 3:24).

The experience of the Holy Spirit is thus described in terms of power, of intoxication, of hope, of freedom, of love. Throughout the literature of spirituality from biblical times onwards, a recurring symbol for the divine activity is the symbol of fire. The fire is one of the earliest symbols of divine presence and action. In the covenant with Abraham, a smoking fire pot and a flaming torch were the signs given (Genesis 15:17). In the account of the sin of Nadab and Abihu, the fire of the Lord came forth and devoured them (Leviticus 10:2). Similarly, in Elijah's struggle against false religion, the fire of the Lord fell both on the altar of Baal (1 Kings 18:38) and on the messengers of Ahaziah (2 Kings 1:10, 12). Elijah was particularly seen in later Jewish thought as a prophet of fire (Ecclus. 48:1) who would appear before the great and terrible Day of the Lord, the day burning like an oven (Malachi 4:1, 5).

The fire symbolises the power of God, but it also is used of his glory. The angel of the Lord appeared to Moses in a flame of fire (Exodus 3:2). The Lord descended upon Mount Sinai in fire, and the people were warned not to 'break through to come up to the Lord, lest he break out against them' (Exodus19:18, 24). We are told that 'the appearance of the glory of the Lord was like a devouring fire' (Exodus 24:17). After the encounter with the divine glory, Moses' own face shone with glory (Exodus 34:35). In the writing of Ezekiel, fire is again used as a symbol of God's glory and splendour. Having described his vision of four living creatures, he goes on:

In the midst of the living creatures there was something that looked like burning coals of fire, like torches moving to and fro among the living creatures;

and the fire was bright, and out of the fire went forth lightning. And the living creatures darted to and fro, like a flash of lightning. Ezekiel 1:13-14

He then looked and saw a throne upon which was seated 'a likeness as it were of a human form'.

> *And upward from what had the appearance of his loins I saw as it were gleaming bronze, like the appearance of fire enclosed round about: and downward from what had the appearance of his loins I saw as it were the appearance of fire, and there was brightness round about him. Like the appearance of the bow that is in the cloud on the day of rain, so was the appearance of the brightness round about. Such was the appearance of the likeness of the glory of the Lord.* Ezekiel 1:27-8

In the similar vision in Revelation, there are flashes of lightning, and seven torches of fire burn before the throne of God (Revelation 4:5). God, the Scriptures assert, is a devouring fire (Deuteronomy 4:24; Hebrews 12:29). And when, on the Day of Pentecost, the Spirit of God fell upon the apostolic community, it was in tongues of fire (Acts 2:3). Fire symbolism is also used in relationship to the last time, the Day of the Lord, the day of judgement, and the experience of hell. In the Old Testament, there are twenty-four occasions on which fire language is used in connection with God's wrath, though there is only one instance where it is used directly of hell (Deuteronomy 32:22). In the Synoptic Gospels, however, *pur is* used twenty-two times, of which fourteen are with reference to eschatological judgement. In these cases, the fire represents the wrath of God, the converse of his glory. In the mystical writers, fire comes to be used of the intensity and burning love of God, while the Pentecostal movements have laid great stress on the power and inexpressible joy brought about through the 'baptism of fire'.

At the heart of the language of fire in relation to God is the sense that any encounter with the divine is marked by terror, awe, and the possibility of being consumed. For no one can see God and live (Exodus 33:20). And yet, in a strange and terrifying way, Moses saw the face of the Lord (Deuteronomy 34:10), spoke mouth to mouth and face to face with him (Numbers 12:8) as one speaks with a friend (Exodus 33:11). In all experience of God there is this mingled sense of terror and intimacy, as we encounter the fire which warms and heals while it holds out the possibility of danger and death. We find the mingling of death and birth, tomb and womb, in the Christian liturgy of baptism.

True God, pp205-207

Baptism by water and fire

In the Christian liturgy of baptism there is a complex symbolic structure, involving water, fire, light, and the strengthening power mediated through anointing and the laying on of hands. Throughout the entire rite, the underlying theme is that of renewal in the Holy Spirit. Baptism occurs once for all just as Christ's death occurred once for all: *ephapax* (Romans 6:10). It is unrepeatable, yet its results are continually manifested in Christian lives. All prayer in fact is a manifestation of baptismal grace, and this grace is daily renewed. So the liturgy of baptism is a microcosm of the entire spiritual path with its threefold process of purgation, illumination, and final union.

The first constituent element in the liturgy is the renunciation of the forces of evil. In the early rites, the candidate faced west, the region associated with darkness, and publicly renounced Satan, his works and pomps. S/he was then anointed with the oil of catechumens, sealed against the powers of evil, and, thus strengthened, s/he made a profession of faith in Christ. Stripped naked, the candidate was then ready for the baptismal death, the plunging beneath the waters of renewal.

And so, secondly, the candidate was baptised in water, and anointed with the oil of chrism. In the early rites, these two elements, later distinguished as baptism and confirmation, were parts of a unified whole. The positive aspect of baptism, the aspect of purification and strengthening by and in the Spirit, is often termed 'illumination' by the Fathers. The verb *photizein*, to enlighten, was used in the mystery religions about saving knowledge, whereas the Fathers used it in relation to baptism. (There may be a hint of such use in the reference, in Hebrews 6:4, to those 'who have once been enlightened, who have tasted the heavenly gift, and have become partakers of the Holy Spirit, and have tasted the goodness of the word of God and the powers of the age to come'.)

Finally, the baptismal liturgy reaches its climax in Holy Communion, in union with God through the sacrament of Christ's body and blood.

Baptism was seen from the beginning as being particularly linked with the activity of the Spirit. In the New Testament there are six references to baptism with the Holy Spirit (Matthew 3:11; Mark 1:8; Luke 3:16; John 1:33; Acts 1:5 and 11:16). The first four are associated with the preaching of John the Baptist. According to him, Jesus will baptise with the Holy Spirit, and Matthew and Luke add the words 'and with fire'. The accounts of Jesus' own baptism are reminiscent of the creation

179

of heaven and earth from chaos as well as of the renewal of the earth after the flood. The dove reappears as a symbol of the hovering and restoring Spirit.[8]

In the use of the phrase 'baptise with the Holy Spirit' by John the Baptist, the context is one of judgement and mercy, as well as of the messianic woes and of the eschatological river of fire and spirit. The association of fire with the final judgement is probably based on Numbers 31:23: 'everything that can stand the fire, you shall pass through the fire, and it shall be clean. Nevertheless it shall also be purified with the water of impurity; and whatever cannot stand the fire, you shall pass through the water.' This, linked with Malachi 3:3 ('he is like a refiner's fire') probably provided the source for the symbolism of 'baptism of fire' as it occurs in John's preaching. Behind this may lie the Persian eschatology in which the mountains, made of metal, melt at the end of the world, and the molten metal pours over the earth, forming a river of fire. All the people pass into this river, and are either purified or destroyed by it. This may well be the source of the river of fire in Daniel 7:10, as well as of the idea of the fiery breath of the Messiah.[9] The baptism of fire was the symbol of entry into a new order:

> *It was an initiatory metaphor – that is, it denoted the means by which the new age would come to birth ('the travail of the Messiah') and the means by which the penitent would enter into the new age and be fitted for the new age, refined and cleansed.[10]*

True God, pp207-208

Charismatic renewal

What has attracted popular attention to the renewal, and drawn more and more people to it, has been the obvious sense of enjoyment and exultation. To those accustomed to somewhat dreary, cerebral, and repressive forms of worship, the renewal has led to a tremendous experience of liberation, freedom in the Spirit, and deep joy. It is the experience generated by the Spirit, which comes first, and the enrichment of the life in Christ which follows. So we see in the charismatic experience precisely the sense of warmth and of power which Christians throughout the ages have described by use of the symbol of fire. And closely linked with the experience of warmth and power is the sense of transcendence of words and concepts. The experience is seen as essentially ineffable. There is a feeling of being devoured, consumed, as by fire, or of being drowned by the waves of God's love. There is a sense of release, and, since this release is the fruit of the resurrection, it is manifested in bodies which are set free to praise, and which experience modes of expression beyond their normal range. The resurrection of the body and the charismatic release of the Spirit are inseparable, just as body and Spirit are inseparable. For the power which enables this renewal of spiritual life is not simply the power of many Spirit-filled persons; it is the power which revives and renews them by virtue of their incorporation into the risen Christ. This experience of incorporation is, of course, the central truth of Christian baptism, and so it is common for those within the charismatic renewal to speak of their experience of the fullness of the Spirit as a 'baptism in the Holy Spirit'. What is happening is the surfacing and revealing of this fundamental truth in the actual, lived experiences of individuals and communities, the explosion of a *dunamis* (dynamite is derived from *dunamis*!) which has often been latent for years. Now fact and realisation are united in one tremendous, exhilarating experience. It has been called a 'baptism of fire'.

True God, pp228-229

Needing a larger towel

In previous sections we have seen how particular moments of a liturgy, or particular liturgical days which come round year by year, can focus someone's spirituality. Maundy Thursday is commonly associated not only with 'feet washing', which may once have been a regular liturgical practice in some parts of the church in association with dealing with post-baptismal sin, but also with the renewal of ordination vows, and the blessing of oils.

A quaint handbook on church needlework, published sometime in the 1950s, contained the instruction: 'The length of the lavabo towel should be 12 inches for Roman Catholics and 18 inches for Anglicans'. It inspired the late S J Forrest to write his poem beginning:

> *O filthy, dirty Anglican,*
> *Needing the larger towel.*

I want to suggest that, as we become more open to the Gospel *mandatum* and to the needs of the world, we will increasingly find ourselves in need of the larger towel.

It is well known that John's account of the feet washing incident replaces the accounts of the institution of the eucharist which appear in the other three gospels. It is a depressing thought that if the Christian liturgy had revolved around feet washing rather than bread breaking, today we might be involved in debates about whether feet should be totally immersed, or whether sprinkling would do; whether the right or left foot should be washed first; about who was authorised to wash feet; about whether women's feet could be washed at all; and about whether women could wash feet. (When I wrote those words, I had not realised that in the Roman Catholic diocese of Pittsburgh, the issue of washing women's feet had indeed assumed the dimensions of a major dispute!) And just as we have invariably missed the point of the eucharistic sharing as a sacrament of a sharing world, so we might have missed the point of the feet washing as a sacrament of the church's servanthood in all of its life.

The feet washing stands as a permanent symbol of Christ's ministry, *diakonia*. Christ whose form is divine assumes the condition of a slave, humbles himself, Christ the Son of Man comes not to be served but to serve. He is among us as one who serves, as a *diakonos*.

The liturgy of Maundy Thursday, a day marked by the renewal of priestly commitment, gives equal attention through the feet washing to the role of the deacon. According to the 1928 Prayer Book, the preacher at the ordination of deacons is to stress 'how necessary that order is in the Church of Christ'. So necessary, comments Reginald Fuller in his Preface to James Barnett's study of the diaconate, that in many dioceses there are no deacons made between Christmas and Trinity. *Diakonia,* service, servanthood, is not and cannot be the sole defining characteristic of the Christian community. The servant church must never replace the prophetic church, the proclaiming church, the contemplative and adoring church. The church is more than servant, but it must never become less so. And the great paschal symbol of servanthood is that larger towel, that dirty towel. What kind of ministry is this to which we are called, and which is symbolised by the larger towel of the Maundy liturgy?

It is *a ministry of lowliness*. St Gregory of Nyssa saw the lowliness of Christ the Servant as the greatest evidence of the divine power.

> *That omnipotence of the divine nature should have had strength to descend to the lowliness of humanity flourishes a more manifest proof of power than even the greatness and supernatural quality of the miracles.*

As a servant church, the disciples of the servant Christ, we are called to a ministry marked by lowliness and humility, not by a triumphalist arrogance, lording it over the community; not by patronising condescension, so often a religious cover for real contempt for people: but by genuine penitential and realistic lowliness of heart.

It is also *a human ministry*. Nothing is more ordinary, more natural, more basic, than washing feet. There is nothing religious about it. It is a human activity. The servant church is called to minister to human beings because they are human, and because that humanity is good and worthy of service. Our ministry is not super-spiritual, in which we stand aloof from human needs, preferring the world of the sanctuary to that of the kitchen and the street. We are called to be fully human.

It is *a dirty ministry*. Feet washing is a messy business. Servanthood is messy. We are called to a messy and potentially contaminating form of ministry, called to be an incarnational people. So much ministry, so much theology, so many priests, are afraid to get their hands dirty, seeking the pseudo-purity and comfort of the study or the sanctuary instead of the untidiness and dirt of the world. In a church committed to the incarnation, gnosticism keeps cropping up. But ministry is a dirty business, a risky business. It is not a pursuit for the fragile, for the precious, for those who will not take risks with their salvation.

It is *a silent ministry*. The ministry of the servant is not an excuse for evangelism. Feet need to be washed because feet need to be washed. It is not an indirect way of preaching or of filling pews. It reduces our excessively talkative ministries to the level of the divine silence. It is, in the truest sense, a contemplative ministry. And that contemplative ministry needs the larger towel to absorb the love which is both received and given in the process of washing the feet of Christ's poor. To wash feet is an act of contemplative prayer.

It is *a cleansing ministry*. The purpose of washing is to be clean, to effect a change. The servant ministry of Christ is a cleansing ministry, a transforming ministry. That transformation may be gradual, painful, feet and hearts may bleed. There will be much dust on the way to glory. We will need the larger towel.

Finally, it is *a ministry of tribulation, passion and tears*. In John, the feet washing occurs between two sayings in which Jesus is said to be 'troubled' in spirit (John 12:27 and 13:21). 'Now is my soul troubled'. 'He was troubled in spirit.' It stands between passover and passion, between life and death. It is a supremely paschal ministry, a ministry marked by suffering and sacrifice. We find that feet are wounded. Through humble service, we are led to the heart of sacrifice.

Fairacres Chronicle 21:1, pp5-7

Racism and the proclamation of the gospel

If anyone wants the experience of tribulation, passion and tears of which Kenneth Leech wrote in that last paragraph, then the struggle against racism is surely where that experience will be endured. The excruciating experience of anti-Semitism in ourselves, and our deep-seated and gut-wrenching terror of those unlike ourselves have to be dealt with inside our ecclesiastical communions before we can have the slightest hope of being believed outside them, if baptismal glory, and ourselves being given a new identity in Christ are to mean very much. These paragraphs need to be read in conjunction with those on the Beatitudes and the Seven Deadly Sins, for self-examination is not just a matter for individuals by themselves, but for groups of people too, since we all so easily learn from one another, for good or for ill.

The parish at worship

Worship is at the heart of the church's life. In worship human persons stretch out their hands and hearts towards God. They do so as a community of equals; redeemed sinners bound for glory. In worship all distinctions of race, class, wealth and so on are done away. Worship cannot be Christian if it is not established on this egalitarian basis. Such worship is a subversive act, rooted in the values of equality and community, the very values which the racist philosophies and practices deny. The greatest care needs to be given to the act of worship, for it creates and demonstrates the church's life and character. How worship is offered reveals more about the self-understanding, the theology, the assumptions of the local church than anything else does.

Good liturgy can be a powerful instrument for instilling the vision and values of the Kingdom of God in the hearts, minds and wills of the worshippers.

To serve Christ in all persons, and to respect the dignity of every human being, are clear anti-racist mandates. Racism is a denial of baptism, a regression to the prebaptismal, unregenerate state.

In the eucharist we assert and enact our solidarity in Christ, our *koinonia* or common life in him. The eucharistic action undermines all ideas of hierarchy based on class, wealth or race. It is an essentially egalitarian and communal act . . . The parish community celebrating the eucharistic memorial of the dying and rising of Christ is performing a fundamental action for humanity and against racism.

The parish needs to take very seriously the consequences of being a eucharistic community, of living out the eucharistic principles in an anti-eucharistic, anti-communal world. Racism is one dimension of this basic world view which is rooted in individualism, competition and division. But if worship and prayer shape us fundamentally, at a gut level, then there is no more important act that we can perform than one in which we commit ourselves profoundly and in the depths of our beings to equality and community.

At the eucharist we are united with the people of God in all ages. The solidarity is not only across geographical, racial and cultural boundaries, but across time and history.

The sacrifice of Christ, in which we share in each eucharistic celebration, must be recognised, proclaimed and manifested as the healing work in which racial and national limitations are transcended and a new humanity is born. But even where this is not apparent, in churches where there is little awareness of the revolutionary significance of the eucharist, there is a subversive power which derives from the sacrament itself and which works to undermine the forces of division. A eucharistic sensibility is bound to develop, often in spite of the prejudices, divisions and wishes of the community present, a sensibility which results from the nature of the sacrament. To celebrate the eucharist is in itself a revolutionary and anti-racist act. It promotes change by its very nature.

Intercession

Moreover, since racial violence and the loneliness and fear associated with it often occur at night, there is a vital place for the praying group which floods the night with intercession and seeks to redeem the night hours for the power of love and gentleness. A network of disciplined systematic intercessors can be of great value in areas infected with racial violence and hatred. It is essential that intercessions are offered regularly for racist groups, their leaders, and those seduced by them; for the perpetrators as well as the victims of racial attacks; and for those in positions to influence the course of events in the field of race relations. Racism is a manifestation of spiritual evil, and it must be fought with the weapons of prayer, fasting and sacrifice.

Proclamation

. . . the parish community confronts racism through its preaching of the gospel . . .

The gospel proclaims a new humanity, a new creation in Christ. The Son of Man was manifested to destroy the works of the Devil. Racism is clearly a work of the Devil. The critique of racism must be seen as a necessary element in Christian preaching and teaching.

If the local church is truly living out the character of the gospel, it will be a focal point of welcome for the stranger and the alien, a home for the homeless and unloved, a place of sanctuary for the refugee. It will be a place which opens its doors to the community. . .

Churches which see themselves merely as refuges cannot hope to combat the evils of racism. And the way in which they see themselves will be visibly manifested and easily recognisable: a closed church, closed against the community, speaks more powerfully than any number of words. A church which is open and welcoming, warm and inviting, speaks powerfully of Christ who welcomes all.

Theology is not an activity for academics, remote in intellectual ghettoes, but an activity for Christian people at street level. It involves a continuous and rigorous process of interrogation and discernment of what God is doing and how the events of the world and of the local community can be understood in relation to the will and purpose of God. It is a process in which mistakes will be made. It has to be a corporate exercise in which there is mutual criticism and correction. It is through the encounter of Christian truths with the conflicts and issues of the day that the meaning of those truths will be recognised and personalised.

Listening

. . . the local church will only be an effective witness against racism if it is a listening church. All pastoral ministry is based on the ability to listen. Christians need to listen to the voices of the powerless and the neglected, to the voices which are silenced or suppressed beneath the clamour of the streets. Often churches are out of contact with the groups and movements which are at work within their neighbourhoods, and even more out of touch with what Martin Luther King called the voices of the unheard. They do not have their ears to the ground. They have become communities of the deaf. As a result, their words are empty and lifeless, for they do not connect with the reality of human need. All pastoral work and all work for social justice must be rooted in contemplative listening.

Repentance

A necessary element in repentance is self-examination. But if the community is to practise self-examination, it must be a corporate discipline. The parish community needs systematically and prayerfully to examine its past and present witness. How far does it reflect the composition of its neighbourhood? Are any groups being excluded? What kind of communication is there with such excluded groups? Are the gifts and insights of groups and individuals within the community being used? Are future ministers being sought from among black Christians? These are only some of the questions which must be asked.

In self-examination and repentance, the church is brought face to face with its own prejudice and hatred. Here is the most difficult and most painful area of the local church's life. For it must be recognised that religious people are often not simply no more loving and open than their neighbours who are outside organised religion; the evidence suggests that they are often less loving, more intolerant and prejudiced, less open to new people and new insights. Churches can be deeply prejudiced and fearful enclaves. In the process of repentance, the pastor needs to teach about the nature of sin and the place of forgiveness and of amendment of life.

Against the principalities and powers

If churches are to become part of the organised struggle against racism, they themselves need to be organised and efficient. The pursuit of righteousness has to be an informed, mobilised pursuit. It calls for discipline and efficiency as well as goodwill and purity of heart.

The local church needs to see itself as part of an international society. Racism is indivisible. It cannot be opposed here and supported elsewhere. Many churches find it easier to support missionaries in Pakistan than to befriend and support an isolated Pakistani in their own parish. Others may respond to incidents of racial discrimination on their own doorstep but fail to make any connection between these incidents and events in South Africa which manifest the same pattern. To recognise that the small parish unit is part of an international community is a valuable way of helping local churches to see their own multiracial and multinational character. The Anglican Church, for instance, is on a world scale a mainly black Church. It is only by seeing it in narrowly English terms that we fail to realise this. It is vital that we learn to think across national and racial boundaries if we are to overcome the racism of our own culture. Anything, including exchange visits and links between parishes, which can help to do this will be valuable.

The parish can only face and overcome racism if it is a community in movement. If the parish sees itself primarily as a preserving body, committed to the defence of the old order, then it is very likely to defend racism as one of the features of that order. The parish needs to see itself as a pilgrim community, constantly on the move, learning new truths, discerning the will of God in the process of movement and struggle towards the Kingdom. If its priorities and its values lie in the new humanity of the future, and not in the preservation of the old order of the past, it will be a force for justice and against racism.

Struggle in Babylon, pp185, 187-188, 190-192, 194-195

The quest for spiritual roots

Here we have paragraphs which present us with some of Kenneth Leech's reflections on the resources we need to take politics seriously, a spirituality of 'adventure and risk'.

To return to the source is to return to a living stream, not to a stagnant pool. It is to a liberating tradition that we return, not to a source of bondage. And much depends on our motives for return. Are we seeking security, safety, a vantage point from which we can stand above the movements and struggles of our age, stand against the currents and tides? Or are we seeking resources of vision and of hope for our own struggles and movements towards a new humanity? In the last resort it is a question of movement. If we are standing still, determined to stay where we are, we will look to the scriptures and the tradition for reinforcement of our rigid positions. And undoubtedly we will find enough to reinforce those positions. But the scriptures are a liberating word, a word of deliverance. They describe, and are rooted in, an exodus tradition, a death and resurrection journey. If they are to convey their liberating power, they must be read by pilgrims on the move. Only the person who is running can read this word (Habakkuk 2:2). For it is the story of a people in pilgrimage, the story of a journey from slavery to liberation.

It is important that we try to avoid seeing faith in terms of intellectual content ('the faith'), and spirituality in terms of devotional attitudes and feelings. Faith is the way of the spirit, the 'spiritual life' is simply the life of faith nourished by the powerful wind (*ruach*, spirit) of grace. These are not two worlds, two levels, but one. If we hold on to the word 'spirituality', it should only be because we recognise that we all stand under the guidance, and often under the devastating judgement, of the divine *ruach*, the wind of God, which is the framework within which faith can blossom and grow. Spirituality is life-giving movement, life driven and energised by God. Spirituality is life in Christ: to be 'spiritual' is to be in Christ, to know Christ and the power of his resurrection, sharing his sufferings and death (Philippians 3:10). Spirituality is life within the love and continual life-renewing power of God.

The Eye of the Storm, pp207-208

The quest for spiritual roots and the Old Testament

Pilgrimage

Christian spirituality is rooted in the spiritual history of Israel, and specifically in the Jewish understanding of God acting in the upheavals of history. Among those upheavals the exodus from Egypt holds a crucially important place. The exodus is more than a historic event: it became for Israel an ever-present reality, a paradigm of salvation history. To the individual Jew the regular celebration of the Passover was an enactment of 'what Yahweh did for *me* when *I* came out of Egypt' (Exodus 13:8). Joshua addressed the people of a later generation, reminding them that 'your eyes saw what I did to Egypt, and you lived in the wilderness a long time' (Joshua 24:7). The exodus is the account of a divinely guided journey. In the ancient world, only Virgil's *Aeneid* is in any way comparable to it. Through this journey a fearful and disorganised mob of slaves is moulded into a people – the phrase 'people of Israel' is first used in the exodus story. It undermined slavery within the new covenant community, for those who had been liberated from Egypt must never again be enslaved (Leviticus 25:39, 42). The events recalled here are events of spiritual and political transformation.

The wilderness experience was to remain central to Israel's faith experience. God is a wilderness God (Jeremiah 2.6ff), and it is from the early Sinai revelation that the call 'Set my people free' is heard. The exodus, that great movement of liberation, grew from the encounter with God in the cloud and thick darkness. That which began in mysticism ended in politics: contemplation led to liberation. And any spirituality which is formed by Jewish and Christian understandings must be a spirituality of movement, movement motivated by the encounter with mystery. It will be a spirituality of the liberating journey. The spirituality which will service and nurture the Christians of the twenty-first century will be a spirituality which recognises God's liberating work in human history, in the upheaval and turmoil of nations, communities and individuals. The spirituality of exodus is not a spirituality of comfort and security, rather does it call us out of security into an encounter with God in the wastes of uncertainty and wilderness. Such pilgrimage is of the very stuff of faith.

The desert

Today Christians of all traditions are rediscovering the place of the desert in their lives. Christians of the future who seek to follow Christ in the way of the Kingdom will need also to follow Christ in his desert prayer, in his solitude and his attention to God. We will see a new approach to community which will emphasise both solitude and solidarity, recognising that the inner life of persons is necessary if humankind is to become a true communion.

The spirituality of the future must be a contemplative spirituality. It must lay stress on stillness, silence and attention to God. If this contemplative spirit is missing, religion is bound to become another form of restless activity, an appendage to the life of power, business and competition. We are in a period when a mutant of spirituality itself, a spirituality of a private and conformist type, is being utilised by big business for its own purposes. The times are indeed upon us, as Daniel Berrigan predicted years ago, when the pursuit of contemplation is likely to become subversive activity.[11] Only a contemplative Church, a praying Church, a Church which attends to the skies, to the hidden voice of God in the movements of history, can hope to respond to the deepest needs of humankind in this terrible phase of its history.

Closely related to contemplation is solitude, that deep encounter with the self and with God which is so threatened by the present dominance of technology and by the noise which seeks to enforce superficiality and conformity. Against such demonic distortions of human destiny, only the recovery of solitude can prevail. Solitude is not opposed to solidarity but is its necessary counterpart and complement. There will be no spiritual renewal unless Christian people recognise that their quest for union with God in the ground of their being is a vital part of their discipleship. And such a recognition is of crucial importance in pastoral work, for only those who have discovered themselves in solitude can hope to be of service to others.

Cloud and darkness

A spirituality which takes the symbolism of cloud and darkness with seriousness will be a mystical spirituality. Not in the sense that it will be élitist or separate from the common life, reserved for a group of initiates, a refuge from the hurly-burly of life. But mystical in the sense that it will seek to enter into the deep and dark mystery which is at the heart of God. The eastern Christians of the early centuries spoke of this spirituality of the cloud as *agnosia*, unknowing, a knowledge beyond conceptual limits. It is this tradition of unknowing which we need to recover and reaffirm. Rejecting the pseudo-certainty of the false lights, it will be ready to stay within the cloud, within the darkness and unclarity which is the very stuff of faith.

In an age of false certainties, of rigid fundamentalisms of various kinds, the renewal of mystical theology, rooted in the *agnosia*, the unknowing, of the negative tradition, is of the greatest importance. Only a renewal of the mystical spirit can overcome the gulf between fundamentalism and the emptiness which is pervasive in our culture. The Christian of the future will, as Karl Rahner observed, either be a mystic, or will not be at all.

Keep on walking

There is nothing quite like the experience of walking to promote comradeship. The Church is meant to be a people on the march, moving forward in solidarity, a pilgrim people. Sadly it often becomes a static backward-looking people. To stand still in the spiritual life is to go backwards. The pilgrim community is one which is oriented towards the future, a community marked and motivated by a divinely inspired restlessness. As the Jewish Passover was to be eaten in haste by people ready to move on, so the pilgrim community must always be moving forwards. Lot's wife looked backwards and became one of God's frozen people.

Our spiritual pilgrimage is not within an artificial religious world, but within the real world in which coal is mined and lemon meringue pie is made, the world in which companies are taken over and homeless people die in the streets, the world in which wars are declared and millions long for peace and for justice. Many Christians have been encouraged by a distorted spirituality to see this world as no more than a 'vale of tears and woe'. But the gospel calls us to proclaim that God loves the world, and that salvation is about its transformation. We need therefore in the future more worldly Christians, Christians who will renounce the false values of 'the world' in the biblical sense of the fallen world order, but who will love and cherish the world in the sense of the material creation, the work of God and the sphere of his redeeming activity.

The pilgrim community will often travel in the dark. One of the most serious accusations levelled against religious people is that they think they have God taped. They are too cocksure, they have all the answers. We need, as a pilgrim community, to accept that we do not have all the answers, that we will often be marching into the darkness, and will be puzzled and confused as to the direction we should take. A pilgrim community will often travel in half-light, in uncertainty and bewilderment. We need to be at home in this night of faith if we are to progress.

The pilgrim community of the future, like its predecessors, will be confronted by monsters, by forces of evil and oppression. Confronted by such monsters, we will need all the spiritual resources we can get. This is not the time for spiritual striptease: we will need more adequate resources and a richer and deeper interior life. For we are called to a spirituality of combat. It is no accident that the march is often a symbol of protest. The Christian pilgrimage is a march against oppression, a march from the oppressive realm of Babylon to the new Jerusalem, the home of peace and justice. There is no way to escape this conflict with the forces of evil within the fallen world order.

Walking wounded

The pilgrim community will often be limping and wounded. Jacob wrestled with God all night, and at the end of the night he still did not know the name of God. He emerged from that struggle wounded. Jesus showed his wounds to his disciples, while Paul spoke of carrying those wounds in his body. A pilgrim Church is a church of the wounded. The best pastors, the best spiritual guides, are those who have experienced wounding, pain, dereliction and suffering. As we are healed by Christ's wounds, so will others be healed by our wounds – or rather, by our sharing in the wounds of Christ. We are called to be wounded healers.

A community of pilgrims needs to abandon clutter and to recover fundamentals. It needs to be set free from the obsession with trivia, to discriminate between things that abide, and passing fashions and fads. The sacraments of the pilgrim Church deal with basic things – bread, water, oil, the clasp of our sister's and our brother's hands. They are the food, provisions and resources for a people on the move.

A community of pilgrims who are rooted and grounded in Christ's resurrection will be characterised by joy. Not the bogus cheeriness of the hearty, jolly, back-slapping Christians, but the deep joy of those who have attained an inner assurance, a confidence and trust in the power of the risen Christ. A pilgrim Church must be a joyful confident Church, which sings the songs of freedom in the midst of its bondage, 'Sing Alleluia and keep on walking', says Augustine in one of his most memorable sermons.[12] As we move into the heart of the storm we will sing but we will keep on walking.

The Eye of the Storm, pp210-211, 220, 221, 231-232, 232-233

God's death is crucial to our life

This is the first of two pieces originally written for a newspaper. It focuses on suffering and was one of a series responding to Margaret Spufford's Celebration.

The early Christian writer Irenaeus claimed that one characteristic of all heretics was their rejection of paradox. Simple, one-dimensional accounts and explanations have their attraction in all generations, not least in our own. The orthodox Christian approach to its central mysteries of incarnation and passion is one which is rooted in awe and wonder, in the amazement and astonishment which is intrinsic to the idea of *doxa*, glory.

The articulation of this amazement at the manifestation of the divine glory takes the form of paradox, of contradiction, of a precarious and risky *via media* which seeks to hold together truths which are apparently incompatible. Transcendence and intimacy, changelessness and birth within time, passionlessness and suffering, immortality and death on a cross. Such paradoxes lie at the heart of Christian faith and Christian theology.

No belief is more paradoxical, more scandalous, more incredible than the belief that God took human flesh: the dogma of the incarnation. The Christmas carol puts the paradox crudely and starkly.

> *O wonder of wonders which none can unfold:*
> *The Ancient of Days is an hour or two old;*
> *The Maker of all things is made of the earth,*
> *Man is worshipped by angels and God comes to birth.*

To contemplate the truth revealed in these words is to open oneself to utter amazement.

Yet it is in the crucifixion that the paradox of God in the flesh is even more apparent and that the amazement become acute and painful. The Japanese theologian Kazah Kitamori has said that the church exists 'to keep this astonishment alive' and ceases to exist when the astonishment is lost. For it is in the cross that the issue of the pain of God is posed in its clearest and most perplexing form. If God is infinite, beyond time and space, *totaliter aliter*, 'without body, parts or passions', the unmoved mover, how can that God experience change, pain, anguish and the negation of Calvary? Many have sought to avoid the horns of the theological dilemma by claiming either that the crucifixion was illusory, or that Jesus was simply a human being in whom God-consciousness was most intensely focussed. Yet orthodoxy has insisted that the whole deity was in the passion and death of Jesus.

So in the very beginnings of the Christian era, Ignatius of Antioch spoke of the suffering of God. But the crucial step towards understanding the identity of Christ's pain with the divine pain was the assertion of the Council of Ephesus in 431 that Mary was *Theotokos*, Mother of God. She was the mother of the flesh of God. There could be no division of Christ into human and divine elements. Indeed the whole work of salvation depended, as the fourth century Greek fathers saw most clearly, on the truth that the whole deity was involved in the lowliness of incarnation and the pain of the cross.

As Gregory of Nazianzen put it so memorably, 'We needed a God made flesh, a God put to death that we might live again'. Gregory speaks of the blood of God and of the crucified God, a term which was later taken up by Luther and more recently by Jürgen Moltmann. It was this assertion which, after centuries of reflection, led to the Theopaschite (literally God-suffering) formula, the claim that, in the words of the Orthodox liturgy, 'one of the Holy Trinity, you died on the cross'.

It was in the nineteenth century that theologians such as F D Maurice and P T Forsyth took the next step of recognising that if God was in the pain of Calvary, then there must have been, and must be, something in the very nature of the divine which is open to pain and suffering. Forsyth expressed it by saying that 'there is a cross in God before the wood is seen upon Calvary'. The whole deity was in it from eternity. Some years later G A Studdert Kenedy ('Woodbine Willie' of the First World War) spoke of God as the greatest sufferer of all.

In her book *Celebration* (Collins, 1989), Margaret Spufford rightly rejects the superficial explanations of her own suffering. For her the central paradox of God's death, and our sharing in it through the eucharist, is, in the most literal sense, crucial. It is only through entering into that central mystery, and living – and dying – within it, that pain begins to make any kind of sense. When that central mystery is lost, the proclamation of the cross becomes a form of propaganda, of oppression, of religious welfare. The crucified mind gives way to the crusading mind. Those who have suffered greatly know only too well the cruelty and oppression of those who prophesy smooth things and who seek to heal the wounds of people lightly by words of explanation. The cross does not explain anything. It cannot be received by the head, cannot be accepted as an intellectual proposition.

The cross is a message of brokenness at the heart of the universe, and can only be received in the brokenness of being. It is a manifestation of power through weakness. That is what Luther meant when he spoke of the cross as the left hand of God. The straightforward, direct, forceful right hand may be outstretched in power and assertion as it often is in conventional religion and conventional politics. But at the heart of the mystery of pain it is the left hand, the sinister, the indirect, the odd and the strange, which comes into play.

The cross is 'God's strange work', a work beyond analysis and conceptual thinking, beyond reason. And yet in the experience of so many who are drawn to that naked and forsaken figure, it is only in the deepening and intensifying of pain to breaking point, the point at which we see that 'to be restored, our sickness must grow worse', it is only there that the roots of redemption are found. So the cross is seen liturgically not as a gallows but as a life-giving tree whose leaves are for healing. The tree of defeat has become the tree of victory. It is the 'one and only noble tree' on which the Creator of the world was hung. To use such language is to stretch language to breaking point also. Yet such stretching of language is merely the external form of a deeper and more fundamental breaking process apart from which the cross has no meaning. Those who are, perhaps in spite of themselves, brought into the mystery of that brokenness, become sharers in that most basic and most terrible form of priesthood: the sharing – ritually, inwardly, perhaps physically, literally – in the dying and rising of Christ of which all theology is a reflection and a record.

The Independent, 30 September 1989

198

Holy night, holy light

The saving power of the Christmas celebration depends upon the truth that Christ is risen from the dead. It is the presence of the risen Christ in the eucharistic mystery which transforms a nostalgic memorial into a source of life and glory. The powerful symbolism of light shining out of the winter darkness must inspire the Christian who worships at this time to cry out: 'Christ is Risen!'

It is the joy of the resurrection, of the Christ who is present through his conquest of death and decay which enters our hearts at Christmas. This recognition that it can only be the risen Christ whom we encounter seems strange and wrongly timed, yet the atmosphere of the liturgy drives us to make the connection. For this is above all else the day of light.

The collects for the Midnight Mass of Christmas and for the Easter Vigil have a close, almost uncanny resemblance. 'You have made this night holy with the splendour of Jesus Christ our Light.' 'You have brightened this night with the radiance of the Risen Christ.' Both nights are referred to as 'holy night' and the readings of each liturgy focus on light and glory.

The celebration of what we now call Christmas was not in origin concerned with the birth of Christ at all but with his baptism. In his descent into the waters and his rising up, was seen both his manifestation, his *epiphaneia*, and also the prefiguring of his resurrection, and ours. While the conventional focus on 25 December has, since Constantine, weakened the original emphasis on light and resurrection, the Christmas season still reaches its climax on the Feast of the Baptism.

To see the centrality of the symbol of light as common to both incarnation and resurrection is to see how inseparable are the Christmas and Easter mysteries. Together they constitute the basic framework of God's activity in and beyond history and time, as they form the heart of Christian faith and hope. Without Easter, Christmas has no point; without Christmas, Easter has no meaning. Both incarnation and resurrection have significance because in these events God is glorified in the flesh. The flesh becomes the source of light, the raw material of glory.

So at midnight on the feast of the incarnation we celebrate Christ as God of God, Light of Light. But the Christ whom we greet is the adult, mature Christ, the rabbi, the friend of Galilean and Jerusalem outcasts, the leader of the attack on the Temple, the rebel hanged in the outer darkness. He does not stay an infant but shines with his mature and transformed humanity.

The light of Christ is a persistent light. It shines through the most powerfully oppressive darkness, shines in the midst of devastation, disaster and upheaval, yet without explaining them, justifying them, or making sense of them. The gospel of incarnation and resurrection is not the answer to a set of questions. It is a persistent and defiant light. And its persistence is paradoxical. For the truth of the gospel of incarnation and resurrection stands in contradiction to, and seems to be contradicted by, the realities of a world in which there is still no room, and where the dead bodies pile up, inexplicably, meaninglessly, in Somalia, Bosnia, Ireland.

Is the light of Christ then no more than an illusory comfort, a false reassurance that all is well when in fact all is clearly unwell in the 'demented inn' of the world? Certainly religious light is often of this illusory kind. But the gospel of incarnation and resurrection cannot be preached in an authentic and truthful way unless it faces the terrible reality of homelessness and meaningless death.

It is these two realities which provide the only possible material context for the light of Christ. For it is as the homeless unwanted Christ of Bethlehem and as the naked condemned Christ of Golgotha that the light shines with its strange persistence and its baffling power to draw people to its shining, enabling them to become dynamic agents in the historical process, lights in the world.

The light of this holy night is not a light of explanation. Yet it is a simple light, a light which penetrates to the heart of humanity and of creation. And it is only as it penetrates, simultaneously drawing and repelling, illuminating and blinding, that we come to understand the power of that light. As Paul says, we are being changed into the likeness of the Lord whose glory we have seen.

The Independent, 29 December 1992

SELECT BIBLIOGRAPHY

The Priest and the Drug Scene, London: SPCK, 1970.

True Prayer: An Invitation to Christian Spirituality, London: Sheldon, 1980.

'Interrogating the Tradition', *The Way* Supplement 54 (1981), pp10-20.

True God: An Exploration in Spiritual Theology, London: Sheldon, 1985.

'Needing a Larger Towel', *Fairacres Chronicle* 21:1 (1988), pp5-7.

Struggle in Babylon: Racism in the Cities and Churches of Britain, London: Sheldon, 1988.

The Eye of the Storm: Spiritual Resources for the Pursuit of Justice, London: Darton, Longman and Todd, 1992.

'Why God's death is crucial to our life', *The Independent*, 30 September 1989.

'A strange, persistent and defiant light', *The Independent*, 29 December 1992.

NOTES

1 Peter Selby, *A World Come of Age*, Cambridge MA, Cowley, 1984, pp20-21, 8, 88.

2 Centre for Christian Spirituality, General Theological Seminary: New York, *Requirements of the Practicum in Spiritual Direction*, MS, Michaelmas 1984, p2.

3 Jean Daniélou, *The Lord of History*, London: Longman, 1958, p77.

4 Peter Selby, *op cit*, p3-4.

5 Carolyn Osiek, 'The spiritual direction of "thinking" types', *Review for Religious* 44,2, 1985, pp209-219.

6 D E Jenkins, *The Contradiction of Christianity*, London: SCM Press, 1976, p83.

7 Sheila Rowbotham, *Dreams and Dilemmas: Collected Writings*, London: Virago, 1983, p66.

8 Cf C K Barrett, *The Holy Spirit and the Gospel Tradition*, London: SPCK, 1947, p39.

9 See C H Kraeling, *John the Baptist*, New York: Scribners, 1951, p117.

10 J D G Dunn, 'The birth of a metaphor: Baptized in the Spirit', *Expository Times* 89.5 (1978) p136.

11 Daniel Berrigan, *America is Hard to Find*, London: SPCK, 1973, pp77-78.

12 Augustine, Sermon 256, in *Patrologia Latina*, ed. J P Migne, 38:1191-93. The sermon is read at Matins on the Saturday of the thirty-fourth week of the year in the Roman Breviary.

ACKNOWLEDGEMENTS

Helen Oppenheimer 'Fellowship' was first published in *Theology* 1968 and in ed. G R Dunstan *The Sacred Ministry 1970* with the title 'Head and Members', reprinted by permission of SPCK; 'Friendship' is reprinted from *Marriage* Mowbray 1990 (an imprint of Cassell); 'Grievances' was first published in *Theology* 1988, reprinted by permission of SPCK. 'Temperance' was first published in *Theology* 1962 and in ed. A R Vidler *Traditional Virtues Reassessed* 1969, reprinted by permission of SPCK; 'Spirit and body' was first published in *Theology* 1990, reprinted by permission of SPCK; 'Christian flourishing' was first published in *Religious Studies* 1969, reprinted by permission of Cambridge University Press; 'Called to be saints' is reprinted from *The Character of Christian Morality Faith Press* 1965, 1974, by permission of the author; 'Jesus Christ his only Son our Lord' was first published in *Theology* 1993, reprinted by permission of SPCK; 'Heaven' is from *Looking Before and After* 1988, reprinted by permission of HarperCollins Publishers Ltd.

Janet Martin Soskice 'Women's problems' was first published in *Priests and People* 1992, reprinted by permission of the publishers; 'Just women's problems?' is reprinted from an essay in eds H D Regan and A J Torrance *Christ and Context* 1993, reprinted by permission of T & T Clarke; 'Annunciation' was first published in eds H Walton and S Durber *Silence in Heaven* 1994, reprinted by permission of SCM Press; 'Incarnation and trinity' is from an essay in ed. James M Byrne *The Christian Understanding of God Today* 1993, reprinted by permission of Columba Press; 'Creation and relation' was first published in *Theology* 1991, reprinted by permission of SPCK.

Margaret Spufford 'Work', 'Pain', 'Suffer the little children', 'God suffers with us', 'Riches' and 'Communion' are all taken from *Celebration* 1991, reprinted by permission of HarperCollins Publishers Ltd; 'A revelation of divine love' was first published in *Theology* 1992, reprinted by permission of SPCK; 'On joy' was first published as 'The most beautiful thing imaginable' in *The Independent* 15 April 1992, reprinted by permission of the author and *The Independent*.

Carlo-Maria Martini 'Ruth – in five scenes' was first published in *David, Sinner and Believer*, reprinted by permission of St Paul's (UK); 'Job, grief and lamentation' was first printed in *Perseverance in Trials* 1992, reprinted by permission of The Liturgical Press; 'From lamentation to praise' was first published in *What am I that you care for me?* 1990, reprinted by permission of St Paul's (UK); 'From praise to sacrifice' was first printed in *The Woman Among her people* 1989, reprinted by permission of St Paul's (UK); 'Death and the revelation of love' was first printed in *Promise Fulfilled* 1994, reprinted by permission of St Paul's (UK).

Jacques Pohier, 'Decomposition', 'No longer being able to preach', 'On Jesus Christ and his resurrection', 'The Word made flesh', 'The renunciation of God', 'To be where God can come', 'A Holy Week', 'Jesus' attitude to sinners and to sin', 'God is God so God is not Everything', 'Breaking the rock', are taken from *God in Fragments* 1985, reprinted by permission of SCM Press.

Kenneth Leech 'The priest and the drug scene' is from the book of the same title 1970, reprinted by permission of SPCK; 'On the Beatitudes' and 'On the Seven Deadly Sins' are from *True Prayer* 1980, reprinted by permission of SPCK; 'Spirituality for today and tomorrow' was first printed as part of 'Interrogating the tradition' *The Way Supplement* 1985 and is reproduced by permission of the Editors, Heythrop College, Kensington Square, London; 'Holy Spirit experienced as profound liberation', 'Baptism by water and fire', 'Charismatic renewal' are from *True God* 1985, reprinted by permission of SPCK; 'Needing a larger towel' was first printed in *Fairacres Chronicle* 1988, reprinted by the permission of SLG Press; 'Racism and the proclamation of the gospel' is from *Struggle in Babylon 1988*, reprinted by permission of SPCK; 'The quest for spiritual roots', 'The quest for spiritual roots and the Old Testament' were first printed in *The Eye of the Storm* 1992, reprinted by permission of Darton, Longman and Todd; 'God's death is crucial to our life' was first published in *The Independent* 30 September 1989, reprinted by permission of the author and *The Independent;* 'Holy night, holy light' was first published as 'A Strange, Persistent and Defiant Light' in *The Independent* 29 December 1992, reprinted by permission of the author and *The Independent*.